Parsing Strategies of Japanese Low-proficiency EFL Learners

Parsing Strategies of Japanese Low-proficiency EFL Learners

AMMA Kazuo

Hituzi Syobo Publishing

Copyright © AMMA Kazuo 2009

First published 2009

Author: AMMA Kazuo

All rights reserved. Except for the quotation of short passages for the purposes of criticism and review, no part of this publication may be reproduced, stored in a retrieval system, or transmitted in any form or by any means, electronic, mechanical, photocopying, recording or otherwise, without the written prior permission of the publisher.
In case of photocopying and electronic copying and retrieval from network personally, permission will be given on receipts of payment and making inquiries. For details please contact us through e-mail. Our e-mail address is given below.

Hituzi Syobo Publishing
Yamato bldg. 2F, 2-1-2 Sengoku Bunkyo-ku Tokyo, Japan
112-0011

phone +81-3-5319-4916 fax +81-3-5319-4917
e-mail: toiawase@hituzi.co.jp
http://www.hituzi.co.jp/
postal transfer 00120-8-142852

ISBN978-4-89476-437-8
Printed in Japan

Abstract

This research investigates low-proficiency language learners' performance in written syntax tests. We attempt to identify a strategy of analysing and comprehending sentences taken characteristically by low-proficiency learners.

A special emphasis is placed on the cognitive constraint which restricts the span of the text to be processed at a time. Observations of low-proficiency learners' test performance indicate a coherent response pattern for certain items. In this research we clarify both learner characteristics and item specifications in terms of cognitive constraint.

A grammaticality judgement test was conducted against 1152 Japanese university EFL students. From the matrices of item association network calculated by logistic regression analysis and contingency table analysis, a cluster of items with mutual association was observed which became stronger as we went down on the test takers' proficiency scale and weaker as we went up on the scale. A common factor among the items in the cluster was identified as the strategy of local parsing; low-proficiency test takers tend to isolate a quasi-meaningful segment within a sentence as a target of comprehension and abandon the rest of the sentence.

In the confirmation study stage, we compared the mean strengths of association between two groups of items: one with sentences allowing local parsing and the other without. The result indicated a highly significant difference in strength of association between the two groups, ie., local parsing operated as differential item functioning in separating low-proficiency from high-proficiency learners. Finally, we calculated the individual participants' tendency to employ the local parsing strategy. Its significantly high correlation with the proficiency measure proved our hypothesis that low-proficiency learners' span of text to be processed is more limited than that of high-proficiency learners.

The research result not only revealed a special mechanism of sentence processing used by low-proficiency language learners, but also suggests the need for practice in low-level input processing to help automatise processes and leave more room for higher-level sentence and discourse processing in EFL.

Acknowledgements

This publication is based on my doctoral research at the University of Reading from 1996 to 2003 and on some subsequent studies in Japan. Throughout this research I was immensely indebted to numerous people: from my supervisors at Reading University to colleagues at Tamagawa University and Dokkyo University and to anonymous students from various institutions. Their selfless assistance was invaluable to my research. In particular, I owe my special thanks to the following people:

Mr Don Porter ... my first supervisor, who always stimulated me and helped me extend my interest ever since my conception of this research topic

Dr Barry O'Sullivan ... my second and 'finish-up' supervisor, who kept my research on schedule and helped me develop it

Ms Amanda Horn ... who facilitated my communication with Reading University, particularly from faraway places

My research colleagues ... who kindly filled in for me during my absence from campus and provided insightful suggestions

Gabriel Lee and Tania Hossain ... who proofread parts of this work

Tanabe Harumi ... who at home kept encouraging me both physically and morally with limitless affection and support.

The publication of this research work was funded by the Academic Publication Grant, Dokkyo University, 2008.

Contents

Abstract	i
Acknowledgements	ii
LIST OF TABLES	vii
LIST OF FIGURES	viii

Chapter 1   Introduction — 1

1.1 General introduction	1
1.2 Purpose of study	3
1.3 Research questions	4
1.4 Research design	6
1.5 Overview of methodological framework	7
1.6 Significance of research	8

Chapter 2   Literature survey — 11

2.1 Proficiency	12
2.1.1 Models of language proficiency	13
2.1.1.1 Componential view	13
2.1.1.2 Cognitive view	17
2.1.1.3 Evaluation	18
2.1.2 Variability in proficiency	19
2.1.2.1 Dimensionality in language proficiency	19
2.1.2.2 Indeterminacy	20
2.1.2.3 Summative evaluation of variability in interlanguage	22
2.2 Qualitative differences in performance between high-proficiency and low-proficiency learners	22
2.2.1 Characteristics of 'poor language learners'	23
2.2.2 Cognitive learning strategies	26
2.3 Input processing strategies	29
2.3.1 Semantic strategy	30

2.3.2 Parsing strategy	32
2.4 Memory and knowledge	36
2.4.1 Working memory	36
2.4.2 Long-term memory and other factors	42
2.5 Test formats	44
2.5.1 Grammaticality judgement	45
2.5.2 Alternative formats in grammaticality judgement	46
2.5.3 C-test	50
2.6 Summary of literature review	52
2.7 Hypotheses	54
2.7.1 Setting up of hypotheses	54
2.7.2 Steps of testing hypotheses	55

Chapter 3   Research design — 61

3.1 Review of background research	62
3.1.1 Grammaticality judgement test: a preliminary study	62
3.1.1.1 Outline	62
3.1.1.2 Procedure	63
3.1.1.3 Results	64
3.1.1.4 Discussion	66
3.1.1.5 Summary of the preliminary study	68
3.2 Main study	69
3.2.1 Participants	69
3.2.2 Materials	69
3.2.2.1 Grammaticality judgement test	70
3.2.2.1.1 Test items	70
3.2.2.1.2 Format	74
3.2.2.2 C-test	76
3.2.2.2.1 Test items	76
3.2.2.3 Questionnaire	77
3.2.3 Test procedure	78
3.2.3.1 Grammaticality judgement test	78
3.2.3.2 C-test	78
3.3 Statistical methodology	79
3.3.1 Logistic regression analysis	79

    3.3.2 Contingency table analysis   85
        3.3.2.1 Contingency table analysis using probabilities   85
        3.3.2.2 Association measure   88
    3.3.3 Multidimensional scaling   89
    3.3.4 Contour plot analysis   90
3.4 Summary   90

Chapter 4   Results and discussion   93

4.1 Results   94
    4.1.1 Data filtering   95
    4.1.2 Basic statistics   97
        4.1.2.1 Grammaticality judgement test   97
        4.1.2.2 C-test   98
        4.1.2.3 TOEFL ITP   99
    4.1.3 Distribution of association measures   100
    4.1.4 Multidimensional scaling analysis   101
    4.1.5 Contour plot analysis   105
    4.1.6 Model mapping of association links   106
4.2 Interpretation   110
    4.2.1 Exploratory phase   110
    4.2.2 Confirmatory phase   113
        4.2.2.1 Test of the difference of item groups with inherent structural attributes   113
        4.2.2.2 Test of the correlation between local parsing measures and proficiency measures   118
4.3 Discussion   121
    4.3.1 Unidimensionality in the C-test   121
    4.3.2 The local parsing strategy   122
    4.3.3 The relationship between general proficiency and parsing ability   125
    4.3.4 Methodological reminders   127
4.4 Summary   129

Chapter 5   Conclusion   131

5.1 Summary of research   132

  5.1.1 Summary of research procedure   132
    5.1.1.1 Preparation   132
    5.1.1.2 Experiment   133
    5.1.1.3 Confirmation   134
  5.1.2 Summary of cognitive mechanism   135
  5.1.3 Limitations   136
 5.2 Originality   137
 5.3 Contributions to academic research   139
  5.3.1 Test development   139
  5.3.2 Data mining   139
  5.3.3 Research in second language development   140
  5.3.4 Suggestions for TEFL   141
 5.4 Future orientations   142

Notes   146
Bibliography   147

Appendices

 A Parsing strategies (Amma, 2001)   161
 B Test material (Grammaticality judgement test)   163
 C Test material (C-test)   177
 D Contour plots of LinkScores at $Cz = -2.0$ to $+2.0$ 179

LIST OF TABLES

Table 2.1	Bachman's model of communicative competence	14
Table 2.2	Path coefficients in simplified causal model with 3 ability variables	25
Table 2.3	Correlations between English working memory scores and English reading comprehension scores for the four segmentation conditions	38
Table 3.1	Matrix of association measures (phi) for 7 responses in Form A	64
Table 3.2	Matrix of association measures (phi) for 5 pairs of responses in Form A in 5 ability levels	65
Table 3.3	Original classification of stimulus sentences and their criteria	71
Table 3.4	Parameter estimates of the logistic probability plot of the combined categories of target option (v) and other options as a collective category (x) in item a5 and h3	84
Table 3.5	Model of 2x2 (two-level two-category) contingency table	88
Table 3.6	Association measures (phi) of a5 and h3 in 9 proficiency levels	89
Table 4.1	List of sums of item association measures in 9 proficiency levels	100
Table 4.2	List of Chi square statistics of item association measures in 9 proficiency levels	101
Table 4.3	Stress values of MDS in 5 trials in 9 proficiency levels	102
Table 4.4	List of stimulus sentences	111
Table 4.5	List of 'accessible' stimulus sentences	114
Table 4.6	LinkScores of items with the label of local parsing in 9 proficiency levels	115
Table 4.7	Parameter estimates of approximation formulae and degrees of fitness	120
Table 4.8	Frequencies of local parsing responses in 3 proficiency levels for items h3, g7, and a5	127

LIST OF FIGURES

Figure 2.1	Candidate's 'proficiency' and its relation to performance	15
Figure 2.2	Range of contextual support and degree of cognitive involvement in communicative activities	17
Figure 2.3	Simplified causal model with 3 ability variables	24
Figure 2.4a	Structural equation modelling representations of cognitive and metacognitive use in relation with SLTP performance among high-ability group	28
Figure 2.4b	Structural equation modelling representations of cognitive and metacognitive use in relation with SLTP performance among low-ability group	28
Figure 2.5a	Correlations between L2 proficiency subtests and working memory tests	41
Figure 2.5b	Correlations between processing efficiency and prediction subtests	41
Figure 3.1	Configuration of 6 responses based on association measures	65
Figure 3.2	Transition of association measures of 5 response pairs shown as the change of ability measure	66
Figure 3.3	Logistic probability plot of all options in item a5 by Cz	80
Figure 3.4	Logistic probability plot of all options in item h3 by Cz	81
Figure 3.5	Logistic probability plot of the target option (v) and other options as a collective category (x) in item a5 by Cz	82
Figure 3.6	Logistic probability plot of the target option (v) and other options as a collective category (x) in item h3 by Cz	82
Figure 3.7	Logistic probability plot of the combined categories of target option (v) and other options as a collective category (x) in item a5 and h3	83
Figure 3.8	Mosaic plot of the combined categories of target option (v) and other options as a collective category (x) in item a5 and h3 at Cz = -1.0	86
Figure 3.9	Mosaic plot of the combined categories of target option (v) and other options as a collective category (x) in item a5 and	

	h3 at Cz = 0.0	87
Figure 3.10	Mosaic plot of the combined categories of target option (v) and other options as a collective category (x) in item a5 and h3 at Cz = 1.0	87
Figure 4.1	Distribution of the original C-test scores and their normal quantile plot	96
Figure 4.2	Distribution of the C-test scores after filtering and their normal quantile plot	96
Figure 4.3	Distribution of the Grammaticality judgement test scores and their normal quantile plot	97
Figure 4.4	Distribution of the TOEFL ITP scores by self report and their normal quantile plot	99
Figure 4.5	Two-dimensional distribution of items by MDS at Cz = -1.5	103
Figure 4.6	Two-dimensional distribution of items by MDS at Cz = 1.5	104
Figure 4.7	Model map of clusters of items at Cz = -1.5	107
Figure 4.8	Model map of clusters of items at Cz = 0.0	108
Figure 4.9	Model map of clusters of items at Cz = 1.5	108
Figure 4.10	Core clusters of items indicated on a model map	110
Figure 4.11	Transition of Linkscores of items in which local parsing is 'accessible'	116
Figure 4.12	Transition of Linkscores of items in which local parsing is 'inaccessible'	117
Figure 4.13	Approximate cubic formula applied to LinkScore plots of a5	119
Figure 4.14	Approximate cubic formula applied to LinkScore plots of h2	119

Chapter 1

Introduction

This chapter introduces the research topic in six parts

1.1 General introduction
1.2 Purpose of study
1.3 Research questions
1.4 Research design
1.5 Overview of methodological framework
1.6 Significance of research

1.1 General introduction

This thesis investigates the use of sentence parsing strategies characteristic of low-proficiency language learners. To begin with we need to define two fundamental notions. First, throughout the thesis we refer to **high-proficiency** and **low-proficiency** learners as the systematic variation of learners with the same study history — their performance in overall language proficiency tests being either high or low. We deal with a cross-sectional, rather than developmental, dataset, which is used to make a qualitative as well as quantitative contrast between the two groups of learners. We assume that they take different approaches to language learning — and in particular, performance in language tests — thus resulting in non-random differences on the proficiency scale; otherwise all learners would be equally efficient after the same span of time. Second, by **parsing** we mean a process of identifying and analysing a sentence structure into meaningful units. A special emphasis is placed on the cognitive constraint that restricts the span of the text to be processed at a time.

What keeps low-proficiency learners behind? Why do they gain little progress, and if any, in an unpredictable manner? These questions have been repeatedly asked by teaching practitioners and researchers. In my own observation of Japanese EFL learners at the university level quite a few number of them understood the sentence

The girl who ate with Cathy loved ice cream

as entailing "Cathy loved ice cream" in a multiple-choice comprehension test. This phenomenon was observed more frequently among low-proficiency learners than among high-proficiency learners. The contrast is merely relative; there is no absolute criterion for categorising learners as *low* or *high* proficiency. But if the tendency is proven and theoretically explained it will lead to a better understanding of human nature as well as the advancement of pedagogical techniques in EFL.

The previous literature indicates that working memory capacity and/or efficiency determines the rate and accuracy in reading, and that it predicts a learner's success in the second language. This theory seems to best explain the phenomenon we have investigated. In contrast with the sentence level analyses that previous studies have dealt with, we shall go further, to examine a constraint operating inside sentences and to clarify the restrictions commonly found among low-proficiency test takers.

We hypothesise that a common cognitive constraint operates when low-proficiency learners take grammaticality judgement tests and their responses against a certain type of test items reflect this constraint. By examining the test responses we aim to identify and characterise the problem. It is expected that the findings will be applied not only to test development but also to second language research and pedagogy.

This thesis is made up of five chapters. Chapter 1, the current chapter, presents an overview of the research, including descriptions of the purpose, rationale, and significance of the research, followed by the research questions. In Chapter 2 we review previous literature relevant to our research. For each topic a short summary of the literature in view of our research direction is provided at the end of the section. Then, based on the accumulation of past knowledge we postulate three hypotheses. Each hypothesis is followed by explanations of how each step of the analysis should be carried out in order to confirm the hypotheses. Chapter 3 describes our experiment in terms of participants, materials, and methodology. As the background of our research design a preliminary research in grammaticality judgement test is summarised at the outset. In the subsequent part for our main research, the research design is described in detail. Chapter 4 reports the results of our experiment in detail. We also expand directional arguments in the discussion section. Chapter 5 concludes our research. We first summarise our research, as we confirm the significance of each step and procedure. Then we indicate the contributions of the current research to related academic fields, including teaching English as a foreign language (TEFL) in the classroom. Finally we discuss the implications for future research.

1.2 Purpose of study

The purpose of this research is to investigate the nature of university-level EFL (English as a foreign language) learners' comprehension of sentences in written language as judged by their performance in grammaticality judgement. Our particular interest lies in the differential behaviour of low-proficiency learners in comparison with high-proficiency learners. Little research has been made to describe the performance of low-proficiency learners with reference to their mechanism of sentence-level comprehension. General research has indicated, nevertheless, that there are some qualitative as well as quantitative differences between learners in high and low proficiency levels (Fowler, 1981; Payne & Holtzman, 1983; Upshur & Homburg, 1983; Holmes, 1987; Oltman, Sticker, & Barrows, 1988; de Jong & van Ginkel, 1992; Purpura, 1998). Thus we hypothesise that these groups of learners will use different strategies of parsing (or analysing a sentence into functional units and identifying their grammatical roles) while taking a grammar test. It can be confirmed by examining whether the response patterns of each learner group constitute psychometrically meaningful units and whether they differentiate the proficiency levels with statistical significance. To illustrate this point, let me indicate the following sentences (an asterisk indicates that the sentence is ungrammatical). Each of them is one of the multiple-choice options for a grammaticality judgement test in our preliminary research (Amma, 2001).

(1.1) *We went to the lake to swimming.
(1.2) *Grandma went to shopping.

As the proficiency level goes down, an increasing proportion of Japanese university EFL learners judge (1.1) as grammatical. It is these learners who judge (1.2) also as grammatical. It is considered that they take an *-ing* form for a noun of action and the preposition *to* for an indicator of purpose. If a similar pattern is observed in other stimuli we can infer that these learners tend to assign a simplistic role to the syntactic units, and this tendency characterises part of the nature of low-proficiency learners as distinct from high-proficiency learners.

Our goal in the current research is to identify a cognitive constraint working negatively on low-proficiency learners. Since the constraint(s) is unknown, our approach is mainly exploratory. The interpretation of the output of the experiment is made to reflect the premise (cf. Amma, 2001) that
- Test takers prefer a cognitively undemanding, rather than demanding, processing task.
- Test takers work in their processing capacity.

Therefore we presuppose no a priori established work domain in syntax and semantics. Categories in grammar books such as 'tense', 'pronominalisation', 'agreement', etc. do not constitute our major criteria of taxonomy.

1.3 Research questions

Previous research indicated that low-proficiency learners and high-proficiency learners have different proficiency structures (Sang, et al., 1986; Milanovic, 1988; Skehan, 1988; Tsuda & Yule, 1985; Upshur & Homburg, 1983) and use different cognitive strategies (Purpura, 1998). Suggestions were made that low-proficiency learners' reading ability was more strongly related to the meaning of individual words than to grammar (Upshur & Homburg, 1983; Absy, 1995; Holmes, 1987), which was supported by the existence of semantic processing strategy (Clark & Clark, 1977; VanPatten, 1996) in contrast with structural processing strategies (Frazier & Fodor, 1978; Frazier & Rayner, 1987; Rayner & Pollatsek, 1989; Frazier & Flores d'Arcais, 1989). Extending the arguments over the nature of the levels of proficiency, we postulate the first part of our research question as follows:

Q1. What is characteristic of the sentence parsing strategy of low-proficiency learners?

Sentence parsing ability is vital in reading and listening comprehension. Though it has a relatively small role in partial information retrieval (ie., skimming and scanning), it is indispensable for accurate understanding and fluent processing (Juffs & Harrington, 1995; Amma, 1984). If its relationship with overall proficiency is established we can confirm the phenomenon of underachievement in EFL learning. Recent studies in working memory suggest that the capacity and/or efficiency of working memory is a good predictor of success in second language reading (King & Just, 1991; Harrington & Sawyer, 1992; Osaka & Osaka, 1992; Miyake & Friedman, 1999; Walter, 2000). In particular, efficiency in low-level processing is said to be responsible for fluency and discourse inferences (Fowler, 1981; Payne & Holtzman, 1983; Gathercole & Baddeley, 1993; Kadota & Noro, 2001). Though the studies are mainly concerned with reading ability, we can assume that low-proficiency learners are under a stronger cognitive constraint in sentence parsing than high-proficiency learners are.

The second part of our research question is of methodological interest. If low-proficiency and high-proficiency learners have different proficiency structures, there must be a means of representing the difference in their parsing strategies. Since the boundary between low-proficiency and high-proficiency learners is not discrete, the representations must also be indiscrete. Hence

Q2. How is it possible to represent the characteristics of a sentence parsing strategy as a function of proficiency scale?

While the first question concerns learner characteristics, the second is to seek differential item functioning (DIF; cf. Ryan & Bachman, 1992; Swaminathan & Rogers, 1990) of test items. These two issues are mutually dependent; one's performance is low because of certain test items *or* some test items behave characteristically because of certain low-proficiency learners. We aim at finding the means of representing the test takers' interlanguage status. Once it is established, we can identify potential problems that a given learner may have in sentence processing if his/her proficiency measure is known.

In this research we are interested in how low-proficiency learners perceive and comprehend a sentence or sentence fragment. Although the quest deals with various problems of learners' performance, the emphasis is on the *process*, rather than on the *cause*, of comprehension errors.

1.4 Research design

This research is an attempt to characterise low-proficiency learners' performance in syntactic parsing. In particular we focus on cognitive constraints on parsing so that imperfect comprehension of test takers can be explained in terms of limitations in parsing strategy use. Appropriate use of parsing strategies and subsequent comprehension are the very foundation of receptive communication. We expect that what EFL teachers have vaguely understood by experience in teaching low-proficiency learners is objectively explained with substantial evidence. The results, if properly interpreted, will promote our understanding of the nature of language proficiency and language development, and will be beneficial for classroom feedback.

In order to achieve this, we conduct an experiment in the form of a grammaticality judgement test. Particular attention is paid to low-proficiency learners and their performance in the grammaticality judgement test. We expect that some cognitive constraint is operative more strongly among low-proficiency learners than among high-proficiency learners, and it should work behind the performance in certain test items of the same kind. In other words, a certain common feature among test items should be observed more clearly as the proficiency level lowers. Our experiment is an attempt to prove the existence of this common cognitive constraint and to predict its strength as the function of proficiency measure.

As the stimuli of the experiment, we prepare a list of sentences with various grammar violations. If test takers judge one sentence as grammatical and another also as grammatical, and if this tendency is observed more frequently among low-proficiency test takers than among high-proficiency test takers, it is possible that the low-proficiency test takers use a common strategy in grammaticality judgement. The initial classification of the stimuli is a working taxonomy, as we do not know yet what precisely is the nature of the cognitive constraint. Therefore a more strict characterisation of the cognitive constraint has to wait for the exploratory analysis of the data.

The analytical method of our research is basically exploratory. We collect data, identify common factors among responses in clusters, and interpret the factors. In our experiment identifying clusters is done by several statistical procedures: logistic regression, contingency table analysis, multidimensional scaling, and contour plot analysis. We shall describe them in the next section. The data so far are objective. In the next step we attempt to interpret the factors. The interpretation of the factors identified is the same process as a factor analysis technique; we compare stimuli in a cluster and find communality in terms of a cognitive constraint. In examples (1.1) and (1.2) we can tentatively assume that the test takers who judge these two stimuli as both 'correct' have a simplified comprehension strategy: 'as long as the goal ("swimming" and "shopping") is comprehensible and the preposition ("to") indicates an orientation for the goal, the sentences are grammatical.' In this case these test takers prefer semantic comprehension strategy to syntactic parsing strategy. If the same tendency is observed in other stimuli among the test takers of the same proficiency level, we can conclude that the semantic comprehension strategy is characteristic of these learners.

The interpretation of the factors is not the final goal of our research. Because interpretation is merely suggestive, we shall attempt to substantiate it in the confirmatory phase of analysis. We first classify the stimulus sentences into two categories as to whether or not each sentence contains a part which can be analysed by the parsing strategy we hypothesise. Then we compare the objective statistics of sentences representing the degrees of clustering between the two categories. If there is a significant difference between the two categories our hypothetical interpretation is maintained.

1.5 Overview of methodological framework

The participants were 1152 Japanese university students studying a wide range of academic subjects. They had studied English as a foreign language for 6–8 years. The choice of these students as experimental participants was meaningful in that after several years' study they had reached a point where the gap between high proficiency and low proficiency was widest and developmental effects were reduced to a minimum.

Our research consisted of two tests: a grammaticality judgement test used as a dependent variable, and a C-test used as an independent variable. The grammaticality judgement test was intended to collect the test takers' false judgement responses from which their parsing strategies were construed. A C-test was intended to measure the test takers' overall proficiency in English. Two tests put together, we could infer the characteristics of parsing strategies of the test takers at a given proficiency level.

Our analytical procedure followed several steps of statistical treatments.

i. A **logistic regression analysis** — enables one to predict the probability of categorical responses at a given point on a continuous scale. This analysis applies both to dichotomous data (as in true/false questions) and polytomous data (as in multiple-choice questions). It was used in our experiment to estimate the probabilities of occurrence of combined responses in all pairs of items. In each item in a multiple-choice format the response we focused on was either the one reflecting a cognitive constraint or any of the others.

ii. A 2x2 **contingency table analysis** — determines the degree of association between two categorical variables. The estimated probabilities which come from logistic regression analysis are used in this contingency table analysis. The result, in the form of a matrix of degrees of association between test items, tells us which items are strongly associated with others.

iii. A **multidimensional scaling analysis** — attempts to provide a two-dimensional solution of the plotting of test items based on a matrix of association measures. A plot of items may change as the proficiency level changes. Items that cluster together represent a meaningful common factor.

iv. A **contour plot analysis** — illustrates the depth or strength of items plotted on a two-dimensional space. We use association measures as the third variable, apart from horizontal and vertical location measures. We can observe the change of the strength of item clustering by the change of contours when the proficiency level changes.

1.6 Significance of research

Our research is significant in research and practice. So far, research on low-proficiency language learners has been rare. Likewise, attempts to develop structure tests that take into consideration those learners who cannot even comprehend target texts are virtually unknown. The result of our research is a first firm step to proposing a more reliable measure and framework in language testing as well as in second language research.

To be more illustrative, our research has potential implications in three directions. First, the probing of a cognitive constraint on learners will provide a deeper understanding of the nature of L2 (second language) development. If we can identify the sources of errors in learners' test performance, it will be made clear what characterises the different status of the learner language.

Secondly, our research will contribute to language testing in the validation of test items. Understanding potential pitfall factors in candidate test items can help us avoid incorrect estimation of learner performances. Test writers should always be aware that some test takers cannot comprehend the stimuli or respond to them properly because of cognitive constraints.

Thirdly, the result of our research will also benefit classroom teaching. We claim that there is a qualitative difference in the proficiency structure between low-proficiency learners and high-proficiency learners. If teachers realise what is lacking among low-proficiency learners, which high-proficiency learners already have, they can arrange a special programme for low-proficiency learners by providing practice for raising awareness of structure and for improving processing efficiency.

Chapter 2

Literature survey

This chapter introduces the literature relevant to our research questions. Because the focus of our research is the qualitative difference between high-proficiency learners and low-proficiency learners, it reviews and discusses the nature of the variability in proficiency. Our argument also deals with the factors that make the difference — processing strategies and capacity. Finally, we critically review the past practices in grammaticality judgement (GJ) tests. Based on an objective appraisal of the traditional framework, a new format in a GJ test is proposed.

   2.1 Proficiency
      2.1.1 Models of language proficiency
         2.1.1.1 Componential view
         2.1.1.2 Cognitive view
         2.1.1.3 Evaluation
      2.1.2 Variability in proficiency
         2.1.2.1 Dimensionality in language proficiency
         2.1.2.2 Indeterminacy
         2.1.2.3 Summative evaluation of variability in interlanguage
   2.2 Qualitative differences in performance between high-proficiency and low-proficiency learners
      2.2.1 Characteristics of 'poor language learners'
      2.2.2 Cognitive learning strategies
   2.3 Input processing strategies
      2.3.1 Semantic strategy

  2.3.2 Parsing strategy
 2.4 Memory and knowledge
  2.4.1 Working memory
  2.4.2 Long-term memory and other factors
 2.5 Test formats
  2.5.1 Grammaticality judgement
  2.5.2 Alternative formats in grammaticality judgement
  2.5.3 C-test
 2.6 Summary of literature review
 2.7 Hypotheses
  2.7.1 Setting up of hypotheses
  2.7.2 Steps of testing hypotheses

The first section on *proficiency* defines the premise of the current research. Attempts are made to clarify the nature of general language proficiency by comparing different views. Then based on our understanding of proficiency we discuss in the section of *qualitative differences* what proficient learners prefer to do in learning language. The knowledge of successful learners could lead to more efficient teaching/learning. The third and fourth topics, *input processing strategies* and *memory and knowledge*, are presented in relation to the mechanism of language processing: strategies and memory factors. We examine major causes for the difference in proficiency. Finally, we review the literature on data eliciting methods in *test format*. Here, we consider whether our two test formats are reliable and valid, and discuss how we can compensate for inadequacies. Then, following the accumulated knowledge of background studies we set up hypotheses corresponding to the research questions.

2.1 Proficiency

Discussions on what constitutes language proficiency have largely been overlooked, as researchers have been more attracted by organisational models of language (Bachman, 1990). There are two views concerning the notion of proficiency. A **componental** view attempts to define the construct of proficiency in terms of the repertoire of competences as potential abilities that an idealised language user has. In other words, it describes what is included in language proficiency. On the other hand, a **cognitive** view reflects on learners' cognitive factors/environment and attempts to define language proficiency in terms of the achievement of language use.

Apart from theoretical constructs, a psychometrical interest has been focused on what can be identified as language proficiency. Early research from the 1920s to 1970s by Thurstone, Carroll, Guildford, Spearman, and other psychologists was interested in identifying a single mental structure and language proficiency was part of it. Oller's Unitary Competence Hypothesis (Oller, 1979, 1983) was basically on the same continuum. The past two decades saw the proliferation of psychological models. Language science was no exception. In language testing, in particular, we have moved from a unitary proficiency view to a multidimensional, multifaceted view of proficiency structure. We shall summarise the arguments concerning dimensionality and variability in L2.

2.1.1 Models of language proficiency
2.1.1.1 Componential view

A landmark in applied linguistics, Canale & Swain (1980) are still the central figures in the study of communicative competence. They clearly stated the need to establish the rules of language behaviour which would no longer be restricted to the syntactic rules in theoretical linguistics. Much emphasis was laid on sociological aspects of language use. The conditions for successful communication must include such factors as situational appropriateness of speech, background knowledge of the world, and rules of communication. Their model of communicative competence comprised three kinds of competence:

1. Grammatical competence
2. Sociolinguistic competence
3. Strategic competence

Grammatical competence means knowledge of lexical items and rules of morphology, syntax, sentence-grammar semantics, and phonology (p.29). *Sociolinguistic competence* includes two subcomponents: *Sociocultural* and *Discourse rules*. *Sociocultural rules* deal with appropriateness of language use, eg., topic, setting, attitude, and register. *Discourse rules* are sensitive to cohesion and coherence. *Strategic competence*, alias communication strategy, is required when communication breaks down due to the incompetence in the language being spoken. It consists of verbal and nonverbal strategies that help overcome the communication gap, eg., paraphrasing, coinage, gesture, and abandoning.

Canale (1983a) slightly modified this model. Stressing the need to separate two distinct features of the *Sociolinguistic competence* in Canale & Swain (1980), he proposed a new framework:

1. Grammatical competence
2. Sociolinguistic competence
3. Discourse competence
4. Strategic competence

His new *Sociolinguistic competence* referred to the mastery of appropriate use and understanding of language in sociocultural contexts (p.7), and *Discourse competence* referred to the mastery of the unity of texts, namely, cohesion and coherence.

Bachman's (1990) whole work was devoted to the construction of the model of communicative competence and its measurement. His model included the following components (Table 2.1).

[Table 2.1: Bachman's model of communicative competence (after Bachman, 1990: 85, 87)]

Strategic competence
    Assessment component
    Planning component
    Execution component
Language competence (knowledge of language)
    Organizational competence
        Grammatical competence (vocabulary, morphology, syntax, phonology/graphology)
        Textual competence (cohesion, rhetorical organization)
    Pragmatic competence
        Illocutionary competence (ideational function, manipulative function, heuristic function, imaginative function)
        Sociolinguistic competence (sensitivity to differences in dialect or variety, sensitivity to differences in register, sensitivity to naturalness, ability to interpret cultural references and figures of speech)
Knowledge structures (knowledge of the world)
Psychophysiological mechanisms
Context of situation

Compared with Canale & Swain's (1980) model, components were arranged more rationally so that theoretical doubts were cleared. First of all, *Grammatical competence* along with *Textual competence* came under *Organizational competence*. This made a clear demarcation of both domains. Secondly, Canale & Swain's *Sociolinguistic competence* was renamed as *Pragmatic competence* which included various functions under *Illocutionary competence*. Thirdly, *Strategic competence* became independent of *Language competence*, as it dealt with communication strategies. This view was a development of Canale (1983a). Finally, para- and non-linguistic features such as *Psychophysiological mechanisms*, *Knowledge structures*, and *Context of situation* came newly into the domain of communicative ability in a wider sense. This enabled us to consider the effect of cultural background, for instance, on the performance in communication or tests.

More recent models of language competence take into account the sociological consequence of language use. McNamara (1996) presented a performance-based model of language assessment. He contended that a valid assessment of a candidate's proficiency is represented by an actual performance of a task which is measured by a rating scale (Figure 2.1)

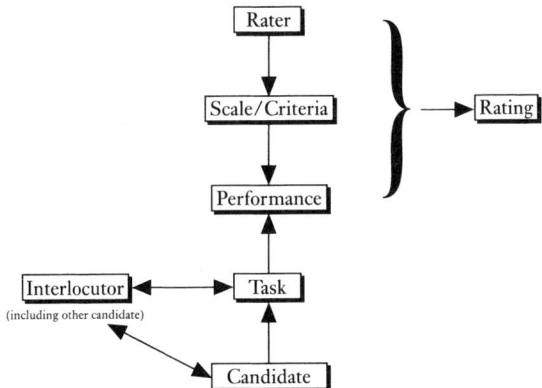

[Figure 2.1: Candidate's 'proficiency' and its relation to performance (McNamara, 1996: 86)]

In his model we understand that the result of an assessment is always relative; the degree of candidate performance is affected by the task difficulty, and the assessment of the quality of performance is affected by the rater's criterion. This was an interesting and useful model of language assessment. Even in a written syntax test, which we focus on in our main research, the model predicted that the test takers' performance is a result of the interaction between their internal proficiency and task difficulty, and is also a result of the norms and expectations of test writer/developer.

We should be aware, however, that there is a conceptual gap between proficiency as inherent to test takers and proficiency as assessed by raters, which is parallel to the contrast between a static view and dynamic view of proficiency. Performance of a task alone, according to McNamara, is an interaction between the candidate 'proficiency' and task difficulty. What we need in our current research context is the identification of proficiency as static, inherent quality of test takers' constant potential capability. Proficiency, in this sense, does not imply the full-fledged theoretical model of native speaker competence, either. Whereas competence is an exhaustive inventory of what an ideal speaker is capable of doing, proficiency denotes the degree to which an individual test taker performs in an idealised, standardised task. In other words, competence is a universal model within the language, whereas proficiency pertains to test takers' individual quality.

Under the definition of proficiency as representing the degree of achievement in the target language use, it is reasonable to assume two aspects of proficiency which would delimit our scope of discussion. First, the actual performance is the result of the interaction between the test taker's proficiency and the difficulty of the target task. We cannot correctly estimate the test taker's proficiency without considering the task difficulty, and vice versa (Henning, 1987). According to the Item Response Theory, a test taker's ability is comparable to the difficulty of test items on the same scale. That is, one is 50% likely to respond correctly when his/her estimated ability measure is equal to the difficulty measure of the item.

Second, when we say someone is high or low in proficiency, we normally refer to other candidates who took the same test. This is the *synchronic* aspect of proficiency; one is good or poor at a language test in reference to the rest of the test takers — *at a certain point of time*. On the other hand, the same person's proficiency may improve or wane *in the course of time*. This is the *diachronic* aspect of proficiency. Ingram (1985) pointed out that development in proficiency is intrapersonal by nature, and thus ASLPR (Australian Second Language Proficiency Rating) was based on this developmental view of learner language. Despite the fact that synchronic (or cross-sectional) differences among individuals appear parallel to diachronic (or developmental) differences (cf. the use of semantic strategy in Section 2.3.1), we shall keep the two constructs apart, since we cannot ignore non-developmental language learning factors such as aptitude, motivation, and learning style which may affect the performance in language use, and deal with the cross-sectional aspect of proficiency alone.

2.1.1.2 Cognitive view

In contrast with these componential views, Cummins (1983), Canale (1983b), and Sang, et al. (1986) presented a cognitive view of language ability. Cummins (1983) developed his previous model of BICS (basic interpersonal communicative skills) and CALP (cognitive/academic language proficiency), and proposed a new set of dimensions, namely, contextual embedding and cognitive demand (Figure 2.2):

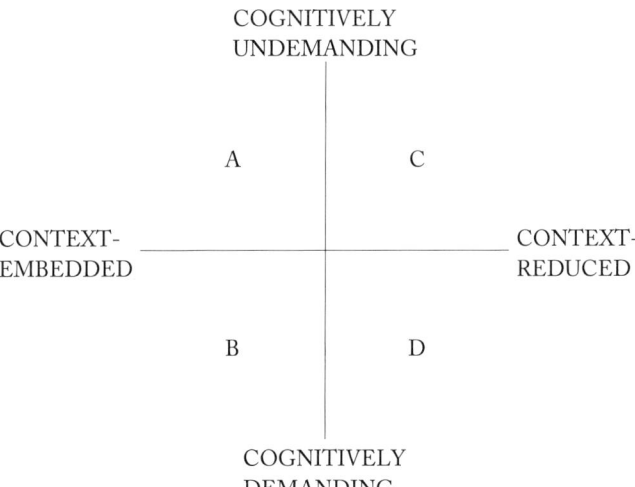

[Figure 2.2: Range of contextual support and degree of cognitive involvement in communicative activities (after Cummins, 1983: 120)]

The horizontal axis represents a situational variation. From left to right, one's recourse to context decreases, eg., from interpersonal communication in which non- and para-linguistic elements play an important role, to academic reading or writing in which "linguistic message must be elaborated precisely" (p.120). The vertical continuum represents the development of language. The same amount of linguistic information is processed with much demand when the language is at a primary stage, but it becomes less burden as one can manage the language automatically (from bottom to top).

Canale (1983b) and Sang, et al. (1986) presented a proficiency-oriented view. In Canale (1983b) three levels of proficiency were proposed:

1. Basic language proficiency
2. Communicative language proficiency
3. Autonomous language proficiency

In Canale's framework, *Basic language proficiency* is the product of universal development in biological and linguistic faculties such as grammatical competence, sociolinguistic universals, discourse universals, strategic universals, and perceptual/processing universals (p.339). *Communicative language proficiency* refers to the social, interpersonal uses of language with sociolinguistic knowledge and skills as its kernel. *Autonomous language proficiency* deals with intrapersonal (unlike sociolinguistic language proficiency which is interpersonal) uses of language with grammatical competence and discourse and strategic competences as the main body. Both *Communicative* and *Autonomous proficiencies* require basic proficiency in part, and the rest derives from contribution of individual differences in personality, intelligence, learning style, motivation, and so on.

Sang, et al. (1986) assumed three levels: *elementary, complex*, and *communicative*. As one goes up the level (although it does not necessarily mean development) solid, homogeneous elements of proficiency become integrated into an organic performance. *Elementary level* deals with basic static knowledge such as pronunciation, spelling, and lexis. *Complex level* is concerned with integration of the basic knowledge so that grammar, reading, listening, etc. are managed. *Communicative level* commands interactive use of language (cf. Skehan, 1988, 1989).

2.1.1.3 Evaluation

We have observed basically two orientations in describing of language ability: (1) a componential view, as in Canale & Swain (1980), Bachman (1990), and McNamara (1996) which incorporated both knowledge of language and language use, though emphasis varied, and (2) a cognitive view, as in Cummins (1983), in which one's language performance is an interaction of contextual demand and his cognitive capacity; a level-oriented view, as in Canale (1983b) and Sang, et al. (1986), which regarded that the degree to which learner's command of language approaches to perfection should represent qualitatively unique ability.

In the interest of our current research, the componential view provides the knowledge of target language skills. In particular, *grammatical competence* (and in part *textual competence*) is exclusively relevant to a test-taking situation. The problems with this view are (i) the models are knowledge-based, ie., they imply that an individual is grammatically competent if that person has the knowledge of grammar, (ii) the models are synthetic, ie., no further subcomponents of grammatical competence can be analysed, and (iii) the models are theory-oriented, ie., no empirical data are provided for confirming or disconfirming the models. When we assume an effect of cognitive constraint on grammatical performance, the componential view does not provide any explanations. On the other hand, the cognitive view appears to fit our research orientation because of its reference to proficiency levels and individual differences. Our task therefore is to develop this view in a test-taking situation and incorporate our findings in the model.

In summary, we adopt the notion of proficiency as denoting the extent of individual learners' achievement of a language task. It is constant quality inherent to learners. The actual performance as a reflection of individual proficiency can vary depending on the task difficulty and other people's achievement, and it can also vary as one's language develops through interlanguage stages. Though McNamara's model has a universal appeal, the notion of *ability for use* (Hymes, 1972) in the socio-cultural context and the factor of an interaction between test takers and tasks/raters have a minor influence on the performance in grammaticality judgement.

2.1.2 Variability in proficiency
2.1.2.1 Dimensionality in language proficiency
Dimensionality concerns whether the variation in a given psychological construct, or syntactic proficiency in our context, is represented by a single scale or by mixed scales. As a premise of our discussion it is important to distinguish psychological dimensionality from psychometric dimensionality. According to Henning (1992: 2), psychological dimensionality reflects psychological constructs one assumes in the entire educational programme. Hence it is

sample independent. Psychometric dimensionality, on the other hand, is a data-driven, sample/item dependent concept. Like internal consistency it appears even when the corresponding psychological construct is not present.

Whether a test performance shows uni-dimensionality or multi-dimensionality was studied by a number of first/second language researchers and proficiency test developers. Oltman, Sticker, & Barrows (1988), for example, examined the dimensionality in TOEFL. The results indicated that there are three dimensions corresponding to the three test components plus an 'end of the test' factor, ie., how far the test taker reaches the last item. A greater dimensional differentiation was observed among low-proficiency examinees. Milanovic (1988) reached a similar conclusion, maintaining that a multifactor solution best explains the performance of low-proficiency learners.

Whether a test performance shows uni-dimensionality or multi-dimensionality is not only a matter of test takers' performance; it is also affected by item construction. If some items question the knowledge/skill that only test takers with a special interest or experience have, the entire test will yield low internal consistency and turn out to be multidimensional. Ryan & Bachman (1992) investigated differential item functioning (DIF) against speakers of various native language background. Using Mantel-Haenszel procedure (Mantel & Haenszel, 1959; Holland & Thayer, 1988) they indicated that some of TOEFL and Cambridge FCE items bore distinct DIF in favour of either an Indo-European language group or a non-Indo-European language group. Although they assumed that the performance was even across different ability levels, they expected that, since L1 influenced most at the early stages of L2 development, the DIF would be greater at a lower level than at a higher level. Their participants who took TOEFL showed three dimensions corresponding to three test components plus one dimension of 'end of the test' factor.

2.1.2.2 Indeterminacy

In what way are low-proficiency learners inefficient? Although they make errors in test performance, which causes them to be assessed as low in proficiency, these are errors from the point of view of those who mastered the target language tasks. 'Errors', instead, may simply be a reflection of their current interlanguage system.

Despite the vast accumulation of research in traditional error analyses or interlanguage studies (Corder, 1967, 1981; Schachter & Celce-Murcia, 1971;

Selinker, 1972; Richards, 1974; Schachter, 1974, 1983=1992; Richards & Rogers, 1986; Tarone, 1988; cf. James, 1998 for an overview of the past and present research), the mechanism of individual errors in *reception* has not been investigated at large. The interest of the researchers involved in errors lies mostly in the source of errors and means of remedy in *production*. Here we focus on receptive indeterminacy as one aspect of interlanguage variability.

Some researchers claimed that L2 was indeterminate and therefore liable to errors by nature (Sorace, 1990; Schachter, Tyson, & Diffley, 1976; Arthur, 1980; Gass, 1983; Dušková, 1983; Coppieters, 1987; Johnson, et al., 1996). Oxford (1993a) pointed out that learners' individual differences were caused by the variety of language learning styles. Also, the use of language learning strategies was said to vary according to individual learners (Bremner, 1999) and cultural/ethnic preference (Sheorey, 1999). According to Sorace (1990: 137–138), interlanguage grammar is (1) indeterminate in the initial stage simply because it is incomplete, (2) stable in the intermediate stage, and (3) indeterminate again at a more advanced stage because reconstruction of grammatical knowledge is triggered. Therefore, "it is entirely plausible to assume that the temporary loss of determinacy of a given construction also involves a decrease in the learner's ability to express a definite acceptability judgement about it" (p.138). Focusing on relatively advanced learners alone, she claimed, one finds a statistically significant deviation and variation of nonnative speaker judgements from native speaker judgements. "This suggests, ... that the two groups of informants may have developed significantly different competence grammars for French, despite the fact that they express the same judgements of grammaticality and are nearly indistinguishable in production" (pp.138–139).

However, this indeterminacy may be characteristic of the test procedure she used: dichotomous grammaticality judgement. Normally, the dimensionality of a test decreases as a test taker's proficiency rises. Amma (1997) showed a significant difference in variance of factor scores between upper-level and lower-level participants of a multiple choice grammar test ($F = 117.28$, $p < 0.001$ for factor 1; $F = 80.19$, $p < 0.001$ for factor 2; and $F = 34.30$, $p < 0.001$ for factor 3). The third-dimension factor score plots of individual test takers in the upper level converged into a small cluster, while those of test takers in the lower level diverged widely apart. This result is in agreement with other observations (Sang, et al., 1986; Milanovic, 1988; Oltman, Sticker, & Barrows, 1988).

Apart from the general tendency of indeterminacy, the observation and analysis of individual parsing errors had not been systematically carried out. Among few such studies Amma (2001) reported typical parsing errors of Japanese university students in an EFL syntactic proficiency test. In general, low-proficiency learners tended to (1) rely on the meaning of content words in comprehending stimulus sentences, (2) use an early closure strategy, and (3) avoid complicated structures. However, his data derived partly from multiple-choice judgement in the form of uncontrolled paraphrases and partly from dichotomous grammaticality judgement, neither of which are now considered as having high reliability and validity (Section 3.1.1.4).

2.1.2.3 Summative evaluation of variability in interlanguage

So far we have discussed the fundamental issue of our research: variability among learners. Through the attempts to seek dimensionality in language proficiency, we can conclude that it depends on how much consideration we take into varying factors. The key seems to lie in the question of how the factors are organised. Sorace's (1990) indication about indeterminacy is quite suggestive in this context. If, as she says, variability in interlanguage is mostly random errors, the quest for multidimensional factors will end up in vain. However, if we introduce a new analytical methodology in consideration of cognitive constraints, we may obtain systematic error factors among low-proficiency learners.

2.2 Qualitative differences in performance between high-proficiency and low-proficiency learners

As stated in Chapter 1, our ultimate goal is to describe the qualitative difference between high-proficiency and low-proficiency learners. Before discussing the mechanical issues in Sections 2.3 and 2.4, we shall first review the research in the behavioural aspects of these learners. In both studies in 'good language learners' and studies in cognitive strategies the main concern is what high-proficiency learners do or choose to do. Whether controllable factors such as motivation and attitude can have a positive influence on the 'given' capacity (eg. working memory) is unknown, but we can extract effective teaching/learning orientations from these studies.

2.2.1 Characteristics of 'poor language learners'

Despite a number of studies of 'good language learners' (Stern, 1975, 1976; Rubin, 1975; Reves, 1978; Naiman, et al., 1978=1995; Cohen, 1987; Chamot, 1987; Mollica & Nuessel, 1997), there have been virtually no systematic studies of low-proficiency learners. Among the former studies, it became gradually popular to consider individual differences that might override the uniform characteristics (Nation & McLaughlin, 1986; Skehan, 1989; Rees-Miller, 1993). Ridley (1997), for example, claimed that 'good language learner' was not a single construct. She observed that her three university-level novice learners of German as a foreign language developed different patterns of language skills which were influenced by the success/failure experience in their previous foreign languages.

Sang, et al. (1986) found that high-proficiency learners marked higher correlations between the subtests of their test battery, while low-proficiency learners marked lower correlations in the same tests. According to their model, integration and interaction of ability elements were the characteristics of the communicative level. The research results meant that the upper-level participants had more integrated proficiency. Skehan (1988) reported Milanovic's (1988) research which indicated that multidimensional factors were found with lower-level participants while fewer dimensions were assigned to upper-level participants. Skehan (1988: 213) summarised the above two phenomena:

> It would seem, to generalise about these results, that with instructed students, higher levels of proficiency have a more integrated structure, with the different skills coming together, either because of the cumulative effects of instruction itself, or because of the inherent qualities of acquisitional processes, or perhaps because of the way different abilities can compensate for one another at higher levels.

Ingram (1985) highlighted a contrast between ESL learners and EFL learners. The ESL learners who received fluency-oriented teaching in Australia marked a high correlation between communicative tests and structure-based tests. The EFL learners, on the other hand, who received code-oriented teaching in China marked a low correlation for the same tests. This fact indicated that ESL learners had more balanced and integrated proficiency. High-proficiency learners, in this sense, appeared to be closer to ESL learners than to EFL learners.

On the other hand, studies of 'poor language learners' are scarce. It is much more difficult to detect the factors of learners' low performance than to discuss the factors of high performance. As we go up on the proficiency scale the factors of success converge, and eventually reach the native-like status in which the learners are equally proficient (Sang, et al., 1986). In contrast, as we go down on the proficiency scale the factors of partial success diverge, because each individual learner has different problems ranging widely in vocabulary, grammar, pronunciation, communication strategy, background knowledge, and so on (Amma, 1997: 114–117).

Upshur & Homburg (1983) in their attempt to verify the subfactors found the relationships between reading, grammar, and vocabulary for different levels of ability. They calculated the path coefficients of grammar and vocabulary upon reading (Figure 2.3). Path coefficient represents the influence of one component upon another. In Table 2.2, P_{RG} indicates the influence of grammar upon reading, and P_{RV} indicates the influence of vocabulary upon reading.

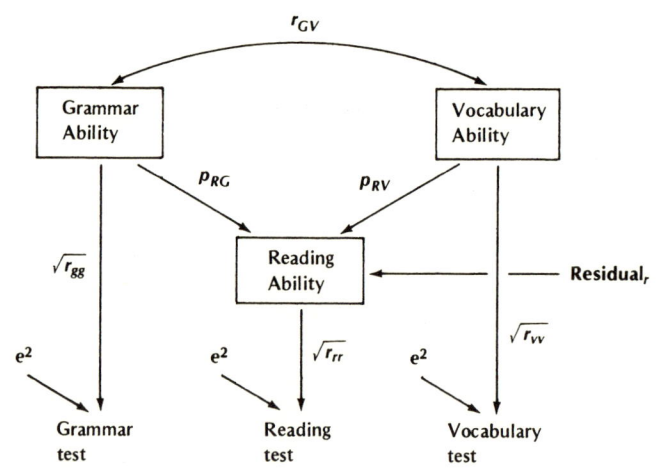

[Figure 2.3: Simplified causal model with 3 ability variables (Upshur & Homburg, 1983: 199)]

[Table 2.2: Path coefficients in simplified causal model with 3 ability variables (after Upshur & Homburg, 1983: 199)]

	Path coefficient	
Sample	P_{RG}	P_{RV}
Total	.35	.46
Level 5 (low)	.26	.62
Level 6	.26	.45
Level 7	.45	.27
Level 8 (high)	.55	.30

Table 2.2 shows that lower-level subjects tend to rely more on vocabulary than on grammar, while higher-level subjects tend to use more grammatical judgment than vocabulary knowledge. The authors remarked: "... at lower ability levels most of the comprehension of a text depends upon knowledge of the meanings of content words employed in the text" (p.199). Further, "in order [for low-ability readers] to achieve fuller comprehension of the text, something which higher-ability readers can do, grammatical knowledge must be relied upon to provide relationships among concepts which cannot be simply or unambiguously inferred" (p.200).

Looking at the methodological aspect of these studies, we find that there are two kinds of limitations. Firstly, most of the studies of 'good language learners' were based on 'self-descriptive' data (Cohen, 1987); information was obtained by introspective questionnaires or by think-aloud protocol. Hence, they tended to fall short of accuracy, especially when researchers had to consider the verbal expressions by the low-proficiency learners who may not be good at verbalising their internalised thoughts. Few involved a solid measurement of learner behaviours (cf. Purpura, 1998, for an exception). Secondly, language educators discussed learner characteristics in terms of cognitive and/or metacognitive strategies that learners use. These were global strategies that applied to learning a target language as a whole. Meanwhile, cognitive psychologists were more interested in parsing strategies that applied to particular milieux of problem-solving tasks in reading. What judgement learners actually make in taking a test has not been widely discussed. For example, Reiss (1983) focused on unsuccessful language learners but after reviewing major articles she merely showed a direction of aids for them by proposing (1) using good learners as tutors, and (2) giving practices of think-aloud techniques.

In sum, the general finding was that high-proficiency or successful learners command a wide range of language learning tasks and skills and as a result their language performance is close to unidimensionality. On the other hand, performance of low-proficiency learners is not explained by the factors applied to high-proficiency learners. Further research is required in identifying the actual mechanism of variability factors influencing low-proficiency learners' performance.

2.2.2 Cognitive learning strategies

One possible source of variability in low-proficiency learners' performance is cognitive orientation; their judgement may be affected by particular learning strategies and in turn by the psychological principles that operate when dealing with memory, attention, inference, and other tasks in learning.

Studies of strategy use in second and foreign language learning sprang in the 1980s to 1990s (Rubin, 1981, 1987; O'Malley & Chamot, 1990; Oxford, 1990, 1993b; Wenden, 1987, 1991; Faustino, 1996). Use of language learning strategies was predominantly observed both in L1 and in L2 (Palacios-Martinez, 1995; Simmons, 1996; Scevak & Moore, 1997). Numerous articles appeared discussing the close relationship between cognitive/metacognitive strategy use and target language proficiency (Ehrman & Oxford, 1990; Carrell, 1991; Oxford, et al., 1993; Flaitz, et al., 1995; Green & Oxford, 1995; Oxford & Ehrman, 1995; Taillefer, 1996; Lin & Hedgcock, 1996; Goh & Foong, 1997; Park, 1997; Sheorey, 1999; Kojic-Sabo & Lightbrown, 1999; Mochizuki, 1999; Halbach, 2000). Some also indicated the application of strategy use to language teaching (Chamot, 1990; Moran, 1991; Wenden, 1987, 1991; Oxford, 1992; Mohammed, 1993; Ayaduray & Jacobs, 1997; Heffernan, 1998). The validity of language learning strategies were examined statistically (Nyikos & Oxford, 1993; Oxford & Burry-Stock, 1995). While mental disposition such as motivation was considered the drive for cognitive strategy use (Guthrie, et al., 1996; MacIntyre & Noels, 1996), psychological constraints such as holistic/analytic processing styles were indicated as part of the cognitive style difference (Littlemore, 1995).

Among recent works Purpura (1998) was most objective, falsifiable, and therefore psychometrically valid. Purpura focused on the effect of cognitive/metacognitive (learning) strategy use on latent SLTP (second language test performance) variables. His participants, 1382 Cambridge FCE test takers in Spain, Turkey, and Czech Republic, were divided into three ability groups: High (N = 234) where the total score was between 34 to 60, and Low (N = 941) where the total score was between 2 to 22. The middle group (15% of the total population) was discarded. The participants took FCE Anchor Test and answered the questionnaire on their cognitive and metacognitive strategy use. The results (Figures 2.4a and 2.4b) indicated that (1) metacognitive strategy use showed small but significant effect on lexico-grammatical ability, reading ability, and cloze with the low-ability group, whereas no effect with the high-ability group (p.371). Low-proficiency test takers used more metacognitive strategies than high-proficiency test takers, because the latter "have achieved a higher degree of automatization, thereby having less of a need to use strategies" (p.374). Moreover, (2) "The effect of the retrieval processes on lexicogrammatical ability was also variant across the two groups" (p.374). But this second finding is dubious, because the loadings were only slightly different (High: 0.659; Low: 0.666). Purpura concluded that "high- and low-ability learners invoke different strategies to read" (p.370).

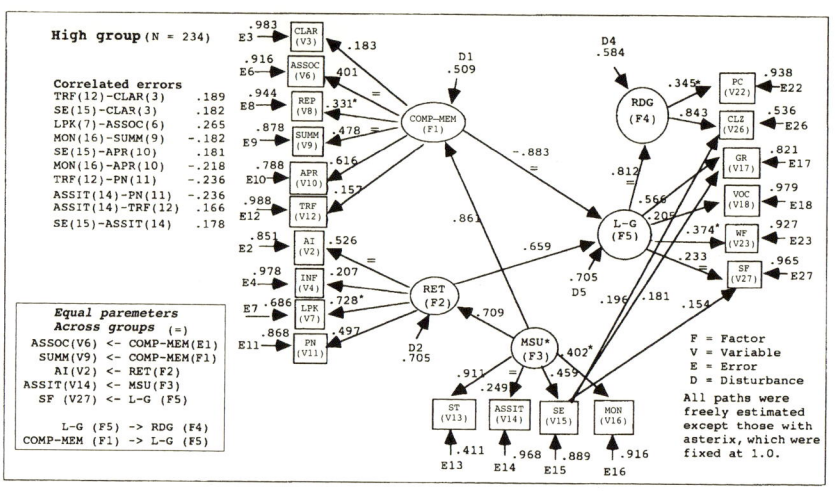

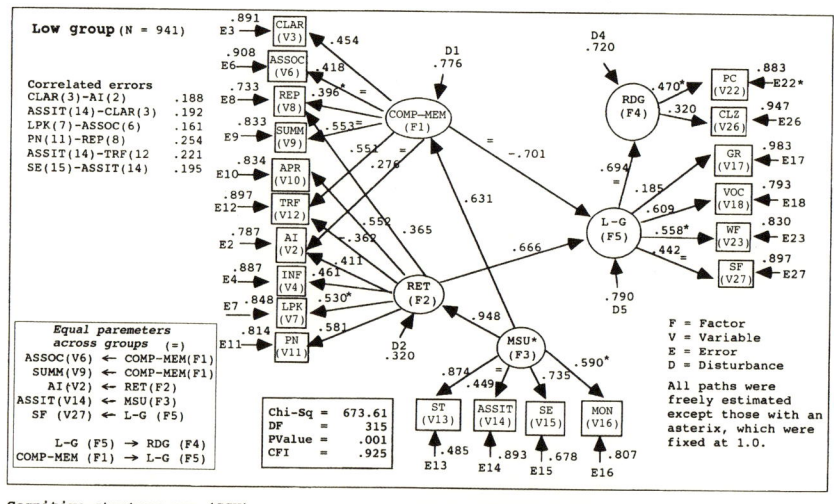

High group (N = 234)

Correlated errors
TRF(12)-CLAR(3) .189
SE(15)-CLAR(3)   .182
LPK(7)-ASSOC(6) .265
MON(16)-SUMM(9) -.182
SE(15)-APR(10)   .181
MON(16)-APR(10) -.218
TRF(12)-PN(11) -.236
ASSIT(14)-PN(11) -.236
ASSIT(14)-TRF(12) .166
SE(15)-ASSIT(14) .178

Equal parameters
Across groups (=)
ASSOC(V6) <- COMP-MEM(E1)
SUMM(V9) <- COMP-MEM(F1)
AI(V2) <- RET(F2)
ASSIT(V14) <- MSU(F3)
SF(V27) <- L-G (F5)

L-G (F5) -> RDG (F4)
COMP-MEM (F1) -> L-G (F5)

F = Factor
V = Variable
E = Error
D = Disturbance

All paths were freely estimated except those with asterix, which were fixed at 1.0.

Low group (N = 941)

Correlated errors
CLAR(3)-AI(2)   .188
ASSIT(14)-CLAR(3) .192
LPK(7)-ASSOC(6) .161
PN(11)-REP(8)   .254
ASSIT(14)-TRF(12) .221
SE(15)-ASSIT(14) .195

Equal parameters
across groups (=)
ASSOC(V6) <- COMP-MEM(F1)
SUMM(V9) <- COMP-MEM(F1)
AI(V2) <- RET(F2)
ASSIT(V14) <- MSU(F3)
SF(V27) <- L-G (F5)

L-G (F5) -> RDG (F4)
COMP-MEM (F1) -> L-G (F5)

Chi-Sq = 673.61
DF   = 315
PValue = .001
CFI   = .925

F = Factor
V = Variable
E = Error
D = Disturbance

All paths were freely estimated except those with an asterix, which were fixed at 1.0.

Cognitive strategy use (CSU)
AI   = Analysing inductively
CLAR   = Clarifying/Verifying
ASSOC   = Associating
REP   = Repeating/Rehearsing
SUMM   = Summarizing
TRF   = Transferring
INF   = Inferencing
LPK   = Linking sith prior knowledge
APR   = Applying rules
PN   = Practising naturalistically
COMP-MEM = Comprehending and memory processes
RET   = Retrieval processes

Metacognitive strategy use (MSU)
ASSIT = Assessing the situation
MON   = Monitoring
SE   = Self-evaluating
ST   = Self-testing

Second Foreign language test performance (SLTP)
RDG = Reading ability
L-M = Lexico-grammatical ability
PC = Passage comprehension
CLZ = Cloze
GR = Grammar
VOC = Vocabulary
WE = Word formation
SF = Sentence formation

[Figures 2.4a (above) and 2.4b (below): Structural equation modelling representations of cognitive and metacognitive use in relation with SLTP performance among high-ability group (above) and low-ability group (below)(Purpura, 1998: 360-361). 'L-M' and 'WE' in the legend should read 'L-G' and 'WF', respectively.]

A closer examination of his data reveals another interpretation. First, the low-proficiency group was disproportionately larger than the high-proficiency group. Although the boundary score was based on the FCE cut-off score, it was not psychometrically validated, if it was psychologically. As a result, the low-proficiency group may have included nonhomogeneous test takers. Second, the latent variable *L-G* (lexico-grammatical ability) had larger loadings on vocabulary, word formation, and sentence formation, but a smaller loading on syntax with the low-proficiency group (Figure 2.4b) than with the high-proficiency group (Figure 2.4a). Here *L-G* should be interpreted more as *rule application* than in terms of Purpura's unhelpful label. Purpura's results suggested that the use of *L-G* is different between the two groups; the high-proficiency test takers are more involved in syntactic processing whereas the low-proficiency test takers tend to use more of vocabulary and idiomatic information. This view is partially supported by another fact that with high-proficiency test takers there was a strong connection between *L-G* and *RDG* (reading ability) (0.812) and between *RDG* and cloze (0.843). On the other hand, with low-proficiency test takers *L-G* was relatively weakly connected to *RDG* (0.694) and *RDG* even more weakly to cloze (0.320), but more strongly to passage comprehension (0.470). The local picture concerning *RDG* would suggest that reading involves a rule-oriented and analytic process more significantly with high-proficiency test takers than with low-proficiency test takers.

In the interest of our research issues, Purpura's observation that low-proficiency learners depended less on rule application strategy than high-proficiency learners did was consistent with the previous studies in language variability. The other observation that low-proficiency learners used more metacognitive strategies than high-proficiency learners seems to bear little relevance to the current research, because it involves basically attitudinal factors. They are a natural source of motivation among beginning-level learners. The picture may change when the learners are unwilling to learn, which is often true with low-proficiency learners.

2.3 Input processing strategies

In this section we shall focus on the strategies learners take in comprehending language input. Our particular emphasis is on the analysis of sentence structures. We take for granted that the ability to analyse a sentence correctly is the basis for receptive accuracy and fluency. If there are individual differences in this analytical ability it will predict in part the success/failure of language learning. The problem, then, is what causes the individual differences.

2.3.1 Semantic strategy

Early in 1977 Clark & Clark (1977) paid attention to how syntactic and semantic information are used in comprehending language. They discussed that native speakers used both syntactic and semantic strategies (pp.59–79). Here are some examples.

> **Strategy 1: Use of function words**
> Whenever you find a function word, begin a new constituent larger than one word.
> **Strategy 2: Anticipating content words**
> After identifying the beginning of a constituent, look for content words appropriate to that type of constituent.
> **Strategy 5: Memory load**
> Try to attach each new word to the constituent that came just before.
> **Strategy 8: Making sense of sentences**
> Using content words alone, build propositions that make sense and parse the sentence into constituents accordingly.
> **Strategy 9: Anticipating constituents**
> Look for constituents that fit the semantic requirements of the propositional function that underlies each verb, adjective, adverb, preposition, and noun.

The first three in this list are syntactic strategies. One makes use of syntactic information in order to analyse and identify a linguistic unit. This view had a long history starting with 'perceptual strategy' (cf. Bever, 1970), but the approach did not reach the detailed description of the syntactic phenomenon that theoretical linguistics had clarified (Clark & Clark: 71–72). A more serious problem was that it took for granted the syntactic role of each word. Take their Strategy 2f (complements) for example, which denoted 'After identifying a complementizer, look for a sentence (as in "Mary knew that I left").' The strategy implied a sequential analysis of the input. Nevertheless the identification of "that" as a complimentiser required the syntactic configuration of the whole sentence. This pseudo-ambiguity led to the difficulty of processing so-called garden-path sentences such as

(2.1) The horse raced past the barn fell.
(2.2) The dealer offered two dollars for the painting refused to sell.

(Clark & Clark: 67) in which one has to reanalyse the sentence when he/she has reached a contradictory point. Clark & Clark did not mention any of such super strategies.

Strategies 8 and 9 are examples of semantic strategies. In particular, Strategy 8 is of great relevance to our research. Clark & Clark argued that the nature of language comprehension was not mechanical; it was not necessarily determined solidly by rigid parsing strategies, but rather it incorporated various *useful* information sources, including semantics as well as syntax. As evidence of this approach they quoted Stolz's (1967) experiment in which the participants were asked to paraphrase two types of double embedded sentences:

(2.3) The vase that the maid that the agency hired dropped broke on the floor.
(2.4) The dog that the cat that the girl fought scolded approached the colt.

Despite the same syntactic structure (2.3) was more correctly paraphrased than (2.4), because in the former one could easily distinguish the semantic role of each word (Clark & Clark: 73). As another piece of evidence they mentioned the developmental strategy use among children. Three-year-olds do not distinguish the semantic roles of a sentence whether it is active or passive (with the actor and object positions *not* reversed), while five-year-olds correctly understand the sentence as they recognise the function words (Clark & Clark: 74).

Similarly, VanPatten (1996: 14) emphasised the importance of semantic information of content words in his input processing principles:

Principle 1:
   (a) Learners process content words in the input before anything else.
   (b) Learners prefer processing lexical items to grammatical items for semantic information.

(c) Learners prefer processing "more meaningful" morphology before "less or non-meaningful" morphology.

In Section 2.4.2 we shall refer to the experiments supporting his meaning-oriented model.

2.3.2 Parsing strategy

Parsing strategy, or how a reader recognises the syntactic structure of a sentence, is of our major interest. Deficiency or inefficiency in parsing causes a delay of comprehension and possibly misunderstanding, resulting in low performance on a syntax test. Parsing strategies were much discussed among psycholinguists in the 1970s and 1980s. Early in 1970s, it was known that cognitive styles such as impulsivity/reflectivity might affect reading skills, the former being more associated with recognition errors (Kagan & Kogan, 1970). Bever (1970) proposed the first model of perceptual strategies based on psychological constraints. He maintained that perception of syntactic structures was influenced by psychologically rational principles. For example, the sequence of noun, verb, and noun tended to be perceived by default as agent, action, and object. Yet his statements were too general and weak to arouse subsequent experiments and discussions. However, attempts were made to pursue universal psychological properties which were operative in language processing (Clancy, Lee, & Zoh, 1986; Frenck-Mestre & Pynte, 1997), and in particular, reading (Frazier & Rayner, 1987; Rayner & Pollatsek, 1989; Frazier & Flores d'Arcais, 1989). Juffs & Harrington (1995) indicated that parsing was the source of difficulty in processing relative clauses among advanced Chinese speakers of English as a foreign language. As an educational application, Amma (1983, 1984) showed that instruction of a parsing pattern with a supersegmental phonological pattern to Japanese high school learners of EFL (N = 158) enhanced accuracy in reading comprehension of ambiguous and pseudo-ambiguous sentences. He taught the intonation pattern of a parenthetical clause in sentences like "The queen said the king is an ugly monster" (commas and quotations are deliberately deleted) before and after a comprehension test of these sentences. Comparison of the post-test with the pre-test revealed that the number of participants who "read with correct intonation" but "comprehended incorrectly" decreased significantly (χ^2 = 5.44, p < 0.05 in one participant group and χ^2 = 4.50, p < 0.05 in another).

On the other hand, limitations of low-proficiency learners' performance may not derive from inefficient use of relevant strategies but from the use of different strategies. Holmes (1987: 598) in his study on reading speed and comprehension, surmised that "The slow average readers may be relying much more on semantic than syntactic information to understand written sentences, while the fast good readers may be using syntactic cues, but not in a 'predictive' way." In a similar vein, Morrison (1996) found that low-proficiency learners used intralingual cues more often than by high proficiency learners whereas word analysis and contextual strategies were more favoured by high proficiency learners. Also, in Absy's (1995) study of Brazilian ESL learners (N = 18), subjects with low reading comprehension scores relied more on finding the meaning of individual words, whereas subjects with high reading comprehension scores used inference to compensate for the shortage of vocabulary.

If we focus on syntactic parsing, we can look back on two major hypotheses: **minimal attachment** and **late closure**. According to Rayner & Pollatsek (1989: 246, 475), minimal attachment refers to the principle of sentence parsing with which "readers attach incoming material into the phrase marker being constructed using the fewest nodes consistent with the well-formed rules of the language under analysis." For example, sentence (2.5) is easier to process than (2.6) because the initial syntactic analysis is not contradicted throughout the sentence, whereas in (2.6) the reader has to reanalyse the sequence "the answer was wrong" as constituting an additional sentence node. Thus, by default the reader prefers a minimal attachment of sentence nodes.

(2.5) The girl knew the answer by heart.
(2.6) The girl knew the answer was wrong.

Late closure applies to a compound sentence. "If grammatically permissible, the reader attaches new items on the phrase or clause currently being processed" (ibid.). For example, in (2.7) "this" is considered as belonging to the subsequent constituent, but in (2.8) the reader has to reanalyse the constituent to which "a mile" belongs, thus causing more difficulty in processing.

(2.7) Since Jay always jogs a mile this seems like a short distance to him.
(2.8) Since Jay always jogs a mile seems like a short distance to him.

Minimal attachment and late closure are simple linear processing strategies. Both of them state the principle that the reader keeps an incoming word/phrase as belonging to the concurrent constituent until it becomes contradictory and needs a reanalysis. In fact, "when *a mile* is encountered, there is no reason to close the phrase, so that *a mile* is incorporated into the phrase as the direct object of *jogs*" (Rayner & Pollatsek, 1989: 248). The only difference between the two strategies is the syntactic attribute; minimal attachment is used with reference to an embedded sentence, whereas late closure is used in a compound sentence. Anyway, the point is that the reader initially hypothesises a parsing strategy that requires a less memory demand. By means of this cognitive constraint Schachter & Yip (1990) attempted to explain the difference in grammaticality of two similar sentences which were both considered grammatical by the standard Government and Binding theory (Chomsky, 1981).

Late closure was at first considered language-independent, but it was soon found that the parsing strategy is affected by (1) specific sentence structures, in particular, the verb preference as to what it requires as subsequent elements (Fodor, 1998; McElree, 1993; de Vincenzi & Job, 1993, 1995; Schriefers, Friederici, & Kuhn, 1995; Trueswell & Kim, 1998) and idiosyncratic NP type (Kaan, 1998; Schütze & Gibson, 1999), (2) discourse context (Britt, et al., 1992; Altmann, et al., 1998), (3) test takers' L1 (Zagar, Pynte, & Rativeau, 1997; Cuetos & Mitchell, 1988), (4) the target language itself (Suh, 1991; Carreiras & Clifton, 1993; de Vincenzi & Job, 1993, 1995; Gilboy, et al., 1995), and (5) memory capacity (Abney & Johnson, 1991).

Minimal attachment involves a reanalysis of the structure or 'garden path'. It was first proposed by Frazier & Fodor (1978) and Fodor & Frazier (1980). Frazier & Rayner (1982, 1987) supported a 'garden path' phenomenon by observing the eye movements of readers when they were met with the need to revise the primarily predicted structure of a sentence. Rayner & Sereno (1994) contended that 'garden-pathing' was generally supported, but regressive eye movements did not necessarily entail in 'garden-pathing'. However, Holmes (1987) provided evidence that 'garden-pathing' was not a universal phenomenon. His results indicated that parsing was influenced by the information of individual lexical items and the level of the reader's skill. The processing time of a sentence varied depending on whether the verb preferred a direct object or a complement structure as an accompanying element.

Fast readers processed potential structures in parallel, and decided on an interpretation at the last moment, thus showing no difference in reaction times when the two types of sentences were presented. Slow readers were insensitive to the structure and relied more on lexical meanings, thus showing no difference either. Only intermediate readers exhibited a significant slowdown, reflecting a 'garden path' effect. Like late closure, minimal attachment is also influenced by ESL learners' native language (Juffs, 1998), and by the context information (Britt, et al., 1992).

In particular, Trueswell, Tanenhaus, & Kello (1993) and Pickering (1999) pointed out that a semantically 'frequent' analysis was preferred to an 'infrequent' one even when the syntactic analysis predicted the opposite way.

(2.9) The spy saw the cop with binoculars but the cop didn't see him.
(2.10) The spy saw the cop with a revolver but the cop didn't see him.

In (2.9) the natural analysis is to connect "with binoculars" to "saw" rather than to "the cop", which is compatible with Frazier and others' minimal attachment hypothesis. But in (2.10) it is improbable to connect "with a revolver" to "saw" instead of "the cop". It contradicts with the prediction of the minimal attachment theory that a high node attachment (as in the structure 2.9) is preferred to a low node attachment (as in the structure 2.10). If we assumed that the two structures involve the same number of nodes we could interpret the preferred analysis of (2.10) (Kayne, 1984). On the other hand, Schütze & Gibon (1999) showed that whether a constituent is an argument or modifier makes a difference in preference. In any case, "the Garden-Path model, like other syntax-based accounts, depends critically on the syntactic assumptions that are made" (Pickering, 1999: 134).

In review of both semantic strategy and parsing strategy, we learn that the meaning of individual lexical items plays an important role in comprehension. Clark & Clark (1977) presented an insightful, but unanalysed, primitive view of comprehension strategy. The parsing strategies that Frazier and his colleagues proposed were analytic but heavily grammar-oriented. What we need instead is the middle point: the effect of semantic factors or other cognitive resources on syntactic analysis.

2.4 Memory and knowledge

We shall consider here the 'resource' of language processing. Working memory and long-term memory are crucial components in any language processing activities. While working memory deals with a dynamic, on-going aspect of processing, long-term memory functions as a static, ready-to-use template for incoming data. Many studies suggest the link between these components with language performance. So, low proficiency can be attributed to the memory problem.

2.4.1 Working memory
Studies in L2 reading ability emphasised the role of working memory (Baddeley & Hitch, 1974; Baddeley, 1986; Baddeley & Logie, 1999; Daneman & Carpenter, 1980, 1983; Carpenter & Just, 1989; Walter, 2000). Researchers used a **reading span** test which was claimed to be a better predictor of reading skill than simple memory load tasks such as number and word matching (Daneman & Carpenter, 1983; Dixon, et al., 1988; Daneman & Merikle, 1996). King & Just (1991), using this reading span test procedure, showed the effect of working memory on processing complex sentence structures. Harrington & Sawyer (1992) found a significant correlation of reading span test scores of Japanese EFL learners with their TOEFL reading scores ($r = 0.54$, $p < 0.001$) and with their TOEFL grammar scores ($r = 0.57$, $p < 0.001$).

In the early stage of research in working memory Osaka & Osaka (1992) found a high correlation between an L1 reading span test and an L2 reading span test ($r = 0.84$, $p < 0.001$) and claimed that the efficiency of use of working memory was language independent (p.288). Their discussion can be misleading in two ways, however. First, their participants were advanced Japanese EFL learners (N = 30). Among them the top score participants "tended to maintain high scores regardless of differences in vocabulary and expression between the ESL and the CMU [Daneman & Carpenter's (1980) original version for L1 speakers]" (ibid.). Language teachers are aware that top learners are teacher independent, textbook independent, and method independent. Their research does not tell us anything about intermediate or beginning level learners. Second, though a strong correlation was observed between L1 reading span test and L2 reading span test, it does not entail that working memory resources are used in the same way in L1 and L2. In fact, Ikeno (2002), to be reviewed later, did not find a significant correlation between L1 reading span test and L2 efficiency tests while there was between L2 reading span test and L2 efficiency tests.

Miyake & Friedman (1999) used a path analysis and found a large coefficient of L1 working memory towards L2 working memory, followed by a coefficient of L2 working memory towards syntactic recognition (identification of thematic roles, ie., who did what to whom in NNV, NVN, VNN structures. They concluded that the capacity of working memory was a good predictor of L2 acquisition: "... those with larger reading spans are more skilled at comprehending complex sentence structures than those with smaller spans" (p.353).

In one of her six experiments Walter (2000) attempted to trace Cromer's (1970) early finding. Cromer presented texts in various ways in short units successively — words, meaningful phrases, meaningless fragments, and sentences. Cromer found that unlike proficient readers poor readers were good at comprehending meaningful phrases only, but poor at comprehending other units. Walter assumed that this was because it was difficult for poor readers to parse text properly (Walter: 118) and build up a meaningful sequence. She used French-speaking EFL learners — 22 collège students who were supposed to be lower in proficiency and 23 Lycée students who were supposed to be higher in proficiency — and compared their performance in reading comprehension under the same condition as Cromer's except that she used computer projections. She presented on the computer screen each line of a passage in various ways of segmentation (ie., by the word, phrase, sentence, or meaningless fragment), and asked the participants to complete the summary of the passage as a means of measuring reading comprehension ability. In the case of meaningful phrases, the units of presentation were "It was market day", "in Souk Teniet,", "and the street was full of people.", "Under the hot sun,", "men went towards the market", and "with their goats and their cows.". In the case of nonsense fragments, they were "It was market", "day in Souk Teniet, and the", "street was full of", "people. Under the hot", "sun, men went towards the", "market with their", and "goats and their cows." (p.121). If Cromer was correct, she could predict good reading comprehension scores among high-proficiency learners under all segmentation conditions, but among low-proficiency learners a better result with meaningful phrases than with meaningless phrases. The results showed no significant effect of segmentation method (ie., whether the unit of presentation is by the word, phrase, sentence, or meaningless fragment), but highly significant correlations between low-proficiency (collège) students' working memory capacity and their reading comprehension scores (Table 2.3). It indicated that working memory was a good discriminator of reading comprehension ability among low-proficiency learners.

[Table 2.3: Correlations between English working memory scores and English reading comprehension scores for the four segmentation conditions (after Walter, 2000: 130) *: $p < 0.05$; **: $p < 0.01$]

	Collège Eng WM scores (N=21)	Lycée Eng WM scores (N=22)
Word	0.33	0.47*
Phrase	0.47*	0.34
Sentence	0.46*	0.27
Fragment	0.60**	0.09
All conditions	0.59**	0.28

Though she did not mention it, the difference in correlation coefficients is highest for meaningless fragments between low-proficiency (collège) and high-proficiency (lycée) students (0.60 - 0.09 = 0.51). It would appear that low-proficiency students' comprehension process was severely impeded by the fragment condition while high-proficiency students were able to judge the ungrammaticality of the fragment and abandon the attempt without consuming the working memory. Walter's failure in obtaining a significant difference with ANOVA may be due to the mixing of both subject groups. At any rate, this view goes along with her observation in her later experiment that "what fails to be transferred in the L2 reading threshold phenomenon is the skill of building reliable mental representations of text" (p.188).

MacDonald, Just, & Carpenter (1992) studied the relationship between working memory capacity as was measured by a reading span test and the processing efficiency of ambiguous sentences. They compared high-span readers and low-span readers in their reading time and accuracy of comprehension for a set of sentences including ambiguity, eg. (p.61),

A. [Main verb resolution — unambiguous]
   The experienced soldiers spoke about the dangers before the midnight raid.
B. [Main verb resolution — temporary ambiguous]
   The experienced soldiers warned about the dangers before the midnight raid.
C. [Relative clause resolution — unambiguous]
   The experienced soldiers who were told about the dangers conducted the midnight raid.
D. [Relative clause resolution — temporary ambiguous]
   The experienced soldiers warned about the dangers conducted the midnight raid.

Their results showed, surprisingly enough, that high-span readers took a significantly longer time than low-span readers in reading ambiguous sentences, especially at the last word where the temporary ambiguity was resolved (p.67). At the same time low-span readers marked a higher comprehension error rate for ambiguous sentences (p.71). Thus they concluded that high-span readers could tolerate multiple interpretations, which lead to tardiness in processing at the point of disambiguation; and that low-span readers could only handle a single interpretation throughout, resulting in faster processing but potentially highly erroneous comprehension.

Pearlmutter & MacDonald (1995) were sceptical about this result, saying that the participants who noticed the test design because of the subtle difference in naturalness between unambiguous sentences and corresponding temporary ambiguous sentences (ie., A vs B and C vs D) became more careful about choosing a particular parsing strategy than those who did not notice it (p.524). They argued, rather, that the increased reading time was caused by individuals' sensitivity to plausible interpretations: "... high span subjects were sensitive to some probabilistic frequency or contextual constraints in the stimuli which were ignored by low span subjects, causing the high span subjects to consider interpretations which the low span subjects did not" (p.529). In conclusion, it was not the working memory capacity itself that made a difference in comprehension, but it was what a person did under the capacity that developed into different degrees of performance.

More recent studies have revealed the role of working memory subcomponents, in particular a phonological subcomponent. According to Baddeley & Hitch's original model (1974) working memory consists of the central executive and two 'slave' systems, namely, "the phonological loop and the visuospatial sketchpad, which are specialized for the processing and temporary maintenance of material within a particular domain (i.e., verbally coded information and visual and/or spatial information, respectively)" (Baddeley & Logie, 1999: 29). Thus the phonological loop (or its equivalent by the similar name) handles low-level verbal signals, be they actually sounds or letters. Fowler (1981) and Payne & Holtzman (1983) indicated that poor readers depended on phonological short-term memory. According to Zwaan & Brown (1996) low-proficient L2 readers had difficulty in integrating information in the discourse level as their performance was constrained by inefficient lexical and syntactic processing. Gathercole & Baddeley's (1993) research in L1 phonological working memory is quite suggestive. They observed that children at the age of four who performed well in non-word retention tasks did better in primary reading tests four years later than the other children. This result emphasises the importance of automatisation in lower level processing. As application of this view to L2 learners, the current author's own study (Amma, 1983, 1984) went along the same vein. After the instruction of the intonation of a sentence comprising a parenthetical clause, Japanese EFL learners increased their accuracy in comprehending ambiguous sentences. Kadota & Noro (2001) argued that skilled readers automatised low-level bottom-up processing and could utilise more working memory resources for elaboration of meaning and inferences than poor readers.

Especially worthy of attention is the view that lower level processing consumes the phonological loop subcomponent in unskilled learners, and as a result they have difficulty in semantic and pragmatic processing of texts and contexts. Ikeno (2002) studied the effect of working memory on text structure prediction in L2. He found that L2 reading span test scores were highly correlated with scores of L2 processing efficiency subtests, ie., lexical semantic judgement, grammaticality judgement, and L2 sentence verification (Figure 2.5a). He concluded that "L2 processing efficiency is certainly related to, but of course does not exclusively determine, L2 WM [working memory] capacity and L2 text structure prediction" (p.111). It is interesting, though, that of the three efficiency subtests the grammaticality judgement (GJ) test scores correlated lowest with the L2 reading span test (L2 RST) scores (Figure 2.5a), and did not correlate significantly with the text structure prediction test (Figure 2.5b). Since all the other components, lexical semantic judgement (SEM), sentence verification (SV), and Prediction involve meaning of words/sentences/discourse, it appears that GJ requires abstract manipulation of linguistic units.

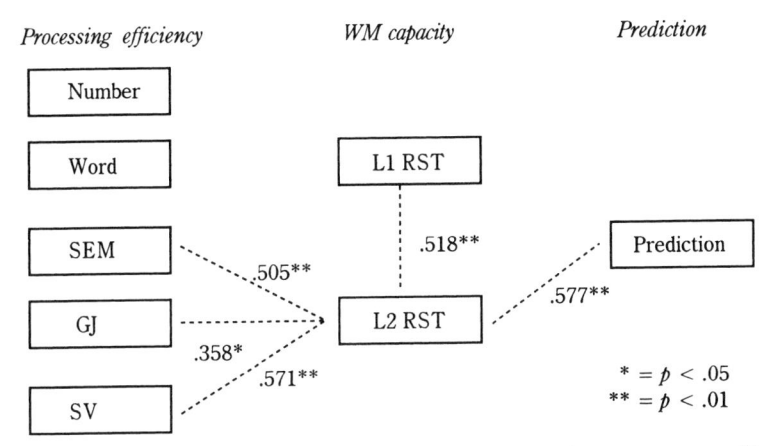

[Figure 2.5a: Correlations between L2 proficiency subtests and working memory tests (Ikeno, 2002: 110)]

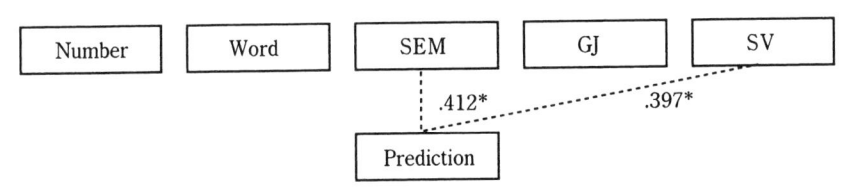

[Figure 2.5b: Correlations between processing efficiency and prediction subtests (Ikeno, 2002: 110)]

Yoshida (2003) studied inference strategies that her participants (Japanese university students, N = 22) employed while reporting their process of reading two short passages. Her learners with larger working memory capacity were better at making textual inferences, especially in global as opposed to local inferences. Her observations of the participants during the think-aloud process in a reading comprehension task suggested that "... lower level processing is resource consuming during comprehension and readers with low working memory are often engaged in encoding processing manifested in a greater incidence of paraphrases, a translation process or repeated reading" (p.9). She remarked that "the low span group spent much of their time for either translating or repeated reading and made fewer inferences" (p.9). Her study emphasised the importance of efficiency in low level processing for lower-proficiency learners.

2.4.2 Long-term memory and other factors

Studies in working memory suggest that it plays an important role in parsing errors. But working memory is not a panacea; too much emphasis on capacity and efficiency fails to recognise the other aspect of input processing, namely, knowledge of grammar. When one's performance in a syntax test is low we don't know what exactly is the decisive cause. It may be either because they are incapable of processing language input efficiently (even for familiar input), or because they lack the knowledge of the formula to follow, or both. While working memory is operative for ongoing processing, long-term memory provides a template (or 'exemplar' in Skehan's term (1998)) with which to automatise the processing.

One solution to the question of the difference in proficiency, in relation with long-term memory, is the Noticing Hypothesis, advocated by Schmidt (1990, 1993a, 1993b). The Noticing Hypothesis, in short, postulates that learning a language takes place if and only if the learner becomes explicitly aware of the formal aspect of the language (in particular morphology and syntax). 'Noticing' is the antithesis of implicit learning or of one of the principles of Natural Approach proposed by Krashen (Krashen, 1985; Krashen & Terrell, 1985). Schmidt contended that noticing or attention was a necessary and sufficient condition for learning a second language. It appeared, then, that learners would never arrive at a correct answer in grammaticality judgement unless they 'noticed' the syntactic structure required. Though the Noticing Hypothesis attempted to explain what constitutes a successful language learner, it was merely a necessary condition; it was not enough to explain the difference of and variability in proficiency levels (see Truscott, 1998, for more critical discussions). On the whole, nevertheless, the fundamental idea of the Noticing Hypothesis supports our present view that less proficient learners tend to disregard syntactic information than more proficient learners.

Skehan (1998: 57) presented a model of input processing relating components of working memory, long-term memory and noticing. In his model, conscious awareness enhances language processing in working memory by focusing on matching, feedback appreciation, recombination, and exemplar generation. It in turn improves the efficiency of the roles of long-term memory: (1) rule-based analytical system, (2) memory-based formulaic system, and (3) schematic knowledge. Skehan envisages that the emphasis of awareness will lead to the automatised use of rules rather than exemplars.

Research has indicated that instruction is effective in second/foreign language development (Ellis, Crystal, & Johnson, 1990; Doughty, 1991), as it entails explicit awareness of linguistic information. VanPatten & Cadierno (1993) and Cadierno (1995) confirmed their hypothesis that formal instruction helps comprehension and production. They taught Spanish-speaking learners that, unlike Spanish in which grammatical roles are assigned by word inflections, the first noun is assigned an agent role in English. The learners in the experimental group who used this processing strategy performed significantly better both in comprehension and production tests than those in the control group.

There are, however, quite a few studies of various kinds in the effect of instruction on acquisition, both pros and cons (Ellis, 1990: 130–173), of which Ellis himself was tentatively affirmative (p.165). Thus although a big caveat must be attached, knowledge of grammar in the long-term memory may facilitate the processing efficiency by providing a template of analysis. In this sense formal instruction is helpful as long as the connection

instruction → acquisition/mastery → automatised use of knowledge

is established. Anderson (1983, 1985) identified three stages of learning:

1. In the **cognitive** stage the learner makes use of conscious activity. The knowledge acquired is typically declarative in nature and can often be described verbally by the learner.
2. In the **associative** stage, errors in the original declarative knowledge are detected and corrected and the knowledge is also proceduralised. During this stage condition–action pairs which are initially represented in declarative form are gradually converted into production sets. The initial declarative representation is never lost, however.
3. Finally, in the **autonomous** stage performance becomes more or less totally automatic and errors disappear. The learner relies less on working memory and performance takes place below the threshold of

consciousness.

The process described here is a transition from an ad-hoc conscious treatment to a rule-governed autonomous processing. The role of knowledge as part of long-term memory is to provide a template for processing and lessen the burden of working memory. The reference to the knowledge system becomes smaller in magnitude and less frequent as the learning stage advances. The effective use of knowledge is possible when it is internalised.

Other factors affecting the efficiency in processing are aptitude, familiarity to the topic, processing style, and general intelligence. For example, familiarity with the language form also improved comprehension (Sasaki, 2000). Unusual word order sentences in German caused more processing time than usual word order sentences (Rösler, et al., 1998). Understanding of the contextual information affected the processing time (MacDonald, Just, & Carpenter, 1992).

In conclusion, we have learnt that memory is one of the crucial elements in cognitive processing of language. Previous studies on low reading span learners can provide a convincing explanation of low-proficiency learners' performance in syntax tests. The only unclear part is that working memory studies use reading span tests which measures the efficiency in reading, and how learners analyse a sentence for the subsequent comprehension has not been discussed. In the actual judgement stage, knowledge of grammar as facilitator of analytical processing is also expected to be at play. Neither memory nor knowledge is within our domain of research, since our main purpose is to identify a phenomenon of isolating a unique set of sentence parsing items in terms of overall proficiency, but the research in this topic indicates a convincing model of the nature of second language learning.

2.5 Test formats

Our final section is concerned with two kinds of tests we use in our experiment: a grammaticality judgement test and a C-test. The former becomes the target or dependent variable in our experiment, so we shall examine possible problems in detail. The latter is the test format we use as the independent variable for predicting the performance in the former. Since many arguments have been made about the validity and reliability of these tests, we need to sort out the discussions in order to find ways to improve the quality of our tests.

2.5.1 Grammaticality judgement

We shall review some literature on grammaticality judgement here. This is the main test method in our experiment, hence we need to know its strengths and weaknesses.

For theoretical linguists, especially generative grammarians, grammaticality judgement has been widely used as an index of language acquisition or realisation of universal grammar (eg. Schachter & Yip, 1990). Among researchers of second language learning, there have been pros and cons as to its validity.

On the one hand, those who focused on concurrent validity tended to agree that grammaticality judgement was both a reliable and stable measure. Hsia (1993) reported a high correlation between grammaticality judgement, paraphrasing, and reading comprehension among ESL speakers of mixed L1 background except for Cantonese speakers for whom grammaticality judgement and paraphrasing did not correlate with reading comprehension. Similarly, Leow (1996) found a high correlation with oral production test in Spanish as a second language. Ito (1997, 1998) confirmed high reliability and moderate level of validity of grammaticality judgement. According to his research, a high correlation between each pair of cloze, grammaticality judgement, and sentence combining tasks suggested that grammaticality judgement was an effective means of measuring test takers' linguistic/metalinguistic knowledge.

On the other hand, people who examined the content and construct validity were on the whole of negative opinions. Yoshitake (1991) concluded that grammaticality judgement was a stable reliable measure of Japanese ESL learners' interlanguage, although some items showed indeterminacy (p.117). Similarly, Gass (1994) remarked that the reliability of grammaticality judgement was inseparable from the indeterminacy of responses. She contended that whereas the judgement in the primary language was to question the fixed language system, that in the second language included indefiniteness or instability, because they were involved in the stage of incomplete learning: "... inferences are being made not about the system they are being asked about, but about some internalized system" (p.305). In Ellis (1991) Chinese learners of English showed inconsistency in 22.5% of the responses. Therefore, according to Ellis, cautions must be taken in using grammaticality judgement. (Note that there were very few participants (N = 21 for the first experiment, N = 8 for the second experiment)). Johnson, et al. (1996), using a grammaticality judgement test against Chinese speakers of ESL (N = 10), indicated that L2 learners were qualitatively and quantitatively different from L1 speakers. In addition, L2 learners tended to answer 'yes' to grammaticality judgements. Furthermore, Hyltenstam (1982), Gass & Selinker (1994: 35–36) and Sorace (1990) doubted if grammaticality judgement was a genuine elicitation procedure. Hyltenstam (1982), in an attempt to investigate the variability of several elicitation measures, found that grammaticality judgement alone showed a disorderly pattern. Sorace (1990: 140–141) pointed out that the dichotomous nature in grammaticality judgement was incompatible with the accretive nature of the learner's interlanguage status:

> Let us consider the case in which a learner is asked to produce an absolute judgement ('correct' vs. 'incorrect') on a construction that is not yet — or no longer — determinate in his/her interlanguage grammar. Any sentence exemplifying that construction will be marked as either correct or incorrect without having such a status in the interlanguage grammar: the learner's choice will be random. If there are different versions of the same test sentence, judgements may or may not be inconsistent. If they are not, the researcher is left with the deceptive impression that the construction is determinate. But if judgements are inconsistent, there can be no unambiguous interpretation of such inconsistency. ... The validity of judgements obtained through dichotomous judgements is therefore highly questionable.

2.5.2 Alternative formats in grammaticality judgement

A large part of the problems indicated so far seems to derive from the test format. Conventional grammaticality judgement tests require a dichotomous response to each stimulus. Since the response is either 'Yes, it is correct' or 'No, it is not correct', there is a high level of chance error, which results in low reliability and inconsistency. The major source of error is the unsystematic interlanguage status (or indeterminacy, according to Sorace (1990)), but even if so test takers may judge the stimuli for some different reasons. Take (2.13), for example.

(2.13) What is a baby cat like? — It's soft.

In my preliminary research (Amma, 2001) about 60% of the test takers judged it as incorrect, even though the grammar involved was very fundamental. It suggested that they took the main verb of the first sentence "is" to be "does" and judged the second sentence as inconsistent, although the originally intended grammar was the use of "like".

In an attempt to correct this irrelevant factor, one can request error correction. If test takers are highly cooperative and motivated to participate it may still work, but otherwise the extra load on the choice of 'incorrect' judgement discourages such judgements, causing the participants to avoid an 'incorrect' judgement (underestimation), and prefer a 'correct' judgement (overestimation). Even without such task it is far easier to simply say 'Yes, it is correct' than to refer to one's intuition and judge the sentence as 'No, it is not correct'. Ellis's (1991) observation mentioned previously that L2 learners tended to say 'Yes' may have reflected this imbalance of cognitive load.

An alternative format, multiple-choice completion (cf. van Susteren, 1997), does not work properly, either. In this format test takers are presented with multiple options as potentially replaceable elements of a slot in a stimulus sentence. Since the correct form is definitely included in the options high-proficiency test takers benefit by the presence of the correct answer and low-proficiency test takers are puzzled by the presence of distractors.

Another alternative (Amma, 2004) is still multiple-choice, but test takers are told to locate the error. In the sample format (2.14), they are first asked to judge whether the stimulus sentence is grammatically correct or incorrect. If the judgement is 'incorrect', they are asked to choose one of the options which indicates the *location* of the error. In this example, the underlined part indicates that it should be corrected or deleted, and the brackets indicate that a word or short phrase should be inserted there.

(2.14) For badly wounded, the soldier stopped fighting.
   a. <u>For</u> badly wounded, the soldier stopped fighting.
   b. For badly <u>wounded</u>, the soldier stopped fighting.
   c. For badly wounded, < > the soldier stopped fighting.
   d. For badly wounded, the soldier stopped <u>fighting</u>.

The advantage of this format is that there is no extra load of error correction, and at the same time test taker's irrelevant responses can be excluded. Amma

(2004) compared this format with a traditional dichotomous judgement format using the same set of stimuli, and concluded that this multiple-choice error indication format is much more reliable than a dichotomous judgement format. Participants (N = 156) took a grammaticality judgement test first in this multiple-choice format, then took another comprising the same set of stimuli (i = 38) in a dichotomous judgement format 5 months later. The KR20 index of the multiple-choice format was $r = 0.559$ ($p < 0.001$) while that of the dichotomous judgement format was $r = -0.213$ (n.s.). A further item-by-item analysis revealed that the test takers' responses in some items are quite distinct in two formats. In the case of (2.14), the multiple-choice format predicts an increasing probability of correct answer as the proficiency (measured by a C-test) rises, while the dichotomous judgement format predicts a flat probability across all proficiency levels.

As for the actual inventory of test items, most studies using grammaticality judgement tests as measures of general L1/L2 development prepare a structure-oriented list of sentence samples. Johnson & Newport (1989) and Johnson, et al. (1996), for example, used 12 pairs of grammatical and ungrammatical sentences (after Johnson, et al., 1996).

SAMPLE TEST ITEMS FOR EACH OF THE 12 RULE TYPES

Past tense	1a.	Yesterday the man make a chocolate cake.
	1b.	Yesterday the man made a chocolate cake.
Plural	2a.	The farmer bought two pig at the market.
	2b.	The farmer bought two pigs at the market.
Third person	3a.	Every Friday our neighbor wash her car.
	3b.	Every Friday our neighbor washes her car.
Progressive	4a.	The little boy is speak to a policeman.
	4b.	The little boy is speaking to a policeman.
Determiners	5a.	Larry went the home after the party.
	5b.	Larry went home after the party.
Pronominals	6a.	The girl cut himself on a piece of glass.
	6b.	The girl cut herself on a piece of glass.
Particles	7a.	Kevin called Nancy for a date up.
	7b.	Kevin called Nancy up for a date.
Auxiliary rules	8a.	Leonard should has written a letter to his mother.
	8b.	Leonard should have written a letter to his

		mother.
Wh-questions	9a.	Where Ted is working this summer?
	9b.	Where is Ted working this summer?
Yes/no questions	10a.	Will be Harry blamed for the accident?
	10b.	Will Harry be blamed for the accident?
Subcategorization	11a.	The boy put the book.
	11b.	The boy put the book in the kitchen.
Basic word order	12a.	The boy the rabbit feeds carrots.
	12b.	The boy feeds the rabbit carrots.

Note. The a version of each pair is ungrammatical and the b version is grammatical.

The items were collected so they could cover basic syntactic and morphological rules in English. This empirical sampling may be good for collecting responses in an already established structural framework. However, the aim of our research is to seek a cognitive constraint on the learner's parsing or syntactic analysis, so the items must reflect the question. In the above example, items 1–4 and 8 concern word morphology; item 5 either the use of "the" or categorisation of "home"; item 6 identification of a semantic feature of "the girl"; item 7 constraints on a particle movement, hence the complexity of phrase structure; items 9–11 word order. Because it is difficult to characterise these items in terms of cognitive constraint (and what kind of constraint the learner is seized by), the obtained results would be far from a cognitively meaningful interpretation. Ideally, two solutions are conceivable. One is to prepare an exhaustive list of sentences which represents the general use of English properly, ie., proportionately and without any bias on particular usage. This will not only be a huge corpus project beyond our present capability, but also be too exhaustive for us to obtain generalisation. Another approach is to limit the target sentences to those reflecting the expected cognitive constraints such as phrase length, modification, and agreement. In that case, we have to conduct another test for obtaining the learner's general proficiency, instead of using the grammaticality judgement test itself as the measure of syntactic proficiency. See Section 3.2.2.1.1 (Grammaticality judgement test) for details of our test materials.

In conclusion, there are two aspects of arguments about grammaticality judgement test: use of the test and its format. As for the use previous studies are more in favour than critical of grammaticality judgement test as an instrument of eliciting intuitive responses. As far as our research is concerned, the procedure of judging whether a stimulus sentence is grammatical or not can at best represent the test takers' parsing of the sentence. Most of the critical views are centred round the format. The traditional dichotomous format gives rise to alleged problems of instability of responses, low reliability, and hence low validity. An alternative format is proposed for solving these problems. The test takers are told to indicate the location of the error by a multiple-choice format. This format increases the reliability of response data.

2.5.3 C-test

As a measure of the test taker's general proficiency in English, we used a C-test. There were several reasons for choosing a C-test: (1) it is a reliable measure with a number of supporting studies, (2) it is an efficient measure for producing a large sum of answers in a short time, compared with a cloze or discrete-point tests, and (3) its scoring is accurate (ie., no alternative correct answers) and quick (compared with a cloze; although machine scoring was beyond our capability). Particularly in our experimental context in which all the tests had to be completed in a class of 90 minutes, choosing an indirect test which produces a fairly large number of answers was a must. As for the validity and practicality issues past literature in C-test has largely been in favour of its use as a measure of general proficiency. Our task, then, was to reduce as much potential disadvantage as possible, including the face validity issue, ie., the problem that a C-test does not look like a familiar language test. Actual steps of test administration will be described in Section 3.2.3.

C-test was first proposed as an improved alternative to cloze (Klein-Braley, 1984, 1985; Raatz & Klein-Braley, 1981). Compared with problematic cloze tests it is still considered as the most economical and reliable integrative test of English proficiency (Klein-Braley, 1997). Klein-Braley indicates its advantages over a cloze test: (1) a C-test can produce more response items than a cloze with the same length of text, (2) C-test scoring is exact and objective, hence avoiding the fuzziness problem with a cloze, (3) C-test scoring is quicker and easier, (4) native speakers can answer a C-test almost perfectly whereas not so with a cloze, (5) it is easier to collect samples of all word classes, and (6) it is possible to collect a wider variety of text samples (p.65).

Confirmation studies followed including a factor analytic investigation of validity (Raatz, 1984), applications to Hungarian EFL students (Dornyei & Katona, 1992), Asian EFL students (Connelly, 1997), students in six European and Asian countries (Klein-Braley & Raatz, 1994), and British native speakers and German ESL students (Köberl & Sigott, 1996). Its construct validity and applicability were discussed (Grotjahn, 1986, 1993, 1995). Variations of C-tests were examined (Kokkota, 1988; Chapelle & Abraham, 1990; Prapphal, 1994; Jafarpur, 1999a, 1999b). Klein-Braley herself has repeated demonstrating the superiority over other test methods. In one of her latest studies (1997) she compared C-tests, cloze tests, multiple-choice cloze tests, cloze-elide tests, a dictation test, and an in-house placement test. As a result, C-tests obtained the highest internal consistency (alpha) with $r = 0.85$ followed by cloze-elide ($r = 0.75$), cloze ($r = 0.66$), and multiple-choice cloze ($r = 0.51$) (p.68). The factor analysis of the same test data named three of the four versions of C-tests as entering the top five subtests bearing high factor loadings (p.70).

On the other hand, limitations were pointed out (Mitchell, 1991; Chapelle, 1994; Jafarpur, 1995). Grotjahn (1987) claimed that C-test is not very effective for advanced learners. Köberl & Sigott (1994) indicated that the frequency of particular words chosen affects the facility of the item. Further, it was often said to lack face validity (Bradshaw, 1990; Oscarson, 1991: 107). In fact, part of the advantages of C-test can turn out to be a disadvantage. The large number of response items, for example, is obtained at the expense of face validity — seemingly too heavily mutilated.

In spite of these shortcomings no serious problem has been pointed out so far, and the benefits far exceed inevitable losses. Klein-Braley and Raatz showed a practical guideline for administering a C-test (Klein-Braley, 1997: 63–64):

(1) The new test should be much shorter, but at the same time should have at least 100 items.
(2) The deletion rate and the starting point for deletions should be fixed, and no longer a matter of personal preference.
(3) The words affected by the deletions should be a genuinely representative sample of the elements of the text.
(4) Examinees with special knowledge should not be favoured by specific texts, in other words, a new procedure ought to use a number of different texts.
(5) Only exact scoring should be used, in order to ensure objectivity.

(6) Adult educated native speakers should normally make virtually perfect scores on the test.

In our experiment we shall follow these principles as much as possible, especially the item size (1), deletion rate (2), and variety of texts (4). See Section 3.2.2.2.1 (C-test) for details of our test design.

In conclusion, the C-test is a reliable measure of learner's overall proficiency. Compared with cloze and other cloze-derived techniques, C-test is most stable and reliable, according to the previous studies. A possible disadvantage is its face validity; test takers may be dismayed at the unfamiliar format. A good amount of practice, therefore, is required before administering the test.

2.6 Summary of literature review

In this chapter we have reviewed major literature relevant to our research. There are five major topics to each of which we shall give a very brief summary and explain how the arguments are relevant to our research.

(1) *Proficiency*
The topic constitutes a premise for our research argument. In this section we considered both theoretical and practical aspects of proficiency. First, to answer the question 'What constitutes language proficiency?', we compared various theoretical models including Canale & Swain (1980), Cummins (1983), Bachman (1990), and McNamara (1996). These are all non-empirical models without scientific evidence. In contrast, the cognitive view including Cummins (1983), Canale (1983b), and Sang, et al. (1986) takes into account some such psychological factors as proficiency levels and individual differences. We concluded that we should tentatively consider proficiency as the degree of the individual learner's state of achievement, in contrast with competence which denotes the constant inventory of a native target language speaker's potential linguistic capability. There is no definite answer to the nature of proficiency by theoretical arguments, but in discussing proficiency as the main criterion of test performance we should be prepared to know the theoretical background: what it means to be proficient in language.

Second, we discussed various aspects of learner variability with a special emphasis on dimensionality in language proficiency. Statistical procedures and data handling were examined. We came to the conclusion that the degree of dimensionality depends on how much in detail we examine the learner performance. Additionally, the interlanguage indeterminacy as indicated by Sorace (1990) is considered as an error factor. With reference to our research, it is important that multidimensionality of proficiency is not excluded from the discussion.

(2) *Difference between high-proficiency and low-proficiency learners*
Research indicates that there is a qualitative as well as quantitative difference between high-proficiency learners and low-proficiency learners in terms of the use of learning and problem-solving strategies. It has become clear that low-proficiency learners depend more on lexical-semantic information than high-proficiency learners, who can also take syntactic information into account (Upshur & Homburg, 1983; Purpura, 1998). This understanding supports our view of the current research that low-proficiency learners employ a characteristic parsing strategy.

(3) *Input processing strategies*
The question now moves on to what strategy learners take in processing linguistic input. The classical semantic strategy (Clark & Clark, 1977) has been supported by many studies, but the claim was too general to be a firm theory. The attempt to theorise the parsing strategy by Frazier and his colleagues, in the form of minimal attachment and late closure, had a heavy emphasis on syntactic rules and ended in failure by the evidence of semantic and discourse factors. However, the significance of these arguments and counterarguments was that they lead to an empirical model of language processing — an alternative to the theory-driven model.

(4) *Memory factors*
Recent development in cognitive psychology has indicated that working memory is a crucial determinant of success in L1 and L2. The most powerful model by Baddeley & Hitch (1974) is convincing in explaining learner differences in proficiency. Worth special attention is the phonological subcomponent. It is considered that low-proficiency learners consume their working memory resource in lower-level processing, such as identifying and storing sound, up to the point where there are no more resources for higher-

level processing, such as inference and ambiguity judgement. Although the relation between working memory and syntactic judgement has not yet been extensively studied as it also involves long-term memory, awareness, and other factors, the framework of working memory provides a working solution to the problems of low-proficiency learners.

(5) *Test format*

Finally, we discussed the validity of two tests we used in our current research. First, grammaticality judgement is the main test method of our experiment. The traditional test procedure had a lot of problems in terms of reliability and validity. We proposed a revised procedure in the form of a multiple-choice error indication format. Second, a C-test was the independent test which measured overall language proficiency in our experiment. Also validity and reliability of the test were discussed. Some practical problems that we did not mention here and the proposed solution will appear in Section 4.1.1 (Data filtering).

2.7 Hypotheses

2.7.1 Setting up of hypotheses

In order to substantially answer the research questions above, we formulate our research hypotheses as follows. Note that all these hypotheses deal directly with Research Question 1, in the sense that they are steps towards characterising the parsing strategies of low-proficiency learners. At the same time, the development of analytical methodologies in dealing with these matters is the reflection of Research Question 2. In other words, while Research Question 1 challenges a qualitative analysis, Research Question 2 a quantitative realisation.

Hypotheses:
1. A cognitive constraint on processing works commonly across certain test items of grammaticality judgement.
2. The performance of test takers at a low proficiency level is more severely affected by the cognitive constraint than that of test takers at a high proficiency level.
3. Test takers with lower proficiency can deal with a relatively shorter span of text than test takers with higher proficiency.

In other words, the length of the text that test takers can process is determined by their general proficiency. This research claims that this tendency holds across different sentence samples, and the contrast between the responses of low-proficiency test takers and those of high-proficiency test takers remains alike for items where the cognitive complexity/difficulty is similar. The hypotheses predict that low-proficiency test takers parse and comprehend a limited length of text within a sentence. Since the constraint derives from the processing capacity/efficiency, it is expected that they use less resource-consuming strategies, such as preference of a partial/localised interpretation of a sentence to the interpretation that involves a wider context, and preference of comprehension cued by lexical meanings of content words to comprehension cued by syntactic structures and function words.

Therefore we expect that the contrast of responses is made clear by sentence types that involves different types of syntactic violations. When a stimulus sentence involves avoidance of necessary inflection and case agreement and yet can be interpreted by content words (whether it is correct or not), low-proficiency learners may recognise it as grammatically correct. When a sentence involves a taught rule of syntax or lexicosyntactic constraint, this tendency is obscured, for the judgement does not derive from cognitive parsing strategies. In sum, our goal is to detect a characteristic cluster of items which forms as a function of the proficiency measure.

2.7.2 Steps of testing hypotheses

Before we describe the steps of research some basic concepts must be explained.

a. Overall proficiency

A C-test is used to measure the participants' overall proficiency in English. The result is a linear continuous measure for each person, and it cannot be analysed any further into possible subcomponents of proficiency. We assume, post-hoc though, that the distribution of the data is normal, in order that our sample should be a good representative of the general population of university level EFL learners in Japan. For the sake of simplicity in subsequent arguments we convert the raw scores to scores of normalised distribution (or z scores) so that the average score will be 0 and the standard distribution will be 1. Thereafter we use the variable Cz which is the normalised C-test score. We also assume the structure of proficiency to be psychologically unidimensional again for the sake of simplicity in subsequent arguments, and therefore expect the entire data set to be psychometrically unidimensional.

b. Elicitation of responses

The main task in our experiment is to elicit responses influenced by cognitive constraint(s). Following the traditional elicitation procedure as we saw in the literature review, we use a grammaticality judgement test. In the test, part of the items are so written that they reflect the hypothesised interlanguage status, eg., low-proficiency test takers do not have enough capacity to judge the redundancy of the subject in the distant location as in

(2.15) Mr Kawase, vice president of Tomato Bank, <u>he</u> will speak to the press this afternoon.

so they should accept the sentence as correct. There are two kinds of expected responses. One is a judgement as 'correct' of an ungrammatical stimulus as (2.15) above. The other is a judgement as correct of a grammatical stimulus but in incorrect comprehension as in (2.16).

(2.16) The fact that the dog hurt <u>the boy scared Linda</u>.

Here the choice reflecting the entailment of this stimulus as "the boy scared Linda" is the expected response.

We now describe the actual steps of research with reference to our hypotheses. First our Hypothesis 1 states

1. A cognitive constraint on processing works commonly across certain test items of grammaticality judgement.

It means there is such a cognitive constraint that operates latently in the grammaticality judgement of an item which also operates in the same way behind other items. If such a cognitive constraint exists, test takers are bound to respond to more than one item in the same way. To prove this we need to (1) find an uneven distribution of association measures across all items, and

(2) identify that the common factor is necessarily and sufficiently a cognitive constraint. As for step (1), we shall first calculate the association measures of expected responses for all item combinations. We expect the distribution of association measures to be significantly dissimilar. However, since association measures (φ) are used instead of strict Chi-square measures (χ^2), the tendency of uneven distribution, if any, is merely indicative. Statistical proof is given in the confirmation phase which we shall explain later. Step (2) is also verified in the same phase in which the factor assumed from our hypothesis of cognitive constraint makes two statistically distinct categories of items. As for the methodological representation, namely Research Question 2, we simply expect to produce a matrix of association measures, so there is nothing new in terms of statistical technology.

Next, our Hypothesis 2 states

2. The performance of test takers at a low proficiency level is more severely affected by the cognitive constraint than that of test takers at a high proficiency level.

This statement claims a non-random relation between the distorted distribution of association measures and proficiency scores. There are three steps to prove this.

2.1 There is a cluster of responses bearing high association measures with one another.
2.2 Members of the cluster stay constant or change gradually as the proficiency measure changes.
2.3 The cluster becomes stronger or weaker monotonically as the proficiency measure changes.

We shall first sort the responses so that items with high association measures come together. A common technique for solving this problem is multidimensional scaling (MDS). However, it has several problems. (1) The solution in the form of multidimensional matrix is difficult to conceptualise. Its two-dimension (or three-dimension, where possible) scatter plot is a visual representation of the matrix, but it normally comprises stress, a measure of contradictory information. The stress changes item by item; it is not constant across all items in the scatter plot. Therefore the graphical representation is not altogether precise. (2) The association measure can in theory take values ranging from -1 to +1. An MDS procedure normally takes positive values as dissimilarity data. When the association is very weak, taking a value near zero or negative, either MDS cannot calculate the data or take it as a missing data. The result is a highly stressful or distorted solution. Therefore we have to first convert the raw association measure to a new measure which satisfies the conditions (i) the new matrix of measure exhibits the least stress of all possible converted measures, and (ii) the new measure fits MDS as a Euclidean distance.

Even after the conversion, the scatter plot of items do not stay consistent because of the fluid nature of stress; a slight change in stress triggers a completely different distribution of items. The largest problem is unnecessary calculation of long distances or weak association. Since very weak association should be ignored in order to focus on the core cluster with a strong association, a moderated handwritten diagram can represent the cluster with visual comprehensibility. Another way to solve the problem of descriptive weakness of MDS is to use third dimension information, a depth variable, onto the scatter plot of items. This is called a **contour plot analysis**. The depth variable represents the strength that the item inherently has in causing association with other items. To obtain such a variable we have to convert the original matrix of association measures which holds between pairs of items into a list of items with their degrees of association with other items. We use a monotonic conversion formula which changes the two-dimensional matrix into a one-dimensional sequence. Having obtained the strength-of-association variable we assign it as the depth variable in the contour plot procedure. The locations of items are based on one typical scatter plot of MDS for one proficiency level and are kept constant across proficiency levels, so we can observe the change of the depth variable or the strength of association. If we observe a cluster of items persistent through some proficiency levels, we will have confirmed step 2.1 of Hypothesis 2. If we observe that the cluster wanes as the proficiency level rises we will have confirmed step 2.3 of Hypothesis 2.

Additionally, we shall draw a diagram of items the distances of which represent the dissimilarity with as little contradiction as possible. It should be a convenient tool to help us conceptualise the configurations of items in different proficiency levels. In the diagram the locations of items are kept constant across proficiency levels so we can observe the changes of association measures.

We expect that the association measures in the diagram change gradually as the proficiency level changes. In other words, if the members of the cluster of strong association change gradually across different proficiency levels, the cluster is characteristic to participants in either high or low proficiency level, thus confirming step 2.2 of Hypothesis 2.

Now the last of our Hypotheses

3. Test takers with lower proficiency can deal with a relatively shorter span of text than test takers with higher proficiency.

attempts to project our picture of low-proficiency interlanguage to the observed phenomenon. It necessarily involves two steps: (1) interpretation of obtained responses and (2) confirmation of a tentative hypothesis postulated as a result of the interpretation. Our core view, supported by the previous literature, is that as proficiency level goes down learners use a 'local parsing' strategy. Based on this view we postulated a working hypothesis on classifying stimuli (to be stated in Section 3.2.2.1.1) and wrote items accordingly. If the results correctly reflect the classification in the working hypothesis, the results should be interpreted according to the original working hypothesis. If they don't, we have to adjust our interpretation so it best fits the observation. Note that the minor categories in the working hypothesis are based on syntactic rules, so they do not necessarily reflect the strength of cognitive constraint. The interpretation will be made subjectively, in the same way as we interpret factors in factor analysis; we compare items belonging to the cluster of high association measures and seek common syntactic/semantic/cognitive features. If the hypothesised interpretation of 'local parsing' explains the cluster well, it is a good candidate of the factor that differentiates stimuli as a function of proficiency measure.

In our next step, we classify stimulus items according to the postulated 'local parsing' hypothesis with minor alterations made through the exploratory step. The fundamental criterion is whether each item contains elements that cause 'local parsing'. The two new categories are now named **'accessible'** (because the stimuli allow local parsing) and **'inaccessible'** (because the stimuli do not contain a sequence of local parsing). The mean strength of association is compared between the two categories by analysis of variance (ANOVA). If the result shows a significant difference, we can say that the distinctive factor is 'local parsing', thus confirming the hypothesis.

Finally, we apply the item *LinkScore* values to test taker characteristics. If low-proficiency test takers tend to make 'local parsing', the aggregate *LinkScores* of their responses (ie., the sum of item *LinkScores* in the proficiency level corresponding to the test taker's proficiency measure) are expected to be significantly higher than those of high-proficiency test takers. In other words, if there is a significant correlation between test takers' proficiency and their aggregate *LinkScores*, we can say that 'local parsing' is characteristic to low-proficiency test takers (Hypothesis 3).

Chapter 3
Research design

This chapter consists of two major parts. First, the materials and procedures of the two main tests — a grammaticality judgement (GJ) test as a dependent variable and a C-test as an independent variable — are described in detail. Our main concern is the rationale of the design of the GJ test. So, this part also consists of part of the background history of developing the test design. The second part is devoted to explaining four powerful statistical methods. Logistic regression analysis and contingency table analysis are used to extract the latent tendency among test items and quantify it in an original procedure. Multidimensional scaling and contour plot analysis are used to represent the quantified variable in the way that we can easily conceptualise the latent tendency.

3.1 Review of background research
    3.1.1 Grammaticality judgement test: a preliminary study
        3.1.1.1 Outline
        3.1.1.2 Procedure
        3.1.1.3 Results
        3.1.1.4 Discussion
        3.1.1.5 Summary of the preliminary study
3.2 Main study
    3.2.1 Participants
    3.2.2 Materials
        3.2.2.1 Grammaticality judgement test
            3.2.2.1.1 Test items

                3.2.2.1.2 Format
            3.2.2.2 C-test
                3.2.2.2.1 Test items
            3.2.2.3 Questionnaire
        3.2.3 Test procedure
            3.2.3.1 Grammaticality judgement test
            3.2.3.2 C-test
    3.3 Statistical methodology
        3.3.1 Logistic regression analysis
        3.3.2 Contingency table analysis
            3.3.2.1 Contingency table analysis using probabilities
            3.3.2.2 Association measure
        3.3.3 Multidimensional scaling
        3.3.4 Contour plot analysis
    3.4 Summary

3.1 Review of background research

3.1.1 Grammaticality judgement test: a preliminary study
3.1.1.1 Outline
A preliminary study (Amma, 2001) had been conducted in a small scale experiment before the main one was contrived. The purposes of this early study were (1) to confirm the phenomenon of item clustering by means of association network, (2) to explore the analytical procedure for objectively representing the phenomenon, and (3) to prepare a list of possible parsing strategies that were expected to cause the phenomenon.

The participants were 346 first and second year university students in Japan. Their nationality was Japanese, their first language was Japanese, and they had been taught English as a foreign language in Japan for seven to eight years.

The test consisted of one grammaticality judgement test. The result of the item responses of the grammaticality judgement test was analysed as the dependent variable, using the total score of the test as the independent variable representing the general ability in grammar.

The entire test material consisted of 23 multiple-choice and 51 dichotomous judgement items. The items were taken from various sources of tests (mainly from Quigley, et al., 1978). The multiple-choice items had three or four options including one correct answer. In the dichotomous judgement items the participants were simply asked to judge whether the item was correct or incorrect. The test item was either in the form of a single sentence or of a dialogue in two lines. Two versions of an equivalent test, Form A and Form B, were prepared. Some items appeared in the part of multiple-choice format in one version and in the part of dichotomous judgement format in the other version.

3.1.1.2 Procedure

(1) The raw data were first analysed by factor analysis using a statistical package *SAS* using a factor procedure (proc factor) in order to confirm an overall unidimensionality.
(2) The raw data were then analysed by Rasch Analysis using *Big Steps* (Linacre & Wright, 1993) in order to eliminate outfit items and persons.
(3) The data were reanalysed by Rasch Analysis in order to measure item difficulties and person abilities (θ).
(4) Using person ability measure as the independent continuous variable, probabilities of occurrence of options were calculated using a logistic regression analysis procedure of statistical software *JMP* (SAS Institute, 2002). This process was repeated for all items.
(5) Within each Form, association measures (phi = φ coefficients) were calculated for all possible pairs of options except for options with low response rates.
(6) The matrix of phi statistics was sent to multidimensional scaling analysis by *SAS* using an MDS procedure (proc mds).
(7) For the responses forming a cluster, logistic regression analysis was made using *JMP* for all possible pairs of options for their four combinations of response patterns: no-no, no-yes, yes-no, and yes-yes, where 'no' means a negative judgement against the stimulus, and 'yes' means an affirmative judgement.
(8) Based on the parameters obtained in step (7), probabilities of the four categories of combined responses were calculated in 16 ability levels: θ = -2.0, -1.8, -1.6, ... +2.0.
(9) For each pair of options in each ability level in step (8), an association measure (φ) was calculated based on the probability estimates obtained in

step (8).

(10) A two-dimensional plot map of the association measures of the options obtained in step (9) was drawn in each ability level. The transition of the distance which represented the strength of association was examined over different ability levels. Expansion of the distance between two responses meant that the responses became differentiated. Attempts were also made to interpret the options that formed a cluster.

3.1.1.3 Results

(a) Responses of incorrect judgement were collected and classified into three major categories which were interpreted as: (A) cognitive and developmental preferences, (B) semantic preference, and (C) structural generalisation. The complete list of incorrect strategies is shown in **Appendix A**.

(b) 6 responses were selected as forming a core cluster by multidimensional scaling. Table 3.1 shows the matrix of overall phi statistics for these responses in Form A,

[Table 3.1: Matrix of association measures (phi) for 7 responses in Form A]

item	(3)	(6)	(7)	(9)	(12)	(16)
(3)	1.0000	.	.	.	.	.
(6)	0.2440	1.0000	.	.	.	.
(7)	0.1841	0.0210	1.0000	.	.	.
(9)	0.1841	-0.0533	0.1841	1.0000	.	.
(12)	0.0034	-0.0357	0.0034	0.2306	1.0000	.
(16)	0.0924	0.1450	0.0924	0.1988	0.0269	1.0000

where the numbered items represent the following test responses judged as correct (all multiple-choice for the underlined parts):

(3) *I've never found <u>the rich kind is</u> to the poor.
(6) *"What is a baby cat like?" "<u>Milk</u>."
(7) *<u>So the man cried</u> was not surprising.
(9) *Rocky shores that <u>do not</u> beaches are eventually destroyed by the sea.
(12) *We went to the lake <u>to swimming</u>.

(16) *When the girls arrived, Bill came downstairs to see the girls.

The astarisk (*) indicates that the sentence is ungrammatical.

(c) The phi statistics for the six responses were calculated. Table 3.2 shows five the phi statistics for five pairs of responses in 5 ability levels for non-positive θ values.

[Table 3.2: Matrix of association measures (phi) for 5 pairs of responses in Form A in 5 ability levels]

item pair \ θ	-2.0	-1.5	-1.0	-0.5	0.0
(3)–(9)	0.3251	0.2357	0.1255	0.0405	-0.0045
(3)–(7)	0.1891	0.2092	0.2130	0.2021	0.1809
(3)–(6)	0.4700	0.4106	0.3367	0.2543	0.1700
(6)–(12)	0.4290	0.4375	0.3690	0.2055	0.0239
(12)–(16)	0.1566	0.2142	0.1494	-0.0472	-0.1246

Figure 3.1 indicates symbolically the configuration of six responses. The thickness of the lines connecting items indicate the strength of association between items, relative to the magnitude of φ. The arrow indicates that the association between the items become weaker as the ability level rises.

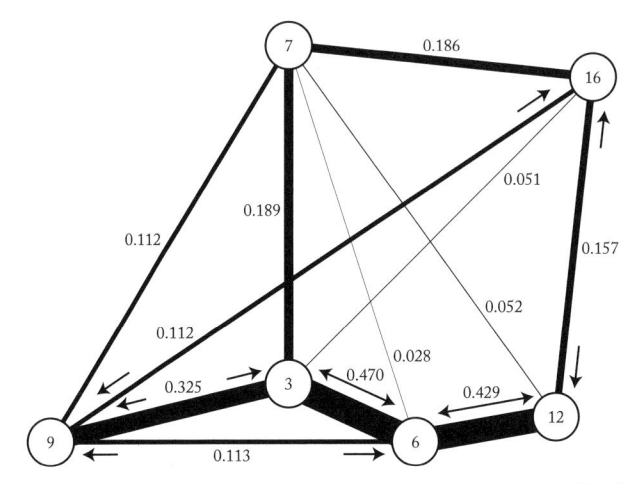

[Figure 3.1: Configuration of 6 responses based on association measures. The figures beside the connecting lines indicate the phi statistics at θ = -2.0.]

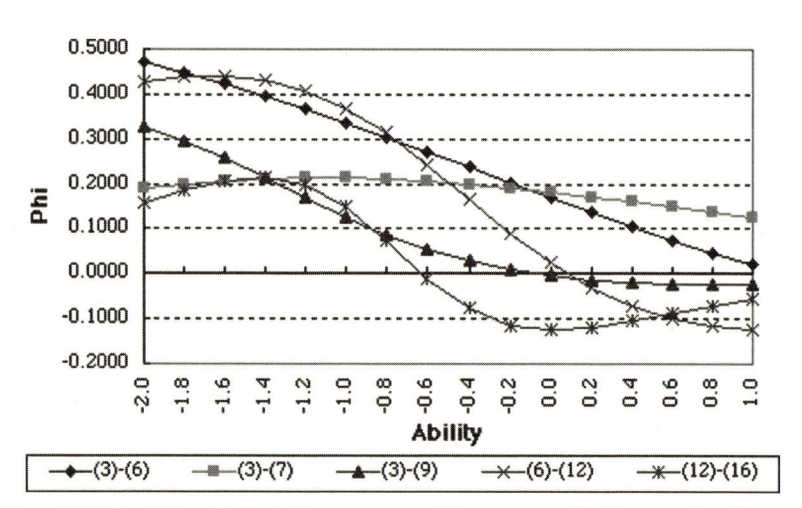

Figure 3.2 shows the transition of association measures of five pairs of responses.

[Figure 3.2: Transition of association measures of 5 response pairs shown as the change of ability measure]

As far as these responses in the core cluster were concerned, we concluded that there is a tendency of association within the cluster becoming stronger as the reference point on the ability scale lowers and weaker as it rises. In other words, test takers in a low ability level tend to make a similar kind of grammatical judgement against these items in common.

3.1.1.4 Discussion
(a) Some items clustered together reflecting the strength of association, and this tendency was strongly observed among low-proficiency test takers. Therefore our research purpose (1) 'to confirm the phenomenon of item clustering by means of association network' was attained. The overall tendency of clustering did not altogether hold true in each ability level. For instance, (6) and (12) were unrelated by the aggregate raw frequency (φ = 0.0357), but there was a strong association φ = 0.4290 at θ = -2.0 and it existed until θ = 0.0. On the other hand, another pair of items which were not included in the core cluster above appeared to be related by the aggregate raw frequency (φ = 0.2790), but the φ exceeded 0.2 only above θ = 0.5. Therefore, the clustering of responses in each ability level was quite different from that based on the totalled raw frequencies. It suggests that the world of association between items in a lower ability level is

non-homogeneous in contrast with that in a higher ability level.

(b) A close examination of local pairs of responses revealed that a strong association among items in the lower level was considered as the result of applying semantically/cognitively oriented rules rather than syntax. For instance, the incorrect option in (6) could have been judged as 'correct' by the participants by disregarding the function word "is" and by preferring the lexical meaning of the content words. A similar strategy could be inferred with (3) where the embedded verb and the preposition were ignored. (9) could have been interpreted in a similar fashion. It could make sense by assuming an existential verb "have" after "do not".

(6) *"What is a baby cat like?" "Milk." → [interpreted as] "What <u>does</u> a baby cat like?" "Milk."
(3) *I've never found the rich kind is to the poor. → [interpreted as] I've never <u>seen</u> the rich/richness among the poor.
(9) *Rocky shores that do not beaches are eventually destroyed by the sea. → [interpreted as] Rocky shores that do not <u>have</u> beaches are eventually destroyed by the sea.

Thus, what was common among these three was ignoring and free replacement of verbs while retaining the meaning of the content nouns.

(c) There were different degrees of transition of association. Whereas the association measure between (3) and (7) remained constant, as indicated in Figure 3.2, the association measure between (6) and (12) dropped steeply at around the ability level θ = -0.5. Relatively speaking, what was commonly critical in the latter pair (and also in (3)) was the semantic strategy of picking up content words, but it was hard to find a common factor in (7). It was assumed that a different strategy was used for processing (7) from the ones used for (3).

(7) *So the man cried was not surprising.

(d) Based on the distribution of probabilities of incorrect judgement responses, major responses were classified in the taxonomy table in such a way as to maximise the explanatory power of the data. As this process was exploratory some statistical confirmation was required later for the identification of each strategy. Moreover, the taxonomy was based on a simple logistic regression analysis conducted independently for all items; the factor of interaction of responses should be considered in order to draw an organic picture of incorrect strategies. Thus our research aim (3) 'to prepare a list of possible parsing strategies that cause the phenomenon' was only partially attained.

(e) Our analysis ended up with a sample distribution. The fact that it showed a cluster and that the size of the cluster correlated with the ability level indicated that our analytical procedure operated properly. However, the mapping of the core responses (ie., Figure 3.1) was done by manual positioning of responses. This was inevitable due to the failure of appropriate mapping by multidimensional scaling. Thus we need to devise a formula for optimally converting the association measures into Euclidean distance measures used in multidimensional scaling. Thus our research aim (2) 'to explore the analytical procedure for objectively representing the phenomenon' was also partially attained.

(f) The current preliminary experiment included both multiple-choice items and dichotomous judgement items. Although the dichotomous items decomposed from multiple-choice items were excluded from the calculation of test takers' abilities and item difficulties, the mixture of two formats of different nature may have obscured the results. The qualitative difference of the two formats was investigated in a separate paper (Amma, 2004). A multiple-choice format is inconclusive because a particular choice depends on the relative plausibility of other choices. A dichotomous format, on the other hand, is unstable because of its high level of error by chance. An alternative format incorporating the advantage of both a multiple-choice format and dichotomous format should be invented.

3.1.1.5 Summary of the preliminary study

The preliminary study confirmed the existence of the basic phenomenon: responses to a grammaticality judgement test clustered together in terms of association network among low-proficiency learners. The results indicated that low-proficiency learners preferred semantic information in parsing sentences to syntactic information which was more often used by high-proficiency learners. This interpretation is merely suggestive; in order to establish a causal relationship between proficiency level and strategy use we need a confirmatory study with a larger size of participants.

3.2 Main study

3.2.1 Participants

The participants were Japanese university students mostly in their first and second years, aged 18–20 (N = 1152). They had received education of English as a foreign language since secondary school (80%) or since primary school (20%). Their major academic subjects fell into three categories: English language and literature (N = 349, 30%), humanities (N = 549, 48%), and natural science (N = 254, 22%). The data were collected from 21 universities and colleges with a varying range of abilities[1]. The participants' proficiency range was not controlled, but the final set of participants indicated a normal distribution.

Unlike Purpura's participants (1998; see Section 2.2.2), ours were homogeneous, on the whole, having the same first language background and having roughly the same language learning history. The major strength of using homogeneous participants was in controlling potential variables that affected test taker performance. A variety of test takers' background factors might affect parsing and test taking strategies. In return, we were obliged to confine our claim of research conclusion to a limited context — Japanese university-level EFL learners. Once a characteristic tendency of parsing strategy of some of our participants is identified, we hope to confirm the same finding with test takers of other background and of mixed background.

3.2.2 Materials

The participants took (1) a grammaticality judgement (GJ) test, and (2) a C-test. Besides, part of the participants reported their latest scores of (3) TOEFL ITP. The grammaticality judgement test was the dependent, target variable in which systematic variations were sought. The C-test was the independent measure of general language proficiency (Klein-Braley, 1984, 1985). The TOEFL ITP is an institutional programme of TOEFL, consisting of test items recycled from regular TOEFL tests, and is claimed to have the same validity and reliability as a regular TOEFL. This test was included in order to guarantee the concurrent validity of the C-test, and to provide an approximate measure of how good/

poor the participants' performance was in terms of their corresponding TOEFL score. There were 38 items in the GJ test and 122 in the C-test. The entire test materials together with their sources are shown in **Appendices B–C**.

3.2.2.1 Grammaticality judgement test
3.2.2.1.1 Test items

The materials for the GJ test were originally 39 sentences. The number was reduced to 38 before we started the analysis because one sentence (**b7** in the list below) proved irrelevant with respect to the research design. The sentences which fit the taxonomy in the preliminary study by Amma (2001; outlined earlier in Section 3.1.1) were taken from various reference books and textbooks of English grammar. Normally they include grammatically correct language, and some test items were taken from part of these sources as correct stimuli (Quigley, et al., 1978; Pyle & Muñoz, 1986). Some other items derived from other parts of sources consisting of incorrect uses of language (Quigley, et al., 1978; Greenbaum & Quirk, 1990; Swan, 1995; Young & Strauch, 1994). Still some other test items came from a learner corpus as incorrect uses of language (Asao, [2000]). Some of the actual test items were modified from the original in order to create grammatically incorrect stimuli. All the test items including multiple-choice options were examined and verified by two native speakers of English working as ELT teachers at a university.

Stimulus sentences were chosen so that they would clarify the effect of cognitive constraint. First, the original taxonomy (Amma, 2001) was reduced to three major categories: (1) *items subject to cognitive constraints* which included 'local closure' phenomena, addition/omission of obligatory arguments, and violation of structure, (2) *items free from cognitive constraints* which included idiosyncratic vocabulary and syntactic rules, related to developmental errors — errors that typically appear in early developmental stages in L1 acquisition, and (3) *items free from cognitive constraints* which included idiosyncratic vocabulary and syntactic rules, related to acquired rules — grammar items that EFL learners learn in the classroom. We originally expected that, ideally speaking, if all the stimuli in category (1) caused the same parsing error and all the stimuli in categories (2) and (3) did not, then this hypothetical major taxonomy would explain the condition for the parsing error. However, even if we obtained a statistically significant difference between categories (1) and (2)+(3), a detailed identification of the parsing error and its domain would require decomposition of categories and reformulation of stimulus sentences. Thus this three-part organisation was a working framework in which new observations were to be explored.

In writing stimulus sentences, attention was paid to the sentence forms which would reflect the possible parsing strategies in the original taxonomy (Amma, 2001). Table 3.3 shows the criteria of writing stimulus sentences.

[Table 3.3: Original classification of stimulus sentences and their criteria. The word with an asterisk (*) indicates that the word should be corrected into some other form, the word with a double cross (#) indicates that the word should be deleted, the caret (^) indicates that a word/phrase should be inserted in that location, and the word/phrase in square brackets ([]) indicates that it should be inserted there.]

Category (1): items subject to cognitive constraints

Local closure
violation of phrasal boundaries
　… One part of a sequence can form a sentence if we ignore the phrase boundary, eg., "the boy disappeared" in **a1**.
　　a1 (grammatical) ¶ The letter kept by the old woman who we met when we were looking for the boy disappeared.
　　a2 (grammatical) ¶ Vivian knew the police officer under suspicion had received the money.
　　a3 (grammatical) ¶ The fact that the dog hurt the boy scared Linda.
　　a4 ¶ You will find the glasses with red marks on both sides #are quite expensive.
violation of agreement
　… The form of the main verb does not agree with the grammatical subject but with the nearest noun phrase, eg., "Foreign Languages are …" in **a5**.
　　a5 ¶ The Department of Foreign Languages *are not located in the new building.
　　a6 ¶ To grow several kinds of flowers *are the joy of gardening.

Violation of obligatory arguments
addition of verbs
　… Unnecessary verbs are inserted as another operator in addition to the main verb, eg., "is" in **b1**, which should be corrected as "… gardening washes the human heart".
　　b1 ¶ I think that gardening #is *wash the human heart.
　　b2 ¶ Half of the people ([who]) (#)were invited to the party didn't turn up.
addition of relatives to inserted structures
　… An unnecessary relative pronoun is inserted after another relative structure, eg., "that" in **b3**, which should be corrected as "… which I think is least expensive".
　　b3 ¶ Take this flight which I think #that is least expensive.
addition of subjects after appositives
　… The subject is repeated after an inserted appositive phrase, eg., "he" in **b4**, which should be deleted as "Mr Kawase, vice president of Tomato Bank, will speak …".

b4 ¶ Mr Kawase, vice president of Tomato Bank, #he will speak to the press this afternoon.

omission of complementisers

... An obligatory complementiser is missing, eg., "that" in **b5**, which should be corrected as "That you don't know Russian is a pity". It is possible to isolate a pseudo-sentence sequence "You don't know Russian".

b5 ¶ [That] You don't know Russian is a pity.

omission of functional particles

... An obligatory preposition or conjunction is missing, eg., "as" in **b6**, which should be corrected as "... was described as a tall man ...". Note that **b7** is a grammatical stimuli even without a hypercorrection by adding "that" as in "such a nice time that I didn't want to leave". Because of its irrelevant elicitation design this item was later deleted from the data.

b6 ¶ His attacker was described [as] a tall man with a beard.

b7 (grammatical) ¶ I was having such a nice time I didn't want to leave.

Violation of subordinate structures

omission of subordinate conjunctions

... An obligatory subordinate conjunction is missing, eg., "when" in **c1**, which should be corrected as "When most people hear 'endangered species', ...". As a result, the stimulus appears to contain two main sentences.

c1 ¶ [When] Most people hear "endangered species", they think of animals.

omission of complementiser

... An obligatory complementiser is missing, eg., "whether" in **c2**, which should be corrected as "I'm worried about whether you are happy". It is possible to isolate a pseudo-sentence sequence 'I'm worried about you'.

c2 ¶ I'm worried about [whether] you are happy.

Violation of agentivity

... The required agent of the predicate does not correspond to the grammatical subject. **d1** should be corrected as "Diane's nose got extremely cold, as she ran home ..."; **d2** as "The activity I liked most in the Gardening Club was to plan many seeds"; **d3** as "It is difficult for Hiromi to learn mathematics".

d1 ¶ Diane's nose got extremely cold, *running home through the snow.

d2 ¶ The activity I liked most in the Gardening Club was *planted many seeds.

d3 ¶ *Hiromi is difficult ^ to learn mathematics.

Functional reinforcement

addition of functional elements

... An unnecessary preposition or relative pronoun is added which appears to function in the way it does in other grammatical sentences. In **e1**, for example, either "for" should be deleted or "For he/she was badly wounded, the soldier ...". In **e2**, either "whom" should be deleted or "I can't think of anybody whom I should invite".

e1 ¶ #For badly wounded, the soldier stopped fighting.

e2 ¶ I can't think of anybody #whom to invite.

association with familiarity

... A gerund is taken for a verb which together with the preceding preposition forms a familiar sequence, eg., ""I don't like to garden" in **e3**, "how to jump" in **e4**, and "to meet an old friend of his" in **e5**.

e3 ¶ I hate insects — it is the reason that I don't like #to gardening.
e4 ¶ I showed the little boys how to *jumping.
e5 ¶ Yamane visited Kyoto to *meeting an old friend of his.

Category (2): items free from cognitive constraints — developmental errors

Avoidance of case agreement
... The case of the subject noun does not agree with the following verb, eg., "her" in **f1**.
f1 ¶ "Can I see Harriet?" "I'm sorry *her [is/has] gone to school."

Avoidance/violation of inflection
violation of inflection
... The inflection of the operator (verb or auxiliary verb) is not appropriate. **g1** should be corrected as "Catherine does not come ..."; **g2** as "It is my mother who likes ..."; and **g3** as "The children thanked Jim for coming".
g1 ¶ Catherine [does] not come here anymore, because her mother is ill in bed.
g2 ¶ It is my mother *to *like arranging little trees in the garden.
g3 ¶ The children thanked Jim for *come.

violation of mood
... The mood of the predicate (ie., the voice of the verb-derived head predicate) is inappropriate. **g4** should be corrected as "I was very interested ..."; and **g5** as "The policemen were surprised ...".
g4 ¶ I was very *interesting in the lesson.
g5 ¶ The policemen [were] surprised that the girls chased the man in the station.

avoidance of determiners
... An obligatory determiner (ie., article) is missing, eg., "a" in two occasions in **g6**.
g6 ¶ What I want is ^ cup, not ^ glass.

avoidance of pronominalisation/reflexivisation
... An obligatory conversion of word form (ie., pronominalisation and reflexivisation) is neglected. **g7** should be corrected as "... to see him/her"; and **g8** as "... what to do with ourselves".
g7 ¶ When the magician appeared, Bill came downstairs to see *the *magician.
g8 ¶ We did not know what to do with *us.

Category (3): items free from cognitive constraints — acquired rules

Avoidance/violation of inflection
... A word form required by a general lexical/discourse grammar is neglected. In **h1** "spending their free time ..." appears to be grammatical if we ignore the requirement of "looking forward". In **h2** "*hisself" comes from the analogy 'she – her – herself, he – his – hisself'. In **h3** the existence of the preceding subordinate clause "hurried" must be changed to "was hurrying".
h1 ¶ All the students were looking forward [to] spending their free time on the

beach.

h2 ¶ Mr Peters used to think of *hisself as the only president of the company.

h3 ¶ When I last saw Janet, she *hurried to her next class on the other side of the campus.

Violation of idiosyncratic vocabulary/structure rules

...A word form required by an idiosyncratic lexical/discourse grammar is neglected. In **h4** the form "*homeworks" is inappropriate because of the idiosyncratic lexical rule of countability of this noun. In **h5** "Naomi"'s being a human proper noun forces the use of "who" instead of "that". In **h6** postmodification "people playing" is not a usual modification pattern.

h4 ¶ Carl was upset last night because he had to do too many *homeworks.

h5 This is Naomi, *that sells the tickets.

h6 ¶ I watched the match because I knew some of the *playing *people.

3.2.2.1.2 Format

The format of the grammaticality judgement (GJ) test is illustrated below. In order to reduce the chance level of error and to identify the source of judgement, participants were asked to answer a confirmation question, ie., (1) if the judgement is 'correct', they find the correct meaning of the sentence from among four Japanese translations/paraphrases/implications, or (2) if the judgement is 'incorrect', they locate the point at which the error is to be corrected by choosing one option from among four. Instructions were given in the participants' native language. The entire GJ test is shown in **Appendix B**.

<Example>
This picture paints by a famous artist in 1765.

If **correct**, choose the appropriate paraphrase or implication in Japanese.

1. [A famous artist painted this picture in 1765.]
2. [Many artists painted this picture together in 1765.]
3. [A famous artist painted a series of pictures in 1765.]
4. [This picture made an artist famous in 1765.]

If **incorrect**, choose where you can correct the error. The underlined word/phrase indicates that its form should be changed or it should be deleted. The angle brackets (< >) indicate that a word/phrase should be inserted here.

5. This picture < > paints by a famous artist in 1765.
6. This picture paints by a famous artist in 1765.
7. This picture paints < > by a famous artist in 1765.

8. This picture paints by a famous artist in 1765.

In this example, option 6 is the correct judgement. In order to elicit the judgement 'correct' against an ungrammatical sentence, we expect the participants to simply say 'correct', but this would be a relatively easier task than to say 'incorrect' *and* choose the correction (cf. Johnson, et al., 1996). Therefore to balance the task load we added the translation/paraphrase task for the judgement 'correct'. This task in turn confirmed that the test taker had made a grammaticality judgement after having detected the expected meaning.

A combination of the three criteria (stimulus, judgement, and identification of error) produces eight cases in theory:

	originally sentence	judgement as	comprehension/identification
(1)	grammatical	correct	right
(2)	grammatical	correct	wrong
(3)	ungrammatical	correct	right
(4)	ungrammatical	correct	wrong
(5)	grammatical	incorrect	right
(6)	grammatical	incorrect	wrong
(7)	ungrammatical	incorrect	right
(8)	ungrammatical	incorrect	wrong

Logically speaking, (5) does not exist. (2) indicates misinterpretation of the original sentence. (1) and (7) reflect the 'pass' correct response of the participant, ie., the participant has properly responded to the stimulus. In (8) the participant has focused on an irrelevant part of the original sentence, thus this type of response would be named 'misfire'. (3) is committed by a convinced but erroneous learner, and we might call it a 'true parsing error'. (4) involves misinterpretation, although the judgement appear close to (3), thus this response would be named 'false parsing error'. (6) reflects erroneous understanding of the syntax or hypercorrection, thus would be named 'potential parsing error'.

Of the four types of responses against ungrammatical stimuli, only (3) is the parsing error that we intended to collect. The rest of the responses, including the proper response are categorised as 'others'.

Items **a1–a3** were originally grammatical stimuli, so the true parsing error was detected in one of the interpretation/inference options for the 'grammatical' judgement. In item **a1**

a1 ¶ The letter kept by the old woman who we met when we were looking for *the boy disappeared.*

the choosing of the interpretation entailed from the italicised part (which in fact does not constitute a clause) is the evidence that the subject has committed the true parsing error, reflecting her/his tendency to focus on the local context and ignore the rest.

In item **a4** two foci were found after administering the test.

a4 ¶ *You will find the glasses* with *red marks on both sides #are quite expensive.*

We then divided the responses into two groups, one focusing on the first of the italicised parts, which we renamed as **a4l** ('l' for local closure), and the other focusing on the second part, which we renamed as **a4v** ('v' for violation of obligatory arguments (addition of verbs)). If a subject chose the entailment "You will discover the glasses", for example, then this was the sign of the local parsing with the focus on the first underlined part. The two response groups were therefore complementary.

a4l ¶ *You will find the glasses* with red marks on both sides #are quite expensive.
a4v ¶ You will find the glasses with *red marks on both sides #are quite expensive.*

Item **b7** was also a grammatical stimulus. We also found that there were no options representing the true parsing error. So this item was deleted from the data.

3.2.2.2 C-test
3.2.2.2.1 Test items
We wanted to observe Klein-Braley and Raatz's (Raatz & Klein-Braley, 1981; Klein-Braley, 1985, 1997) original suggestion that a C-test should contain several passages from different genres with a total number of items being at least 100. We ended up with four passages containing 122 items. Four pieces of passages was the best we could do in order for each passage to be authentic and self-contained. Meanwhile the total number of items had to be limited as we had to administer the two tests, C-test and GJ test, within a class hour and the participants were not familiar with this test type although there was

a practice passage. We had learned in the trial C-test conducted a year before for Japanese university students (participants: N = 158, items: i = 131) that the valid items and participants were much fewer than the original test size. The result indicated a high internal consistency (KR20: r = 0.958). However, after eliminating the participants with more than 20 consecutive blanks and the items whose discrimination index (DI) was less than 0.20, there were not many items left for actual calculation (N = 130, i = 67). Therefore we assumed that the present size of 122 items was a minimum requirement.

The materials were chosen from EFL textbooks and ESL supplementary readers. They were all narratives, but some of them included dialogues. The themes varied: a travel anecdote, two scientific descriptions, and a fiction. All the passages had similar difficulty set at a late beginner level, roughly corresponding to the reading textbooks the participants had used three or four years before. The materials had been trialled and difficult passages had been replaced with easier ones.

Unlike the GJ test this C-test has only one version — one type of passage order. The entire C-test is shown in **Appendix C**.

3.2.2.3 Questionnaire

Along with the two main tests a questionnaire was given to the participants in order to get the information of their study background. The questionnaire items included (1) "report your TOEFL score if you have taken," and (2) "have you lived in overseas countries for more than three months?"

The first question asked was the TOEFL ITP score. We collected the information by the participants' self report partly because the information was to be used only supplementarily, and partly because we could not administer a TOEFL test to all the participants for time and financial reasons. They were asked to mark a score range by 20 points between 340 and 600. For those who reported that they took only TOEFL CBT, the CBT scores were converted to ITP scores using the official conversion table. Since the majority of the participants were first year students at university/college, not very many of them were expected to have taken TOEFL before. Therefore the information obtained was of secondary importance, compared with the main grammaticality judgement test and C-test. The data, representing part of the participants' ability, were intended to give an independent supplementary measure in converting our C-test scores to more generally acknowledged TOEFL scores provided that the two sets of scores bear a statistically significant correlation.

The second question was the overseas experience. This item was intended to identify participants with heterogeneous background, ie., non-EFL learners. If the size and distribution of these participants on the proficiency scale should affect the dimensionality of the independent variable, C-test, the data must be eliminated. In fact, it did not happen (see Section 4.1.1).

3.2.3 Test procedure
3.2.3.1 Grammaticality judgement test
In order to minimise the effect of the order of items, in particular that of the unfinished items towards the end, the items were randomised and compiled in ten versions.

This Grammaticality Judgement (GJ) test was conducted at 21 universities and colleges in a 90-minute class hour together with the C-test. In each institution a classroom teacher supervised the test: explaining the task, answering questions, timing the test, and collecting the papers. The GJ test was administered in the following steps. (1) Explanation of the test by the supervisor, using an example item. (2) Main test with 38 multiple-choice judgement items, administered for 30 minutes.

All the answers were marked on a separate machine-readable form and were manually corrected for illegible markings and machine-reading errors. Since different versions had different item order, the raw data were sorted in the way all versions follow the same order as shown in **Appendix B**.

Any participant data in which either the GJ test or C-test was missing were discarded.

In return of the data collection, the participants' data were analysed and a grammar diagnosis report was sent back to the participants through the classroom teachers.

3.2.3.2 C-test
The C-test was administered in the following steps. (1) Explanation of the test by the supervisor, using an example passage half already filled in, another half to be filled by the participants. (2) A practice answering session for about 10 minutes, using a short paragraph of 34 words, 12 blanks. (3) Explanation of the practice paragraph by the administrator for about 5 minutes. (4) Main test with four passages and 122 blanks, administered in 25 minutes. (5) In case there

were participants who could not complete the test, they were told to finish it at home for another week's time, but were also told not to use dictionaries and other reference books or to ask others for help.

Originally the C-test was intended to be conducted within a class hour together with the GJ test. We allowed the participants to do the test as a take-home assignment for two reasons. First, we learnt from our trial tests that reaching the end of the test is crucial in maintaining a high reliability. So we considered it was better to let them finish the test at home even if we sacrificed part of the rigor of test administration than to stop the test on time causing participants — presumably mostly low-proficiency test takers — to leave some items unfinished, which might have to be discarded in the end. Second, the participants' proficiency level varied widely. As a result, it was expected that a lot of participants would leave the subsequent C-test unstarted, let alone unfinished. It would incur a loss of the data particularly from low-proficiency learners, who were our main target of study. Additionally, we considered that unlike a grammar test a C-test would not be easily solved unless one asks for others' help, which was prohibited. For these reasons the participants were allowed to take the C-test home. The C-test was then collected and manually scored.

The raw scores of the C-test were normalised so that their mean would be 0 and standard deviation would be 1. The new variable after this conversion was named **Cz**.

3.3 Statistical methodology

3.3.1 Logistic regression analysis

Logistic regression analysis is a measure of estimated probabilities for multiple categorical data as dependent variables, given one type of continuous data as an independent variable. In our research we sought the probabilities of the occurrence of the response options based on the overall proficiency scale Cz.

This statistical measure, like classical item analysis, is item-specific; the result obtained from one item is independent of other items. However, if we combine the occurrence patterns we can relate the responses across items. Let me illustrate the procedure, using the actual data for items **a5** and **h3**.

«a5»
The Department of Foreign Languages *are not located in the new building.
1. [You won't find the Department of Foreign Languages in the new building.]
2. [The building of the Department of Foreign Languages is not new.]
3. [The new department is not Foreign Languages.]
4. [You won't find the new building of the Department of Foreign Languages.]
5. The Department of Foreign <u>Languages</u> are not located in the new building.
6. The Department of Foreign Languages <u>are</u> not located in the new building.
7. The Department of Foreign Languages are not <u>located</u> in the new building.
8. The Department of Foreign Languages are not located <u>in</u> the new building.

A simple logistic regression analysis of item **a5**, for example, yields the probability distributions of its eight options (Figure 3.3)

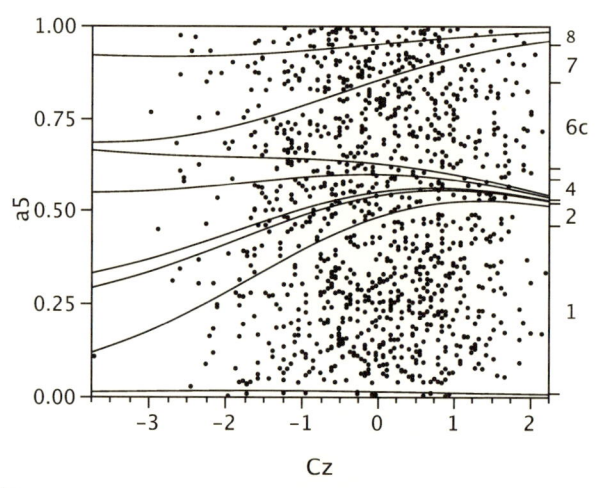

[Figure 3.3: Logistic probability plot of all options in item **a5** by Cz]

where 'c' denotes that option 6 is the correct option. The horizontal axis represents the independent measure of ability by Cz, which follows a normal standard distribution, and the vertical axis represents the probabilities of the dependent categorical measures in 8 levels '1, 2, 3, 4, 5, 6, 7, 8', plus '-' which represents no response. Each level corresponds to the name of the option in the test item. In the graph of multilevel logistic regression the vertical width of a given area of category X at a given proficiency level θ represents the estimated probability of X at that proficiency level. In this example, you can read that at proficiency level Cz = 0 (ie., the average proficiency) the probability of option 1 is approximately 0.474 whereas that of option 6 is 0.221. We also learn that as the proficiency measure rises the probabilities of these two options rise. The dots represent individual responses randomly scattered within the area, indicating that a dense area is more reliable than a scarce area.

Similarly, the probability distributions of responses to item **h3** are as follows (Figure 3.4).

«h3»
When I last saw Janet, she *hurried to her next class on the other side of the campus.
1. [Janet was hurring to the classroom on the other side of the campus.]
2. [Janet had to hurry because she was in the far end of the campus.]
3. [Janet came to the end of the campus as she hurried to the next class.]
4. [Janet was running in a hurry in the far end of the campus.]
5. When I <u>last saw Janet</u>, she hurried to her next class on the other side of the campus.
6. When I last saw Janet, she <u>hurried</u> to her next class on the other side of the campus.
7. When I last saw Janet, she hurried to her <u>next class</u> on the other side of the campus.
8. When I last saw Janet, she hurried to her next class on <u>the other</u> side of the campus.

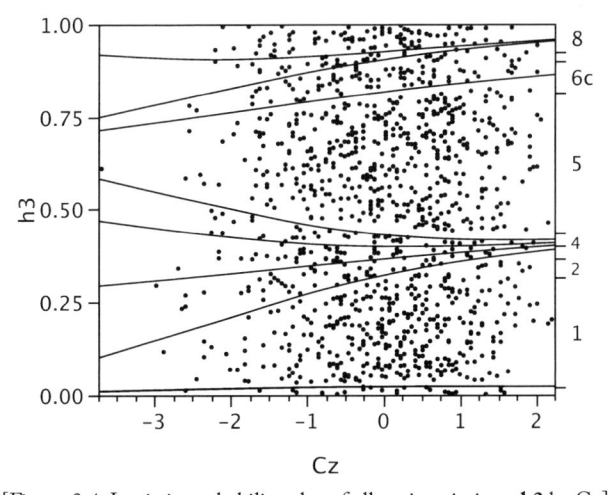

[Figure 3.4: Logistic probability plot of all options in item **h3** by Cz]

Since we want to know the strength of association of error we are interested in the probabilities of the target options reflecting the hypothetical 'local parsing' strategy. In item **a5**, the option in focus is '1'; the rest of the options are irrelevant. We name the option in focus 'v' and the rest combined together 'x'. We then can calculate the distribution of probabilities of two responses by logistic regression analysis (Figures 3.5 and 3.6).

«a5»

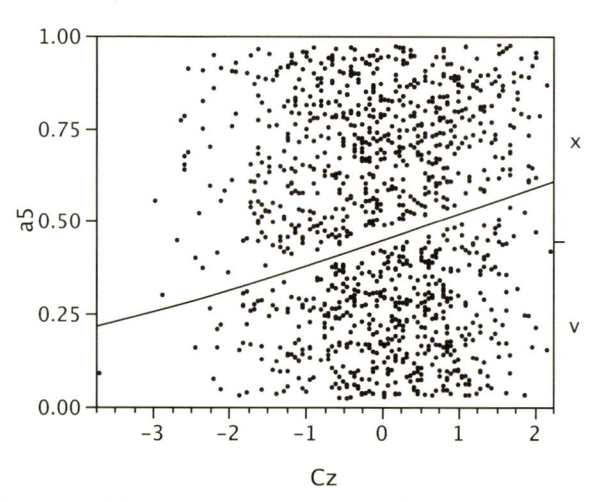

[Figure 3.5: Logistic probability plot of the target option (v) and other options as a collective category (x) in item **a5** by Cz]

«h3»

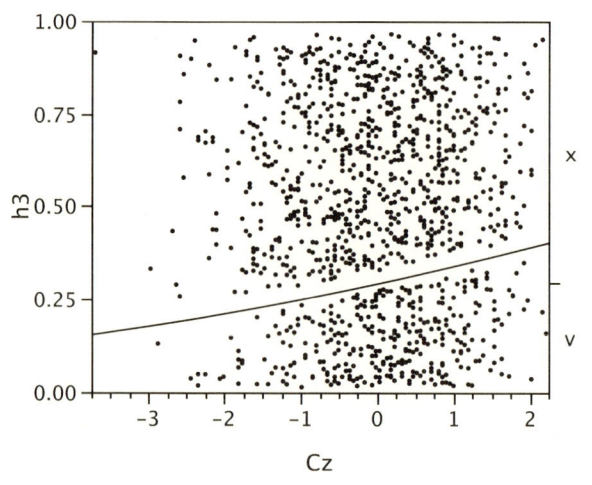

[Figure 3.6: Logistic probability plot of the target option (v) and other options as a collective category (x) in item **h3** by Cz]

By combining the simplified probability distributions of responses in **a5** and those in **h3** we obtain the distributions of four types of responses, namely,

A: **a5** = 'v' and **h3** = 'v'
B: **a5** = 'x' and **h3** = 'v'
C: **a5** = 'v' and **h3** = 'x'
D: **a5** = 'x' and **h3** = 'x'.

A represents the probability of the combined responses of 'v' in both **a5** and **h3**, that is, how much one is likely to choose the assumed cognitively constrained options in both items. *B* represents the probability of the combined responses of 'x' in **a5** but 'v' in **h3**. *C* represents the probability of the combined responses of 'v' in **a5** but 'x' in **h3**. Finally, *D* represents the probability of choosing other options ('x') in both items.

Using the Cz scores as an independent variable, we can estimate the probabilities of the four cases, *A*, *B*, *C*, and *D* by logistic regression analysis (Figure 3.7).

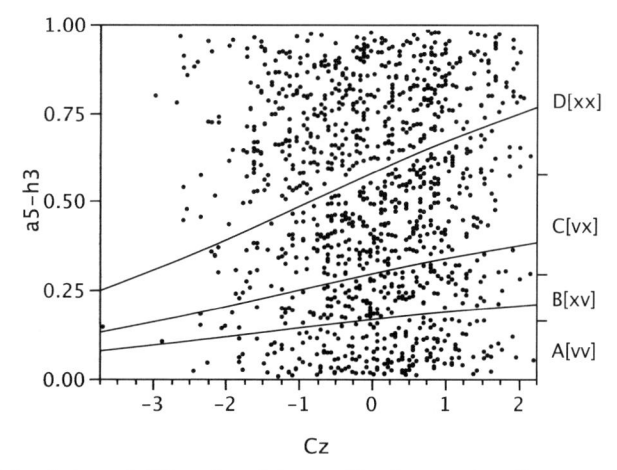

[Figure 3.7: Logistic probability plot of the combined categories of target option (v) and other options as a collective category (x) in item **a5** and **h3**]

[Table 3.4: Parameter estimates of the logistic probability plot of the combined categories of target option (v) and other options as a collective category (x) in item **a5** and **h3**]

Term	Estimate	Std Error	ChiSquare	Prob > ChiSq
Intercept[A[vv]]	-0.9247951	0.0864986	114.31	< .0001
Cz[A[vv]]	0.35850648	0.0883631	16.46	< .0001
Intercept[B[xv]]	-1.185258	0.0954365	154.24	< .0001
Cz[B[xv]]	0.39392785	0.0977654	16.24	< .0001
Intercept[C[vx]]	-0.3950081	0.0728092	29.43	< .0001
Cz[C[vx]]	0.39055267	0.0744996	27.48	< .0001

For log odds of A[vv]/D[xx], B[xv]/D[xx], C[vx]/D[xx]

The three sets of parameter estimates denote, from top to bottom, the intercept for category *A*, the slope (Cz) for category *A*, the intercept for category *B*, the slope (Cz) for category *B*, the intercept for category *C*, the slope (Cz) for category *C*. The intercept and slope (Cz) for category *D* can be calculated as the residue of *A*, *B*, and *C*.

The probabilities of responses *A*, *B*, *C*, and *D*, ie., the vertical widths of the four areas in Figure 3.7, are calculated by Expression 1, using the estimates in Table 3.4 (Hastings, 1986):

$$p_i = \frac{\exp(\beta_{0i} + \beta_{1i}x)}{1 + \exp(\beta_{01} + \beta_{11}x) + \exp(\beta_{02} + \beta_{12}x) + \ldots + \exp(\beta_{0(r-1)} + \beta_{1(r-1)}x)} \quad \ldots(1)$$

$(i = 1, 2, \ldots r - 1)$

where r is the number of options, β_{0i} is the intercept estimate of response i, and β_{1i} is the slope estimate of response i. In our example in Figure 3.7,

$\beta_{01} = -0.9247951$
$\beta_{11} = 0.35850648$
$\beta_{02} = -1.185258$
$\beta_{12} = 0.39392785$
$\beta_{03} = -0.3850081$
$\beta_{13} = 0.39055267$

The probability of case *A* at proficiency level Cz = -1.0, for example, is

$p_1 = \exp(\beta_{01} + \beta_{11} \times (-1.0)) / (1 + \exp(\beta_{01} + \beta_{11} \times (-1.0)) + \exp(\beta_{02} + \beta_{12} \times (1.0)) + \exp(\beta_{03} + \beta_{13} \times (-1.0)))$
$= 0.143$

The probability of case B at proficiency level $Cz = -1.0$ is

$p_2 = \exp(\beta_{02} + \beta_{12} \times (-1.0)) / (1 + \exp(\beta_{01} + \beta_{11} \times (-1.0)) + \exp(\beta_{02} + \beta_{12} \times (1.0)) + \exp(\beta_{03} + \beta_{13} \times (-1.0)))$
$= 0.106$

The probability of case C at proficiency level $Cz = -1.0$ is

$p_3 = \exp(\beta_{03} + \beta_{13} \times (-1.0)) / (1 + \exp(\beta_{01} + \beta_{11} \times (-1.0)) + \exp(\beta_{02} + \beta_{12} \times (1.0)) + \exp(\beta_{03} + \beta_{13} \times (-1.0)))$
$= 0.235$

The probability of case D at proficiency level $Cz = -1.0$ is

$p_4 = 1 - (p_1 + p_2 + p_3)$
$= 0.516$

We have demonstrated in this section that we can calculate the sizes of the four combined response categories as continuous functions of the proficiency measure, given the test takers' proficiency measures and their responses in either 'v' or 'x' to a particular item. The above formulae illustrate the probabilities of the four cases A, B, C, and D at proficiency level $Cz = -1.0$. By providing other proficiency measures we can calculate the probabilities continuously.

3.3.2 Contingency table analysis
3.3.2.1 Contingency table analysis using probabilities

A normal contingency table analysis is a tool to test the dependency of two categorical variables. Its limitation is that it can only take frequency values in integers. So it appears to be useful to test the data in the whole population or grouped population (eg., advanced, intermediate, and beginning). The technique is, regrettably, not directly applicable to a particular point of proficiency level, because the frequency of data can only be obtained from a range of data on the proficiency scale. In other words, we get the *frequency* of particular responses between Cz = 0 and Cz = 1, for example, but cannot get any *frequency* of responses at exactly Cz = 0 or any other point.

However, if we apply the technique described in the previous section, we still can get the estimated probabilities of responses at any point on the proficiency scale. In one step further, we use these probability estimates in a contingency table analysis instead of frequency integers, in order to measure how much dependent the two items are on each other at a particular proficiency level[2].

The following (Figures 3.8, 3.9, 3.10) are three mosaic plots in three proficiency levels (Cz = -1.0, Cz = 0.0, and Cz = 1.0, respectively). In theory we can obtain mosaic plots in any proficiency levels. But these three cases are enough for demonstrating how the dependency of the two items gradually varies as the proficiency level varies.

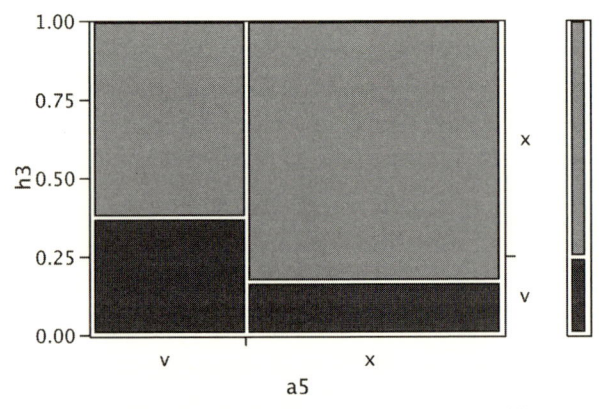

[Figure 3.8: Mosaic plot of the combined categories of target option (v) and other options as a collective category (x) in item **a5** and **h3** at Cz = -1.0]

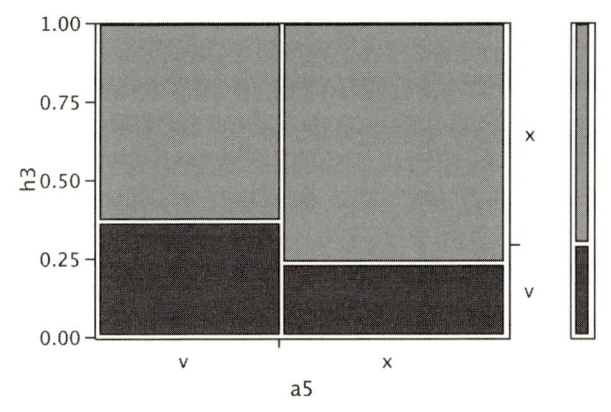

[Figure 3.9: Mosaic plot of the combined categories of target option (v) and other options as a collective category (x) in item **a5** and **h3** at Cz = 0.0]

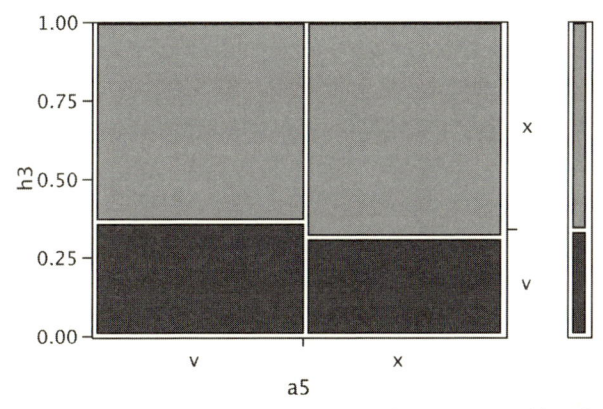

[Figure 3.10: Mosaic plot of the combined categories of target option (v) and other options as a collective category (x) in item **a5** and **h3** at Cz = 1.0]

From these figures we can observe that as the proficiency level rises the distortion of the distribution becomes neutralised. At Cz = -1.0, the size of the combined response (**a5** = 'x') and (**h3** = 'x') (top right) and the combined response (**a5** = 'v') and (**h3** = 'v') (bottom left) are disproportionately large. It means that there is a strong dependency between the two variables **a5** and **h3**. On the other hand, at Cz = 1.0 these two areas are almost proportionate to the corresponding area of the other variable, ie., the proportion of the combined response (**a5** = 'x') and (**h3** = 'x') (top right) is very close to that of the combined response (**a5** = 'v') and (**h3**= 'x') (top left), and the proportion of the combined response (**a5** = 'v') and (**h3** = 'v') (bottom left) is very close to that of the combined response (**a5** = 'x') and (**h3** = 'v') (bottom right). It means that the two variables **a5** and **h3** are mostly independent of each other.

3.3.2.2 Association measure

The contingency or dependency of two categorical variables is usually calculated by a contingency table analysis as a Chi square (χ^2) value. However, a Chi square cannot be used as a measure of association because its significance is subject to the sample size (Lewis-Beck, 1993: 172–173; Sirkin, 1995: 372–375). Instead, phi (φ) is used as a measure of association, where

$$\varphi^2 = \chi^2 / N$$

where 'N' denotes the subject size (Reynolds, 1993).

Once the four probabilities of the four cases of two-level two-category responses are obtained we can calculate the association measure for the two options **a5** and **h3**. Generally speaking, where responses to two dichotomous categories X and Y are obtained (Table 3.5),

[Table 3.5: Model of 2×2 (two-level two-category) contingency table]

		Category X		
		yes	no	
Category Y	yes	a	b	$a + b$
	no	c	d	$c + d$
		$a + c$	$b + d$	

the association measure between the two categories are calculated as Expression 2:

$$\varphi = \frac{ad - bc}{\sqrt{(a + b)(c + d)(a + c)(b + d)}} \quad \ldots(2)$$

It is important here that we use probabilities instead of frequencies for a, b, c, and d. We then can calculate the phi given the proficiency measure. Here are some phi values in 9 proficiency levels (Table 3.6).

[Table 3.6: Association measures (phi) of **a5** and **h3** in 9 proficiency levels]

Cz	φ (a5-h3)
-2.0	0.302
-1.5	0.269
-1.0	0.232
-0.5	0.192
0.0	0.149
0.5	0.103
1.0	0.054
1.5	0.004
2.0	-0.047

In this example we learn that the association measure for the pair **a5** and **h3** decreases monotonically as the proficiency measure increases. Our task then is to make a matrix of phi values for all possible pairs of responses across items (theoretically 38 (items) × (38 - 1) times / 2) for several different levels of proficiency.

For statistical work space it is impractical to calculate a matrix of phi values in very minute differences in proficiency level, so we sample nine proficiency levels at Cz = -2.0, 1.5, -1.0, -0.5, 0.0, 0.5, 1.0, 1.5, and 2.0.

3.3.3 Multidimensional scaling

From the matrix of association, groups of strongly associated items are identified by multidimensional scaling (MDS), using the association measures as proximity data (Romney, et al., 1972; Shepard, Romney, & Nerlove, 1972). This analytic procedure enables us to visualise which responses are closely located to one another. The groups of items judged as significantly clustered are then reinterpreted in the same way as factor analysis. This result might or might not correspond to our initial grouping stated in the tentative taxonomy in Section 3.2.2.1.1.

For the calculation of estimates, the statistics software package *SPSS* was used (SPSS, 1995).

In applying MDS, however, we have several problems. First, though any interval measure can be used as long as it represents Euclidean proximity or distance (Everitt & Dunn, 1991: 67), we are not sure whether the original φ coefficient obtained via logistic regression and contingency table analyses truly represents the proximity. By definition φ takes values between -1.0 and +1.0.

Where there is a strong association between two items the ceiling effect may underestimate the magnitude of association. Second, the treatment of negative values. It is possible that the more likely one considers an item grammatical the less likely one does to another item although the two items in fact belong to the same category. Negative values do not fit an MDS, since a proximity measure only takes a positive value. Finally, if we deliberately ignore low distance values, including negative ones, by equating them with 'missing data', it means they can take any values, hence resulting in irrelevant clustering of remote objects.

We propose a solution in Section 4.1.4 using the actual data obtained by the experiment.

Another problem inherent in MDS is the indeterminacy of apparent distances; since the solution has more or less degrees of stress, a certain distance measure between one pair of items is not necessarily equivalent to the same distance measure between another pair of items. To supplement this weakness, a measure representing the strength of association that each item has is introduced. This measure is applied in a contour plot analysis as the third dimension scale over the MDS plot, so the clustering of items will be observed distinctively.

3.3.4 Contour plot analysis

Contour plot analysis is a graphical tool to show a third dimension scale on the two-dimensional space. An easiest example to conceptualise it is a sea map. Any given point has three types of information: horizontal location, vertical location, and depth. Thus a contour plot analysis visualises salient third-dimension information. In our research the horizontal and vertical locations are the information conveyed by the MDS plot in a two-dimensional space, and the third dimension expresses the strength of association calculated from the phi statistics of association between a given item and its surrounding items.

For statistical analyses and graphical output, a software package *JMP* was used (SAS Institute, 2002).

3.4 Summary

In this chapter we have described the research design and statistical methodology involved. First, the participants were 1152 Japanese EFL learners from 21 universities. The sampling was not controlled but the final data showed a normal distribution of proficiency (Section 3.2.1). Second, as test materials two tests were described. (i) **Grammaticality judgement test** works as a dependent variable in our experiment. It has an original multiple-choice format; after the dichotomous judgement as 'correct' or 'incorrect' they are asked either to choose out of four options the implication or entailment of the stimulus sentence if the judgement was 'correct' or to choose out of four options the one indicating the location of what they think is the error. This format was chosen in order to solve the problem of high chance-level error and consequential indeterminacy which was indicated by the previous literature (Section 3.2.2.1.2). The stimulus sentences are written in such a way as to elicit 'local parsing' responses from the participants (Section 3.2.2.1.1). The history of developing grammaticality judgement test in the form of a summary of preliminary study was also described in order to rationalise our test format and procedure (Section 3.1.1). (ii) **C-test** works as an independent variable in our experiment. It consists of 122 blanks in four passages taken from a variety of sources so that the test takers' overall proficiency will be measured (Section 3.2.2.2.1). The raw scores are normalised into a new variable Cz so their mean is 0 and standard deviation is 1 (Section 3.2.3.2). Additionally, a questionnaire was prepared in order to filter out the participants with peculiar study background and to collect information of their TOEFL scores by self report. The TOEFL scores were intended to prove concurrent validity of the C-test, and to map the distribution of the C-test scores to that of TOEFL scores (Section 3.2.2.3).

Second, as statistical methodology four types of statistics were described: contingency table analysis, logistic regression analysis, multidimensional analysis, and contour plot analysis. Contingency table analysis tests the independence of two categorical data (Section 3.3.2). Since our research aim is to calculate the association measures of two stimulus items as a continuous function of proficiency, phi (φ) instead of Chi square (χ^2) statistic is to be calculated (Section 3.3.2.2). To do so probabilities of occurrence of dichotomous categories, namely the target response and other responses, are estimated by logistic regression analysis (Section 3.3.1, Expression 1). Two items are combined in one logistic regression analysis so the probabilities of four possible cases are calculated as a function of test takers' proficiency at nine sampling levels: Cz = -2.0, -1.5, -1.0, -0.5, 0.0, 0.5, 1.0, 1.5, and 2.0. These probability estimates, which indicate the magnitude of categories, are used in the contingency table analysis instead of frequencies. The contingency table analysis calculates a phi (φ) statistic

(Expression 2). By repeating the calculation for all possible pairs of 38 items, we can get a matrix of phi statistics given a level of proficiency. Since the phi statistics can be used as a basis of psychometric distance, the matrix becomes a map of items in which items of similar behaviour are located in relative closeness. By repeating this process over nine proficiency levels we can observe how the item mapping changes across proficiency levels (Section 3.3.2.2). Using a matrix of association measure, φ, we calculate a scatter plot of items by multidimensional scaling (Section 3.3.3). However, a two-dimensional solution of multidimensional scaling does not necessarily yield proportionate distances between two items of different combinations. Therefore we use a contour plot analysis in which we fix the item locations calculated by multidimensional scaling at a certain proficiency level and add a depth variable to each item which represents the strength of association that the item has with other items (Section 3.3.4). All these statistical steps are involved in an attempt to calculate a cluster of items having a strong association with one another, the strength of which changes as the proficiency level changes.

Chapter 4
Results and discussion

In this chapter we describe the results of our experiment and discuss the problems in the following steps.

First, we report the basic statistics of the data analysed: GJ test (dependent variable), C-test (independent variable), and TOEFL ITP (supplementary reference frame). We confirm here that all these data are not abnormally distributed.

The next stage is to establish the relation between item responses, using **logistic regression anaysis** in an attempt to explore the response behaviour. This stage includes the following two steps: (1) calculating the probability function of the response reflecting the strategy of 'local parsing' in each item, and (2) calculating the association measures of all combinations of items by contingency table analysis. Then the association measures are sent to **multidimensional scaling analysis** in order to obtain the two-dimentional plot of items. The association measures are converted to Euclidean scale measures before applying multidimensional scaling analysis. As this plotting job can be done for any proficiency level, we repeat the process in nine discrete proficiency levels. Because of the limitation in presenting a gradual change in configurations of items in multidimensional scaling analysis, we apply **contour plot analysis**. Here the location of items are fixed and the contour dimension represents the strength of association that each item has, called *LinkScore*, which is converted from the inter-item association measure.

In the confirmatory stage we classify the stimulus items into two categories: 'accessible' and 'inaccessible', depending on whether the sentences contain parts of local semantic interpretation. Then we test whether there is a difference in the *LinkScores* between 'accessible' and 'inaccessible' items. Finally, we estimate individual participants' degree of the tendency of local parsing by calculating the product of item responses and *LinkScores*. Then we test whether the participants' aggregate measures of local parsing inversely correlate with their proficiency measures. Thus we finalise our confirmation of the Hypotheses.

4.1 Results
    4.1.1 Data filtering
    4.1.2 Basic statistics
        4.1.2.1 Grammaticality judgement test
        4.1.2.2 C-test
        4.1.2.3 TOEFL ITP
    4.1.3 Distribution of association measures
    4.1.4 Multidimensional scaling analysis
    4.1.5 Contour plot analysis
    4.1.6 Model mapping of association links
4.2 Interpretation
    4.2.1 Exploratory phase
    4.2.2 Confirmatory phase
        4.2.2.1 Test of the difference of item groups with inherent structural attributes
        4.2.2.2 Test of the correlation between local parsing measures and proficiency measures
4.3 Discussion
    4.3.1 Unidimensionality in the C-test
    4.3.2 The local parsing strategy
    4.3.3 The relationship between general proficiency and parsing ability
    4.3.4 Methodological reminders
4.4 Summary

4.1 Results

We conducted the following analyses in addition to basic statistics.
(1) **Logistic regression analysis** for the grammaticality judgement (GJ) test, where the standardised C-test score was the independent variable and the probability of the response reflecting cognitive constraint was the dependent

variable.

(2) **Association measures** between responses, based on the probabilities of responses from individual items.

(3) **Multidimensional scaling analysis** and **contour plot analysis**, which, combined together, sought to describe the size of the clusters of responses as a function of the test takers' proficiency measure.

4.1.1 Data filtering

We first trimmed the irrelevant parts of the data before we actually started our calculation. Originally we collected data from 1508 participants, but since we intended to pair the data of the GJ test and of the C-test, 156 had to be discarded because they lacked one of the two tests. Of the remaining 1352, another 200 were abandoned as the individual data fit on one or both of the following criteria, in which case they were considered as having a motivational problem or being uncooperative.

i. More than 33% of the answers to the GJ test items were unanswered, whether they were consecutive or discrete.
ii. More than 90% of the answers to any one of the four passages in the C-test were unanswered.

The distribution of the participants in terms of the C-test scores before the filtering is shown in Figure 4.1. Hereafter, the figures of frequency distribution denote the frequency on the horizontal axis, and the variable bands on the vertical axis.

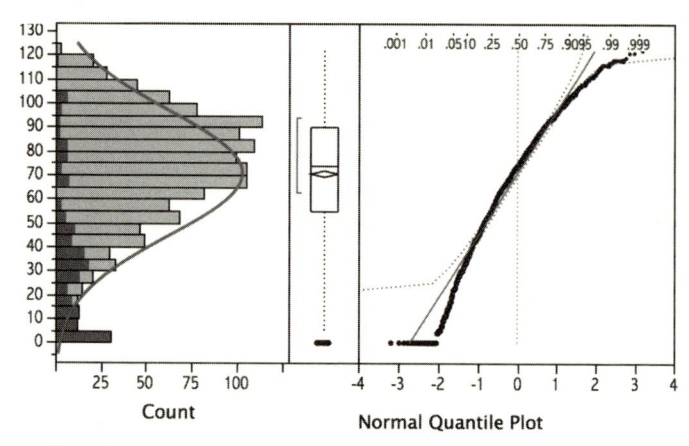

[Figure 4.1: Distribution of the original C-test scores and their normal quantile plot. N = 1352. The dark areas show the participants to be filtered out.]

After filtering the participants of 'incomplete' performance indicated in the dark areas in Figure 4.1, the corrected distribution now looked like Figure 4.2.

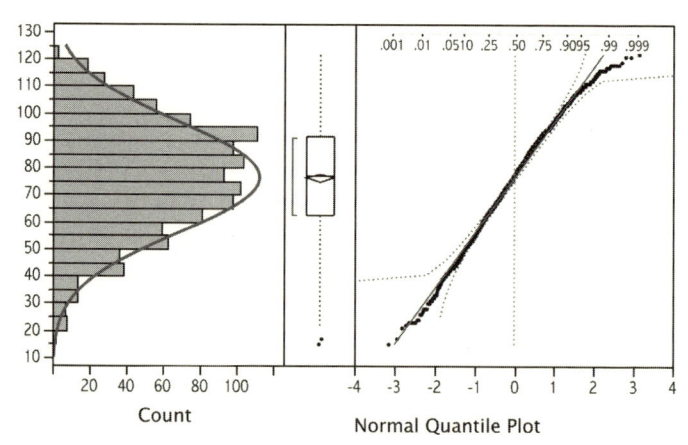

[Figure 4.2: Distribution of the C-test scores after filtering and their normal quantile plot. N = 1152.]

By this filtering the fit distribution index improved from W=0.948 to W=0.974 (Shapiro-Wilk W test). It is also indicated by the linear distribution of data on the normal quantile plot.

We did not eliminate the participants having overseas experience (N = 84) because (1) their relatively high scores on the C-test (mean = 86.47 as opposed to the rest: mean = 75.32; difference: t = 5.496, p < 0.0001) did not, logically speaking, affect the choices of options by low-proficiency test takers, which were our main concern, and (2) a tentative elimination of these participants did not affect the normality of distribution of the C-test scores (W = 0.975 when this set of participants was eliminated).

4.1.2 Basic statistics
4.1.2.1 Grammaticality judgement test
The basic statistics and distribution of the total scores of the GJ test were as follows.

N = 1152
Mean = 10.71
SD = 5.32
Skewness = 0.594
Distribution of the total scores (Figure 4.3):

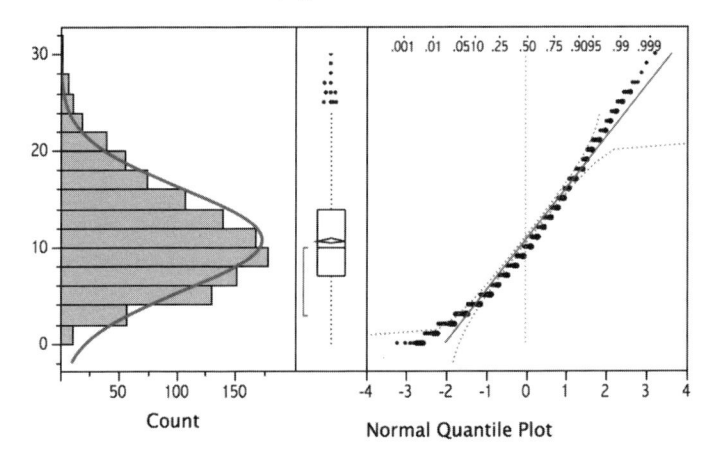

[Figure 4.3: Distribution of the Grammaticality judgement test scores and their normal quantile plot]

The item statistics of the GJ test were as follows.

KR20: r = 0.773
Mean facility value = 0.282
Mean discrimination index = 0.293
Primary eigenvalue = 1.012 (14.458%)
Secondary eigenvalue = 0.297 (4.242%; 18.700% cumulative)

The distribution was positively skewed, which meant that the average difficulty level of the test items was above the participants' average proficiency level, and the internal consistency (indicated by KR20) was not very high. Though the drop rate of the eigenvalues (ie., the ratio of the primary eigenvalue to the secondary one) was approximately 3.41, the percentage of the primary eigenvalue was below 20%. Therefore the data were not considered unidimensional (Reckase, 1979; Holmes, 1982). Note that it was barely unidimensional according to Guttman's (1954) old criterion which counts the number of factors whose eigenvalues are above or equal to 1.

4.1.2.2 C-test

The basic statistics and distribution of the total score of the C-test were as follows.

N = 1152
Mean = 76.384
SD = 20.499
Skewness = -0.251
Distribution of the total score (see Figure 4.2 above):
KR20: r = 0.959
Mean facility value = 0.626
Mean discrimination index = 0.245
Primary eigenvalue = 4.030 (19.480%)
Secondary eigenvalue = 0.732 (3.537%; 23.017% cumulative)

The distribution was quite normal, and the internal consistency was very high. Also, since the drop rate of the eigenvalue was 5.51 and the percentage of the primary eigenvalue was almost 20% the data were considered unidimensional.

The raw scores were then normalised (N(0, 1)), so the frequency distribution now had mean = 0 and standard deviation = 1. Henceforth the normalised measure Cz is used as a measure of the independent scale. By this conversion we can conceptualise the measure with more ease; for example, a person with Cz = 1 has a level of proficiency 1 standard deviation above the average, and is ranked at 16% from the top in the population.

4.1.2.3 TOEFL ITP

The participants' TOEFL ITP (Test of English as a Foreign Language: Institutional Testing Program) scores were collected through the questionnaire. Since the scores were based on their self report the figures were not accurate. Also, because the majority of the entire test takers were first and second year students who were normally not supposed to have taken the TOEFL so far, the TOEFL ITP score reports were limited (N = 183 as compared with the entire population N = 1152). For the participants who only reported TOEFL CBT scores they were converted to ITP scores. The basic statistics of this test were as follows.

N = 183
Mean = 435.027
SD = 51.738
Skewness = 0.614
Distribution of the scores (Figure 4.4):

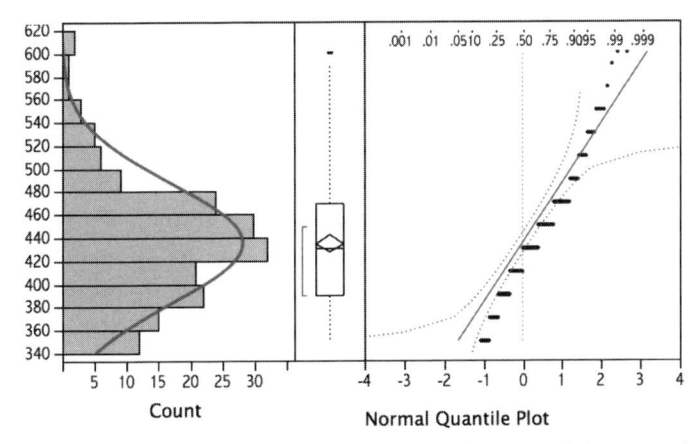

[Figure 4.4: Distribution of the TOEFL ITP scores by self report and their normal quantile plot]

Note that since individual TOEFL ITP data were only single scores without any further information about test items (ie., the self report was in the form "My TOEFL ITP score is xxx"), no summary of the item information (ie., reliability index (KR20), facility values, discrimination, and eigenvalues from factor analysis) is provided here.

The TOEFL ITP scores were then compared with the corresponding

C-test scores (represented by the measure Cz). The Pearson's product moment correlation coefficient was not very high ($r = 0.574$), but the figure shows a highly significant correlation ($p < 0.001$, two-tailed test, df = 182).

Correlation: $r = 0.574$

Linear regression equation: [TOEFL ITP] = [Cz] × 30.009 + 416.623

4.1.3 Distribution of association measures

The matrices of association measures shows that certain pairs of items had higher measures than others. Table 4.1 is a list of sum of phi (φ) values for each item. The sum of φ of a given item at a given proficiency level was calculated by adding up the φ of all pairs in which the item was a member. For instance, the total φ values of item **a1** was the sum of (φ of **a1** and **a2**) + (φ of **a1** and **a3**) + (φ of **a1** and **a3**) + ... + (φ of **a1** and **h6**).

[Table 4.1: List of sums of item association measures in 9 proficiency levels]

Cz	a1	a2	a3	a4l	a4v	a5	a6	b1	b2	b3	b4	b5	b6	c1	c2	d1	d2	d3	e1
-2.00	2.06	-0.64	0.72	-0.58	2.09	2.34	3.29	0.51	2.10	1.12	2.47	-0.56	1.65	2.24	1.63	3.04	1.82	0.11	3.04
-1.50	2.16	-0.55	0.63	-0.13	1.93	2.42	3.16	0.81	2.02	1.30	2.51	-0.47	1.74	2.30	1.74	2.79	1.91	0.31	2.97
-1.00	2.26	-0.45	0.57	0.27	1.72	2.49	3.01	1.09	1.93	1.47	2.54	-0.34	1.83	2.34	1.83	2.52	2.00	0.53	2.88
-0.50	2.36	-0.33	0.51	0.62	1.44	2.52	2.83	1.35	1.81	1.65	2.55	-0.19	1.92	2.38	1.90	2.24	2.08	0.76	2.77
0.00	2.46	-0.19	0.47	0.93	1.11	2.52	2.62	1.59	1.68	1.82	2.55	-0.01	2.00	2.40	1.95	1.95	2.15	1.00	2.62
0.50	2.55	-0.03	0.47	1.18	0.71	2.49	2.39	1.80	1.52	1.98	2.52	0.20	2.06	2.40	1.99	1.65	2.21	1.25	2.46
1.00	2.64	0.16	0.54	1.39	0.26	2.42	2.13	2.00	1.35	2.13	2.48	0.47	2.12	2.39	2.02	1.35	2.27	1.52	2.27
1.50	2.72	0.41	0.80	1.55	-0.22	2.32	1.86	2.17	1.17	2.27	2.42	0.87	2.16	2.38	2.04	1.05	2.32	1.79	2.06
2.00	2.79	0.74	1.33	1.67	-0.72	2.19	1.58	2.33	0.98	2.39	2.34	1.49	2.18	2.36	2.06	0.75	2.36	2.08	1.84

Cz	e2	e3	e4	e5	f1	g1	g2	g3	g4	g5	g6	g7	g8	h1	h2	h3	h4	h5	h6	total	mean
-2.00	2.07	2.07	1.22	0.28	0.92	0.15	1.60	1.38	1.21	3.16	2.88	3.17	3.07	1.38	2.66	3.96	1.81	0.94	2.97	65.34	1.72
-1.50	1.94	2.15	1.46	0.64	1.25	0.58	1.51	1.47	1.26	3.06	2.75	2.96	2.82	1.58	2.61	3.74	1.70	1.13	2.92	67.08	1.77
-1.00	1.81	2.20	1.68	0.98	1.56	0.99	1.42	1.57	1.29	2.93	2.58	2.71	2.53	1.77	2.52	3.48	1.57	1.31	2.84	68.23	1.80
-0.50	1.67	2.24	1.88	1.31	1.84	1.36	1.32	1.67	1.30	2.77	2.39	2.42	2.22	1.96	2.40	3.18	1.41	1.49	2.72	68.71	1.81
0.00	1.54	2.24	2.06	1.61	2.09	1.69	1.22	1.76	1.30	2.58	2.17	2.10	1.89	2.13	2.25	2.85	1.23	1.66	2.56	68.54	1.80
0.50	1.40	2.23	2.23	1.89	2.31	1.96	1.12	1.86	1.29	2.37	1.93	1.74	1.53	2.30	2.07	2.49	1.03	1.82	2.36	67.73	1.78
1.00	1.27	2.19	2.39	2.14	2.51	2.19	1.02	1.95	1.27	2.14	1.66	1.36	1.15	2.45	1.85	2.09	0.80	1.97	2.12	66.42	1.75
1.50	1.13	2.13	2.53	2.35	2.68	2.36	0.93	2.03	1.26	1.89	1.38	0.95	0.77	2.59	1.60	1.66	0.55	2.10	1.86	64.91	1.71
2.00	1.00	2.06	2.66	2.54	2.83	2.48	0.84	2.12	1.25	1.63	1.09	0.50	0.37	2.72	1.32	1.21	0.28	2.22	1.59	63.45	1.67

Assuming the null hypothesis that the distribution of φ was equal throughout the 28 items in each proficiency level, the deviances of observed φ sums were calculated. Table 4.2 shows total Chi square (χ^2) values of the entire set of items for each proficiency level.

[Table 4.2: List of Chi square statistics of item association measures in 9 proficiency levels. ***: p < 0.001, **: p < 0.01, *: p < 0.05]

Cz	a1	a2	a3	a4l	a4v	a5	a6	b1	b2	b3	b4	b5	b6	c1	c2	d1	d2	d3	e1
-2.00	0.04	1.89	0.34	1.79	0.05	0.13	0.84	0.49	0.05	0.12	0.19	1.76	0.00	0.09	0.00	0.59	0.00	0.88	0.59
-1.50	0.05	1.72	0.41	1.16	0.01	0.14	0.63	0.29	0.02	0.07	0.18	1.60	0.00	0.09	0.00	0.34	0.01	0.68	0.47
-1.00	0.07	1.56	0.47	0.72	0.00	0.15	0.46	0.15	0.01	0.03	0.17	1.42	0.00	0.09	0.00	0.16	0.01	0.50	0.37
-0.50	0.09	1.39	0.52	0.43	0.04	0.16	0.32	0.06	0.00	0.01	0.17	1.22	0.00	0.10	0.00	0.06	0.02	0.34	0.28
0.00	0.13	1.22	0.55	0.24	0.15	0.16	0.20	0.01	0.00	0.00	0.17	1.01	0.01	0.11	0.01	0.01	0.04	0.20	0.21
0.50	0.19	1.03	0.54	0.11	0.36	0.16	0.12	0.00	0.02	0.01	0.17	0.79	0.03	0.12	0.01	0.01	0.06	0.09	0.14
1.00	0.26	0.82	0.48	0.04	0.72	0.15	0.05	0.02	0.05	0.05	0.17	0.54	0.05	0.14	0.02	0.05	0.09	0.02	0.09
1.50	0.35	0.57	0.28	0.01	1.27	0.13	0.01	0.07	0.10	0.11	0.17	0.24	0.07	0.15	0.04	0.15	0.13	0.00	0.04
2.00	0.45	0.31	0.04	0.00	2.06	0.10	0.00	0.15	0.17	0.19	0.16	0.01	0.10	0.17	0.05	0.31	0.17	0.06	0.01

Cz	e2	e3	e4	e5	f1	g1	g2	g3	g4	g5	g6	g7	g8	h1	h2	h3	h4	h5	h6	Chi^2	p
-2.00	0.04	0.04	0.08	0.70	0.22	0.83	0.01	0.04	0.09	0.71	0.46	0.72	0.62	0.04	0.30	1.70	0.00	0.20	0.53	17.17	***
-1.50	0.05	0.05	0.03	0.41	0.08	0.45	0.02	0.03	0.08	0.54	0.31	0.46	0.36	0.01	0.23	1.25	0.00	0.13	0.43	12.73	***
-1.00	0.00	0.05	0.00	0.21	0.02	0.20	0.04	0.02	0.08	0.40	0.19	0.26	0.17	0.00	0.16	0.88	0.02	0.07	0.34	9.45	**
-0.50	0.01	0.06	0.00	0.08	0.00	0.06	0.07	0.01	0.08	0.28	0.10	0.11	0.05	0.01	0.11	0.58	0.05	0.03	0.25	7.15	**
0.00	0.02	0.06	0.02	0.01	0.03	0.00	0.10	0.00	0.08	0.18	0.04	0.03	0.00	0.03	0.06	0.34	0.10	0.01	0.17	5.72	*
0.50	0.05	0.06	0.06	0.00	0.09	0.01	0.14	0.00	0.08	0.11	0.01	0.00	0.02	0.08	0.03	0.16	0.18	0.00	0.10	5.13	*
1.00	0.08	0.06	0.13	0.05	0.19	0.06	0.17	0.01	0.07	0.05	0.00	0.05	0.12	0.16	0.00	0.04	0.30	0.02	0.05	5.41	*
1.50	0.11	0.06	0.23	0.14	0.32	0.14	0.21	0.04	0.07	0.01	0.04	0.20	0.30	0.27	0.00	0.00	0.46	0.05	0.01	6.57	*
2.00	0.16	0.06	0.35	0.27	0.49	0.24	0.25	0.07	0.06	0.00	0.12	0.49	0.60	0.39	0.04	0.08	0.69	0.11	0.00	8.99	**

Table 4.2 indicates that in all proficiency levels the distribution of φ was significantly uneven.

Thus Hypothesis 1

1. A cognitive constraint on processing works commonly across certain test items of grammaticality judgement.

namely, the association measures between all pairs of items are uneven, has been confirmed. It implies that a certain factor affects the association measures of some particular items selectively. The identification of this factor had to wait for the confirmatory analysis to be stated in Section 4.2.2.

4.1.4 Multidimensional scaling analysis

Our next step of analysis was to identify the relative positioning of items. Multidimensional scaling (MDS) analysis enables us to configure the locations of responses on a n-dimensional space (usually two- or three-dimensional) when distance or proximity measures between pairs of responses are provided. In our experiment we attempted to plot items on a two-dimensional space based on the information of association measures between items.

In Section 3.3.3 we pointed out a problem concerning the use of φ statistics for multidimensional scaling, ie., incongruity of scales between φ statistics and Euclidean distant measures. It is problematic in two ways: (i) φ statistics cannot represent all the distance measures which take values between 0 and infinite, and (ii) negative values of φ statistics are by default regarded as missing data, which allows distortion of item configuration. In order to solve these problems we converted the φ scale into a new scale while retaining the monotonic function.

$$SDist = \frac{1}{e^{k \cdot \varphi}}$$

This conversion formula does not yield negative values, and the ceiling effect is attenuated. The coefficient k was sought through trials of calculating the stress against the present data (Table 4.3). Since the variability of the data increases towards both ends of the proficiency scale, the average stress was calculated for the range between Cz = -1.0 and Cz = 1.0. By definition Cz follows a standardised normal distribution (0, 1), so this range represents 68% of the total participants.

[Table 4.3: Stress values of MDS in 5 trials in 9 proficiency levels]

Cz	k=10	k=20	k=30	k=40	k=50
2.0	.34328	.33804	.35034	.35034	.35036
1.5	.32824	.32828	.32828	.32827	.32827
1.0	.32007	.31785	.31785	.31784	.31785
0.5	.30282	.29430	.30133	.30127	.30127
0.0	.29533	.29780	.29767	.29765	.29765
-0.5	.30114	.29430	.29411	.31208	.29402
-1.0	.33093	.32711	.32999	.32600	.33008
-1.5	.31783	.37048	.32764	.32820	.32824
-2.0	.33634	.33641	.33639	.33642	.33639
whole range average	.31955	.32273	.32040	.32201	.32046
narrow range average	.31006	**.30627**	.30819	.31097	.30817

Judging from the narrow range average score of the stress values, the stress was considered least when k=20. Regrettably, the overall stress values were not quite satisfactory, since the R^2 of the variance at k=20 and Cz = 0.0, for instance, was 0.5497, which was smaller than the normally accepted critical value of 0.6. However, considering the multidimensional nature of linguistic stimuli, and the fact that we forcefully stretched the stimuli onto a two-dimensional space, deciding the coefficient k based on the relative stress size was meaningful at least for our present purpose of specifying the conversion formula. In conclusion, the new measure (Expression 3)

$$SDist = \frac{1}{e^{20 \cdot \varphi}} \qquad ...(3)$$

was used as the measure of distance.

The results of the analyses were drawn in the form of stimulus configuration. We copy here two representative figures of the item plots at Cz = -1.5 (Figure 4.5) and at Cz = 1.5 (Figure 4.6).

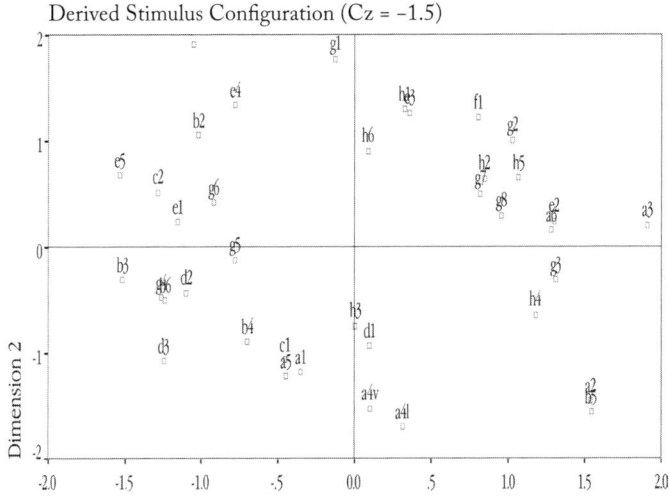

[Figure 4.5: Two-dimensional distribution of items by MDS at Cz = -1.5]

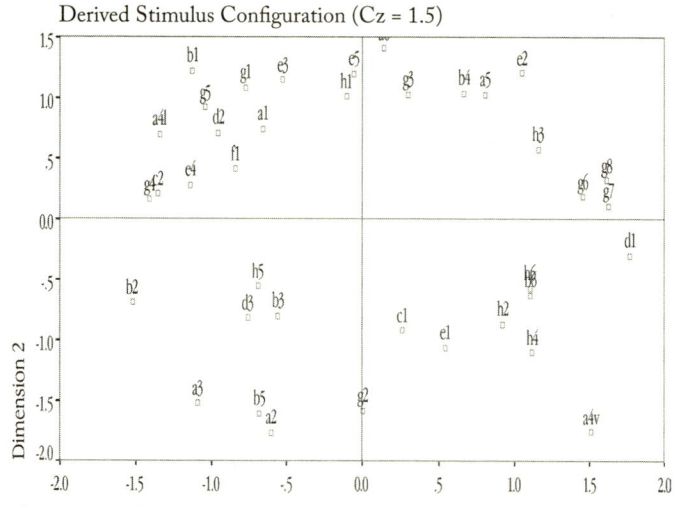

[Figure 4.6: Two-dimensional distribution of items by MDS at Cz = 1.5]

The distribution of items in each configuration figure showed no continuous transition. A slight change in distance between some responses may result in a large difference in configuration. For example, items **a3** and **d3** were found in the top right quarter in the configuration for Cz = -1.0 (ie., both dimensions 1 and 2 were positive), they were in the bottom left when Cz = -0.5 (ie., both dimensions 1 and 2 were negative), top right again when Cz = 0.0, and bottom left again when Cz = 0.5. Also, the Euclidean distance of any two given items on the graph does not necessarily represent the true dissimilarity scale, ie., *SDist* value. For example, locations of items **a5**, **g7**, and **h2** when Cz = -1.5 were calculated by MDS as follows:

a5 (-0.4455, -1.2240)
g7 (0.8170, 0.4941)
h2 (0.8464, 0.6371)

The Euclidean distances among these three items, *SDist*, and φ were:

	Distance	SDist	phi
a5-g7	2.132	0.006	0.258
g7-h2	0.146	0.022	0.192

The real distance by *SDist* between **a5** and **g7** should be much shorter than that between **g7** and **h2**, but the MDS plot did not reflect this fact but was affected by other distances in combination with other items. The problem arises from the fact that an apparent distance between items on a two dimensional configuration does not always retain the same magnitude within a configuration for a given proficiency level and across configurations for different proficiency levels, though the items are plotted in such a way that minimises the entire stress.

Therefore a simple configuration by MDS does not give us a clue as to whether or not some items make a cluster. Instead, we need to fix the location of items and assign to each of them a measure which reflects the strength of association between items.

4.1.5 Contour plot analysis

In order to visualise the measures of the strength of association between items a contour plot analysis was used. Contour plot analysis adds the third dimension, depth, to the conventional two-dimension plotting, and it features gradation of colours over and between the plots. So far we have discussed the association between pairs of items, which does not let us know how much *each item* is involved in the association network. Therefore we had to convert the pair measure into an item measure. As the depth variable the following parameter for item *i* was devised (Expression 4).

$$LinkScore_i = \sum_{k=1}^{n}(\varphi_{ik})^2 \quad \ldots(4)$$

where *n* is the total number of links with positive values.

This parameter reflects the total strength of links of an item with other items. Small association measures ($\varphi < 0$) were ignored so they would not affect the item configuration.

At the same time the location of items had to be kept constant across all proficiency levels, because the raw MDS configurations were unstable. The prototype configuration could be any one of those for the 9 proficiency levels, but because of the relative discernibility the dimensions at Cz = -0.5 were chosen.

The results of the contour plot analyses in the form of stimulus configuration in nine proficiency levels (ie., at Cz = -2.0, -1.5, -1.0, -0.5, 0.0, 0.5, 1.0, 1.5, and 2.0) are found in **Appendix D** (Figures D1–D9). At proficiency level Cz = -1.5 (Figure D2), there was a cluster of items with high *LinkScores* around item **h3**. On the other hand, at proficiency level Cz = 1.5 (Figure D8), there was no remarkable cluster; the contour was levelled. From these contour plot graphs it seemed likely that the contrast of the density of links was strongest at a certain cluster of items when the proficiency score Cz was lowest, and it became weaker as the proficiency level rose.

Hence the first of the three steps of Hypothesis 2, namely,

2.1 There is a cluster of responses bearing high association measures with one another.

was confirmed. The third step of Hypothesis 2, however, needed more clarification.

2.3 The cluster becomes stronger or weaker monotonically as the proficiency measure changes.

The central cluster around **h3** showed the strongest cohesion at Cz = -2.0, weakened gradually as the proficiency level lowered, and disappeared at around Cz = 0.0. In higher proficiency levels there was no apparent clustering of items. In other words, the participants' common erroneous parsing strategy, represented by the major cluster, existed below the middle range of proficiency. It seemed likely that high-proficiency test takers' parsing strategies are more diverse and complex than those of low-proficiency test takers, so the commonality in responses is harder to find among high-proficiency test takers. In the next section we shall focus on particular pairs of items and examine how the actual association measures, instead of the cumulative *LinkScores*, change as the proficiency level changes.

4.1.6 Model mapping of association links

Our next question was to identify the members of the cluster which exhibits a strong link when the proficiency level is low. To help us visualise the transition of association between items, a simplified plot model, instead of the MDS-based plot chart, was postulated. Here the items were plotted in such a way that the association measures (φ) between pairs of items were best read. The location of items and hence the distance among them did not necessarily reflect the strength of association. In order to focus on the core cluster 16 major items were chosen whose association measures with other items were more than 0.18 on the proficiency level $Cz = -1.5$.

Using the same plotting locations, association measures (φ) were added in the map for each of 9 proficiency levels. Below we show three typical maps at $Cz = -1.5$ (Figure 4.7), $Cz = 0.0$ (Figure 4.8), and $Cz = 1.5$ (Figure 4.9).

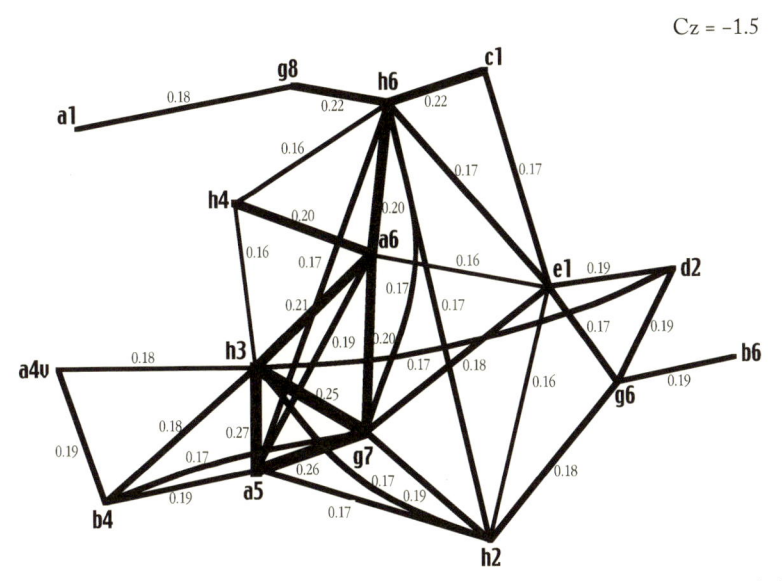

[Figure 4.7: Model map of clusters of items at $Cz = -1.5$. The thick lines indicate major links. Figures indicate association measures.]

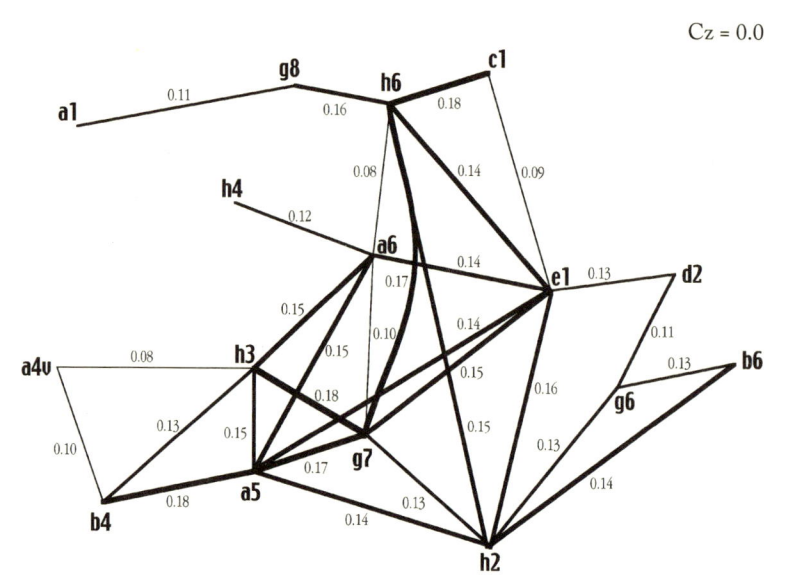

[Figure 4.8: Model map of clusters of items at Cz = 0.0. The thick lines indicate major links. Figures indicate association measures.]

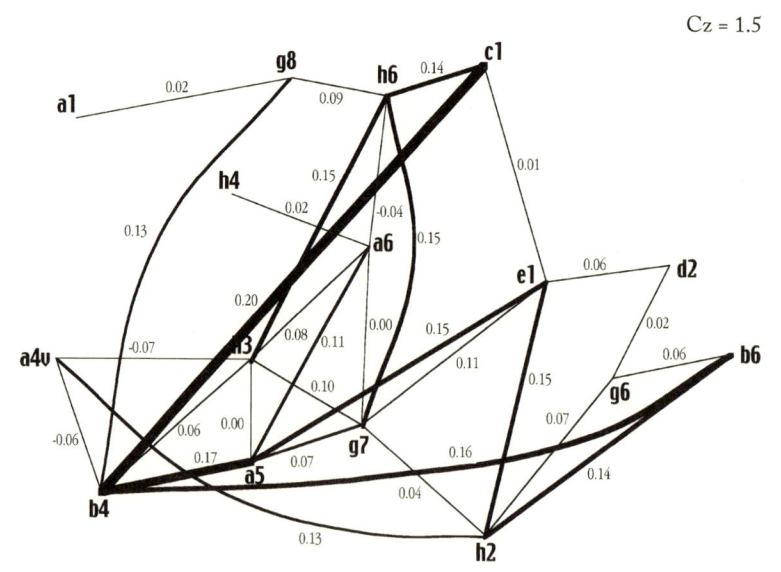

[Figure 4.9: Model map of clusters of items at Cz = 1.5. The thick lines indicate major links. Figures indicate association measures.]

From these maps we found that items **a5, g7,** and **h3** bore the strongest association among other items. The members of this core cluster and items around it changed gradually as the proficiency level changed. The core cluster was strongest at Cz = -2.0 and weakened as the proficiency level rose until approximately at Cz = 0.0 when it was no longer salient. Other items around the core cluster followed more or less the same pattern. Thus we roughly identified a hierarchy of association for low-proficiency test takers. Figure 4.10 represents the hierarchical clustering of items. Note that this hierarchy and inclusion of particular items did not derive from a statistical calculation; nor the identification of levels is strict. The figure indicates that there are different degrees of strength of association among items which form a cluster in gradient magnitudes.

<<Core Cluster Level 1>>
   a5, g7, h3
<<Core Cluster Level 2>>
   Items in Level 1 + **a6, b4**
<<Core Cluster Level 3>>
   Items in Level 2 + **a4v, e1, h2, h4, h6**
<<Core Cluster Level 4>>
   Items in Level 3 + **a1, b6, c1, d2, g6, g8**

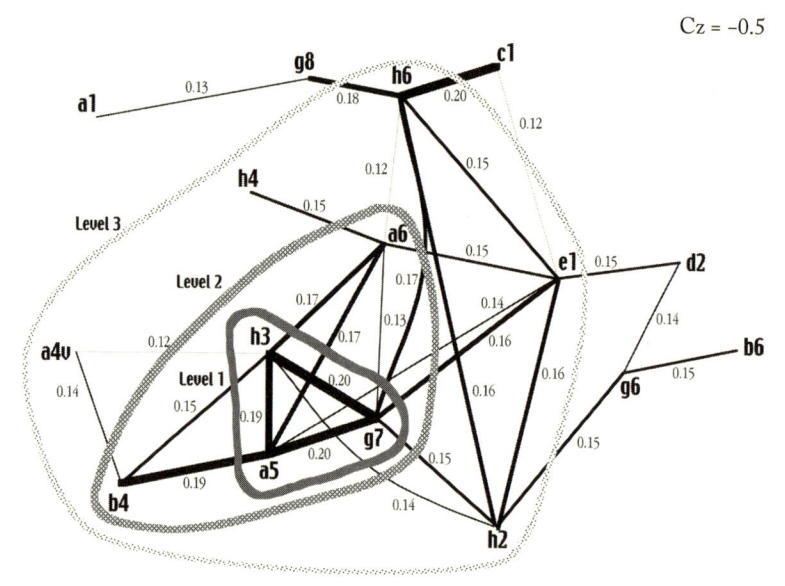

[Figure 4.10: Core clusters of items indicated on a model map. Figures indicate association measures.]

Hence the second step of Hypothesis 2, namely,

2.2 Members of the cluster stay constant or change gradually as the proficiency measure changes.

was partly confirmed. We observed that the deeper we go into the cluster the stronger association the members have. The membership of the core cluster persisted approximately until $Cz = 0.0$, then dissolved gradually as the proficiency level rose further.

4.2 Interpretation

4.2.1 Exploratory phase

Based on the clusters obtained in the previous analyses we considered the cognitive communality of core items. Here is a list of items we cited earlier in 3.2.2.1 now in the order of core clusters.

[Table 4.4: List of stimulus sentences. Italicised parts indicate the sequences of local parsing. The word with an asterisk (*) indicates that the word should be corrected into some other form, the word with a double cross (#) indicates that the word should be deleted, the caret (^) indicates that a word should be inserted at that location, and the word/phrase in square brackets ([]) indicates that it should be inserted in that location.]

<<Core Cluster Level 1>>
a5 ¶ The Department of *Foreign Languages *are not located* in the new building.
g7 ¶ When the magician appeared, Bill came downstairs *to see*the*magician*.
h3 ¶ When I last saw Janet, *she *hurried* to her next class on the other side of the campus.

<<Core Cluster Level 2>>
a6 ¶ To grow *several kinds of flowers *are the joy* of gardening.
b4 ¶ Mr Kawase, vice president of Tomato Bank, #*he will speak* to the press this afternoon.

<<Core Cluster Level 3>>
a4v ¶ You will find the glasses with *red marks on both sides #are quite expensive*.
e1 ¶ #*For badly wounded*, the soldier stopped fighting.
h2 ¶ Mr Peters used to think of **hisself* as the only president of the company.
h4 ¶ Carl was upset last night because *he had to do too many *homeworks*.
h6 ¶ I watched the match because I knew some of the **playing *people*.

<<Core Cluster Level 4>>
a1 ¶ The letter kept by the old woman who we met when we were looking for *the boy disappeared*.
b6 ¶ *His attacker was described* [as] a tall man with a beard.
c1 ¶ [When] *Most people hear "endangered species"*, they think of animals.
d2 ¶ The activity I liked most in the Gardening Club was **planted many seeds*.
g6 ¶ *What I want is* ^ cup, not ^ glass.
g8 ¶ We did not know what to do *with *us*.

<<Core Cluster Marginal>>
a2 ¶ *Vivian knew the police officer* under suspicion had received the money.
a3 ¶ The fact that the dog hurt *the boy scared Linda*.
a4l ¶ *You will find the glasses* with red marks on both sides #are quite expensive.
b1 ¶ I think that gardening #is *wash the human heart.
b2 ¶ *Half of the people* ([who]) (#)*were invited* to the party didn't turn up.
b3 ¶ Take this flight which I think #that is least expensive.
b5 ¶ [That] You don't know *Russian is a pity*.
c2 ¶ I'm worried about [whether] you are happy.
d1 ¶ Diane's nose got extremely cold, **running home* through the snow.
d3 ¶ *Hiromi is difficult ^ to learn mathematics.
e2 ¶ I can't think of anybody #whom to invite.
e3 ¶ I hate insects — it is the reason that I don't like #to gardening.

e4 ¶ I showed the little boys how to *jumping.
e5 ¶ Yamane visited Kyoto to *meeting an old friend of his.
f1 ¶ "Can I see Harriet?" "I'm sorry *her [is/has] gone to school."
g1 ¶ Catherine [does] not come here anymore, because her mother is ill in bed.
g2 ¶ It is my mother *to *like arranging little trees in the garden.
g3 ¶ The children thanked Jim for *come.
g4 ¶ I was very *interesting in the lesson.
g5 ¶ The policemen [were] surprised that the girls chased the man in the station.
h1 ¶ All the students were looking forward [to] spending their free time on the beach.
h5 ¶ This is Naomi, *that sells the tickets.

The phrases in italic letters indicate locally interpretable fractions. We call them instances of 'local parsing'. In item **a5**, for example, many test takers considered the local cohesion as grammatically correct (see the area '1' in Figure 3.3), when they thought that "Foreign Languages" was plural and "are" agreed with it. To be more precise, they did not notice that the head noun phrase of the Subject is "the Department", which is singular, and the verb did not agree. The same agreement error applies to items **a6** ("several kinds of flowers" and "are") and **a4v** ("red marks on both sides" and "are"). In **h3**, the sentence in the main clause ("she hurried to her next class") would be correct without the preceding subordinate clause. The test takers who judged this sentence as correct focused only on the main clause. Likewise a pseudo-sentence in item **b4** ("he will speak to the press") would be OK if we ignored the preceding context which, in fact, includes the subject ("Mr Kawase"). The same parsing strategy must have been applied to item **c1**, where the first of the two unsubordinated clauses ("Most people hear 'endangered species'") were considered grammatical. Item **b6** would sound grammatical as a short sentence ("His attacker was described") if we ignored the last phrase. Finally, item **g8** concerns a command within a phrase ("us" → "ourselves"). This phrase would be grammatical if the preceding part of the sentence did not contain the same subject as "us". The same strategy may have been applied to item **g7** where pronominalisation of "the magician" (→ "him/her") is obligatory.

In items **e1** and **h6** the assumed strategy of local conceptualisation is the same as above, but the within-phrase syntax is incorrect. To low-proficiency test takers, however, the absolute syntactic correctness is inaccessible. It is rather considered that in item **h6** the superficial semantic plausibility ("playing people" like "playing cards") made them judge that the sentence was acceptable. In item **e1** this idea of semantic plausibility was emphasised by the (inappropriately) added preposition "for", which they knew is used for expressing reason.

Items **h2**, **h4**, and **g6** appear to involve somewhat different parsing strategies. They concern lexical form and grammar ("hisself" in **h2**, "homeworks" in **h4**, and "cup" and "glass" in **g6**). They are erroneous within the word. But this kind of error may have been unnoticed by test takers as long as they attended to the meaning. They are considered items of local parsing in the same way as items **h6** and **e1** are.

On the other hand, item **d2** is not considered the subject of local parsing because of the semantic conflict between "the Gardening Club" which contains the feature [-plantable object] and "was planted". Similarly, item **d3** is ungrammatical because the feature [+person] in the subject noun ("Hiromi") is incompatible with the complement ("is difficult").

Items outside Level 4 were relatively unaffected by the proficiency level. Though they included some items of likely local parsing errors (ie., items **a2** ("Vivian knew the police officer"), **a3** ("the boy scared Linda"), **a4l** ("You will find the glasses"), **b2** ("Half of the people were invited"), **b5** ("Russian is a pity"), and **d1** ("running home")), most of the planned errors derive from different causes. In items **b1**, **e3**, **e4**, **e5**, **f1**, **g3**, and **g4**, errors should be corrected against local configurations involving conflicts between adjacent verbs, prepositions, and modifiers (ie., "is wash" in **b2**, "like to gardening" in **e3**, "how to jumping" in **e4**, "to meeting" in **e5**, "her gone" in **f1**, and "for come" in **g3**). Local configuration is disturbed by superfluous elements in items **b3** ("that" in "which I think that is ...") and **e2** ("whom" in "anybody whom to invite"); by lack of necessary elements in items **c2** ("whether" missing in "... about [ ] you are happy"), **g1** ("does" missing in "Catherine [ ] not come", **g5** ("were" missing in "The policemen [ ] surprised"), and **h1** ("to" missing in "... looking forward [ ] spending their free time"); by replacement of necessary elements ("to like" instead of "who likes") in item **g2**.

Overall, it was observed that items involving local parsing errors tended to cluster together reflecting the errors made by low-proficiency test takers.

4.2.2 Confirmatory phase
4.2.2.1 Test of the difference of item groups with inherent structural attributes
To substantiate our categorisation as to whether an item response represents local parsing, we compared items in two groups of different strength of association links: 'accessible' and 'inaccessible'. 'Accessible' is a category of items

containing a 'local parsing' element, ie., a phrase or pseudo-sentence which alone appears grammatically correct and semantically coherent (Table 4.5). 'Inaccessible', on the other hand, is a category of items in which local parsing is blocked by syntactic anomaly. In the contour plot charts in **Appendix D** (Figures D1-D9), 'accessible' items are indicated by circles (o) and 'inaccessible' items by crosses (x). We find that the depth value (*LinkScore*) is higher around 'accessible' items than around 'inaccessible' items.

[Table 4.5: List of 'accessible' sentences (copied from Table 4.4)]

a1 ¶ The letter kept by the old woman who we met when we were looking for *the boy disappeared*.
a2 ¶ *Vivian knew the police officer* under suspicion had received the money.
a3 ¶ The fact that the dog hurt *the boy scared Linda*.
a4l ¶ *You will find the glasses* with red marks on both sides #are quite expensive.
a4v ¶ You will find the glasses with *red marks on both sides #are quite expensive*.
a5 ¶ The Department of *Foreign Languages *are not located* in the new building.
a6 ¶ To grow *several kinds of flowers *are the joy* of gardening.
b2 ¶ *Half of the people* ([who]) (#)*were invited* to the party didn't turn up.
b4 ¶ Mr Kawase, vice president of Tomato Bank, #*he will speak* to the press this afternoon.
b5 ¶ [That] You don't know *Russian is a pity*.
b6 ¶ *His attacker was described* [as] a tall man with a beard.
c1 ¶ [When] *Most people hear "endangered species"*, they think of animals.
d1 ¶ Diane's nose got extremely cold, **running home* through the snow.
e1 ¶ #*For badly wounded*, the soldier stopped fighting.
g6 ¶ *What I want is ^ cup, not ^ glass*.
g7 ¶ When the magician appeared, Bill came downstairs *to see *the *magician*.
g8 ¶ We did not know what to do *with *us*.
h2 ¶ *Mr Peters used to think of *hisself* as the only president of the company.
h3 ¶ When I last saw Janet, *she *hurried* to her next class on the other side of the campus.
h4 ¶ Carl was upset last night because *he had to do too many *homeworks*.
h6 ¶ I watched the match because I knew some of the **playing *people*.

We used the parameter *LinkScore* (defined in Section 4.1.5) to represent the strength of association links for each item, and compared the mean parameter values between the two categories. Table 4.6 shows the transition of *LinkScores* of items along with the change of proficiency measures. In each local parsing category items are arranged in the order of Core Cluster Level list above.

[Table 4.6: LinkScores of items with the label of local parsing in 9 proficiency levels. 'Slope' indicates an approximate rate of rise in LinkScores between Cz = -1.5 and Cz = 1.5. 't' indicates the t-score of the difference of mean LinkScores between 'accessible' and 'inaccessible' categories.]

Item	Local parsing	-2.0	-1.5	-1.0	-0.5	0.0	0.5	1.0	1.5	2.0	Slope
a1	accessible	12.75	11.75	10.5	10.5	10.25	9.5	10	13	14.75	0.42
a2	accessible	1.5	1	0.75	0.25	0	0	0.25	2	4.25	0.33
a3	accessible	3	2.25	1.25	0.75	0.75	1	1.75	5.5	10.75	1.08
a4l	accessible	2	1.5	1	1.75	2.5	4.25	6	6.5	7	1.67
a4v	accessible	13.25	10.5	9.75	7.25	5	3.75	1.75	1.75	2.5	-2.92
a5	accessible	17.25	17.75	16.5	15.25	12	10.75	12	11.25	12	-2.17
a6	accessible	22.5	21.5	21	14.75	11.5	10.5	9.5	8	10.25	-4.5
b2	accessible	14.25	13.5	8.75	6	4.25	5	5.25	5.75	6.75	-2.58
b4	accessible	17.75	16.5	13.25	12.25	11.75	13	13.75	15.25	14.5	-0.42
b5	accessible	3.75	3.25	1.5	1	0.5	0.75	1.5	6	7.5	0.92
b6	accessible	14	13.5	10.25	9	8.25	7.5	8.5	10.75	10.5	-0.92
c1	accessible	14.75	12.75	11.75	12	10.5	9.75	10.25	10.5	11.75	-0.75
d1	accessible	20.75	18.75	12.25	9.5	7.75	8.25	6.5	6.25	6.25	-4.17
e1	accessible	22.5	21	18	14.75	11.5	11	11	10.75	9.75	-3.42
g6	accessible	20.25	17.75	14.25	12.75	10.5	8.5	7.5	7	6	-3.58
g7	accessible	25	23.25	20.25	16.5	12	10.25	7	4.5	3.5	-6.25
g8	accessible	18	13.75	12.5	10	7.75	6	5.25	3.5	3.25	-3.42
h2	accessible	21.25	20	18.25	16.25	11.5	10.25	7.25	7.75	6	-4.08
h3	accessible	29.5	28	24.75	18.75	14.25	12.75	8.75	6.75	6	-7.08
h4	accessible	13.75	12.25	7.25	7	5	3.25	2.75	2.25	2.75	-3.33
h6	accessible	23.25	21.75	19.5	18	12.75	11.75	12.25	9	8.5	-4.25
b1	inaccessible	8	8.75	9	11	10.5	13.5	14	15.25	19	2.17
b3	inaccessible	6.5	5.75	4.75	4	5.75	6.5	8.25	12	13	2.08
c2	inaccessible	8.5	8	7.5	6.5	7	9.25	11.25	11.5	13	1.17
d2	inaccessible	10.25	10	10	7.5	8.5	9.5	11.25	14.25	16.75	1.42
d3	inaccessible	4.75	4	2	2	2.75	3.5	4.75	8.75	10.25	1.58
e2	inaccessible	13.25	10	7.5	5.5	3.75	4.75	5.25	5.5	8.75	-1.5
e3	inaccessible	15	13.5	8.75	8.5	8.5	9.25	9	11	13.5	-0.83
e4	inaccessible	11.5	11	8.75	10.5	11.75	13	15.75	18.25	19.25	2.42
e5	inaccessible	5	5.25	5.75	8	9.25	10	12	14.75	16.75	3.17
f1	inaccessible	6.75	6	5	6.75	8.25	9.75	12	16.25	18	3.42
g1	inaccessible	2.75	3	5.25	6.5	9.25	11.25	13	15.75	17.75	4.25
g2	inaccessible	10.5	9.75	6.5	4.5	4.25	3.25	2.75	3.5	4.5	-2.08
g3	inaccessible	7.75	7	4.25	4.5	4.5	7.25	8	10.25	12.25	1.08
g4	inaccessible	6	5.5	4.75	4.75	3.75	4.25	4.5	5.5	5.75	0
g5	inaccessible	22.25	19.5	14.75	11.25	10.5	12.25	12.75	12.75	13.75	-2.25
h1	inaccessible	6	6.75	7	7.25	7.25	11.75	13	13.5	16.75	2.25
h5	inaccessible	4.75	3.5	2.75	3.25	4.25	5.25	6.25	8.75	9.5	1.75
	t	3.373	3.285	3.138	2.526	0.896	-0.806	-2.018	-3.336	-4.129	
	p	0.0019	0.0025	0.0039	0.0172	0.3763	0.4257	0.0514	0.0022	0.0003	

The mean value of *LinkScores* in the 'accessible' items group was significantly higher than that in the 'inaccessible' items group (t = 3.373, p = 0.0019, df = 33.615, unequal variances assumed) when the proficiency was Cz = -2.0. The difference of the mean values of *LinkScores* became smaller as the proficiency level rose, and the difference became reversed when the proficiency was more than the average. Furthermore, the *LinkScores* marked unequal distributions at three different proficiency levels, Cz = -1.0, Cz = 0.0, and Cz = 1.0 when the items were divided into the 'accessible' group (F = 5.1610, p = 0.0085, df = 2,60) and 'inaccessible' group (F = 4.06, p = 0.0235, df = 2,48), but no significance was observed for the aggregate set of items (F = 1.8301, p = 0.1652 (ns), df = 2,111).

The 'slope' values are a rough index of the transition of *LinkScores* from the point Cz = -1.5 to the point Cz = 1.5. Obviously more 'accessible' items had negative values than 'inaccessible' items. It means the *LinkScore* of items in 'accessible' category tends to decrease as the proficiency level rises. In contrast, more 'inaccessible' items had positive values than 'accessible' items. It means the *LinkScore* of items in 'inaccessible' category tends to increase as the proficiency level rises.

Figure 4.11 and Figure 4.12 show the transition of *LinkScores* of items in 'accessible' and 'inaccessible' categories, respectively, in 9 proficiency levels.

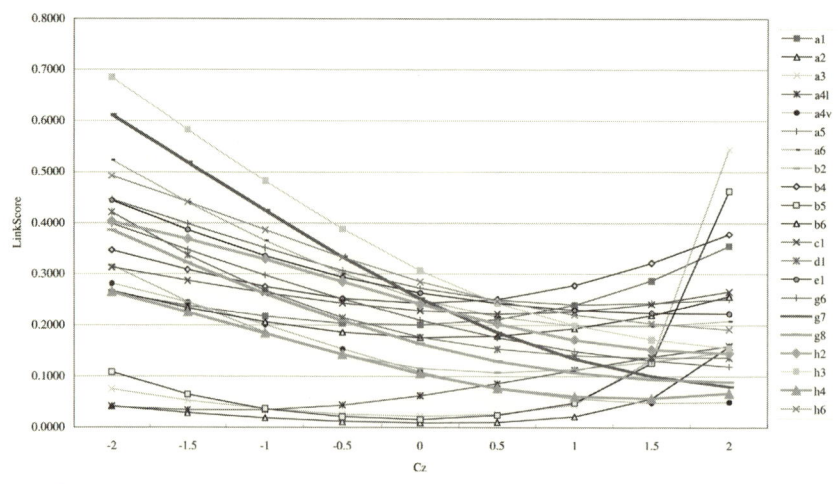

[Figure 4.11: Transition of Linkscores of items in which local parsing is 'accessible']

Inaccessible items

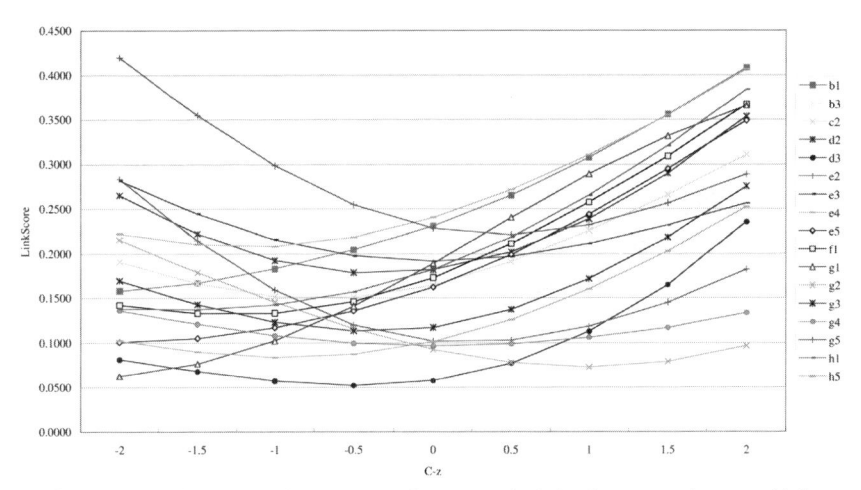

[Figure 4.12: Transition of Linkscores of items in which local parsing is 'inaccessible']

In Figure 4.11 for 'accessible' items, four items exhibited exceptional transition tendencies:

a2 ¶ *Vivian knew the police officer* under suspicion had received the money.
a3 ¶ The fact that the dog hurt *the boy scared Linda*.
a4l ¶ *You will find the glasses* with red marks on both sides #are quite expensive.
b5 ¶ [That] You don't know *Russian is a pity*.

In Figure 4.12 for 'inaccessible' items, one item exhibited a strong exceptional transition tendency:

g5 ¶ The policemen [were] surprised that the girls chased the man in the station.

After all, we observed a statistically significant difference in the *LinkScores* of items across proficiency levels which we obtained by the contour plot analyses in Section 4.1.5 when the items are subcategorised by local parsing types. The local parsing types are the means of differentiating the set of items which cluster together as the proficiency lowers from the set of other items.

This result indicates that low-proficiency test takers have a common error tendency towards the items in which local parsing is 'accessible' while high-proficiency test takers have a common tendency of not choosing the 'accessible' option in their grammaticality judgement. Considering the fact that most 'accessible' items incorporated locally grammatical but globally ungrammatical structures, the span of the text that low-proficiency test takers paid attention to was relatively limited. In contrast, since most 'inaccessible' items incorporated locally ungrammatical structures, high-proficiency test takers must have been sensitive to syntactic anomaly. This is presumably why these items had significantly higher *LinkScores* than 'accessible' items when the proficiency level was high.

Thus step 2 of Hypothesis 1

1. A cognitive constraint on processing works commonly across certain test items of grammaticality judgement.

namely, at least one common factor is operative behind the clustering of items, has been confirmed. We postulated a 'local parsing' strategy reflecting cognitive constraint, and classified the stimuli into two categories accordingly. The index that represents the strength of association with others inherent to individual items showed a statistically significant contrast between a category of items in which 'local parsing' is accessible and the other category of items in which 'local parsing' is inaccessible.

4.2.2.2 Test of the correlation between local parsing measures and proficiency measures

Another means of testing our main hypothesis that low-proficiency test takers use more 'local parsing' strategies than high-proficiency test takers was to estimate the individual test takers' degrees of 'local parsing' tendency and compare them with the test takers' proficiency measures. The former statistic was obtained from the product of individual responses ('v' or 'x') and the magnitude of *LinkScores* that individual items have as intrinsic attributes. Note here that a *LinkScore* is not a fixed constant; the value changes as the proficiency level changes. It is considered that when a test taker has made a 'v' response to a given item, the magnitude of *LinkScore*, which is expected to have affected the choice, is *at least* the size corresponding to the proficiency measure of the test taker. Therefore, given the proficency measure (ie., Cz) of a test taker, we can conservatively calculate the magnitude of *LinkScore* at the point of the proficiency measure. For this purpose we need to establish a formula, with its parameters heuristically deduced, as a continuous function of proficiency measure (θ). In Figures 4.11 and 4.12 we simply observed the transition of *LinkScore* values in 9 discrete proficiency levels.

In the end we found a cubic formula best fits the plots. Figures 4.13 and 4.14 illustrate the approximate formula representing the continuous *LinkScore* of **a5** and **h2**, respectively.

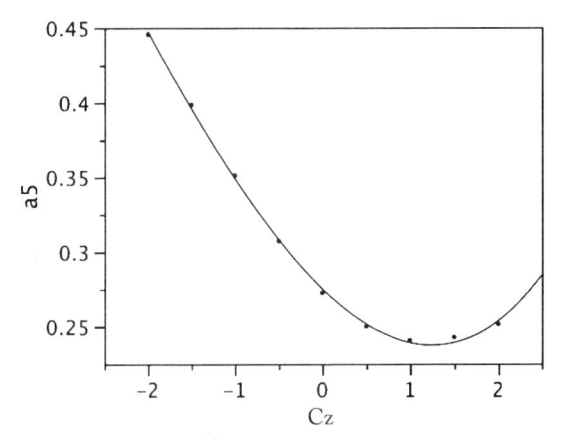

[Figure 4.13: Approximate cubic formula applied to LinkScore plots of **a5**]

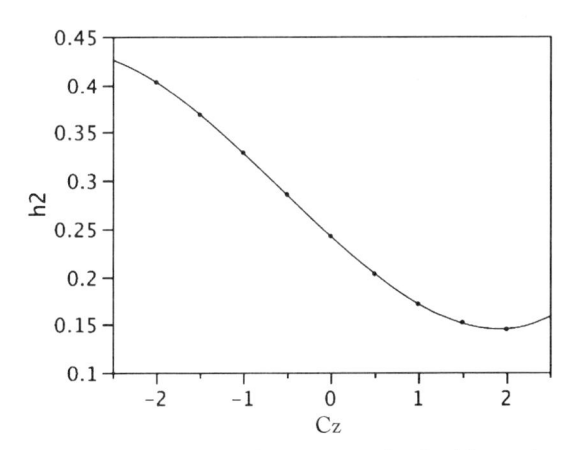

[Figure 4.14: Approximate cubic formula applied to LinkScore plots of **h2**]

The formulae predict the plots with extremely high degrees of fitness in all items except in **a2**, **a3**, and **b5** in which 5th power formulae best fit the plots. Table 4.7 shows the parameter estimates and degrees of fitness (R^2).

[Table 4.7: Parameter estimates of approximation formulae and degrees of fitness]

Item	Local parsing	Parameter Intercept	Parameter Power = 1	Parameter Power = 2	Parameter Power = 3	Parameter Power = 4	Parameter Power = 5	R Square
a1	accessible	0.2007787	0.0071484	0.0272783	0.0039322			0.999884
a2	accessible	0.0096854	-0.0012700	0.0047773	0.0011593	0.0044205	0.0016139	0.999806
a3	accessible	0.0291197	0.0063390	-0.0189380	-0.0149430	0.0221546	0.0106636	0.998755
a4l	accessible	0.0630952	0.0416323	0.0094522	-0.0030180			0.999510
a4v	accessible	0.1120280	-0.0773640	0.0139941	0.0049022			0.999079
a5	accessible	0.2751786	-0.0572130	0.0188147	0.0021902			0.999001
a6	accessible	0.2526570	-0.0842430	0.0285453	0.0013393			0.999789
b1	inaccessible	0.2316089	0.0621826	0.0130227	0.0001124			0.999926
b2	accessible	0.1184663	-0.0340850	0.0290556	-0.0020900			0.998614
b3	inaccessible	0.1265465	0.0263431	0.0228352	0.0028409			0.999192
b4	accessible	0.2452540	-0.0008580	0.0298044	0.0021758			0.997580
b5	accessible	0.0220855	0.0096010	-0.0046290	-0.0138070	0.0175044	0.0083706	0.998596
b6	accessible	0.1772450	-0.0077990	0.0213481	0.0012973			0.998938
c1	accessible	0.2291949	-0.0207740	0.0151581	0.0022763			0.999652
c2	inaccessible	0.1662721	0.0390585	0.0214134	-0.0023220			0.999200
d1	accessible	0.1778973	-0.0614120	0.0253885	-0.0024570			0.999855
d2	inaccessible	0.1828350	0.0233224	0.0318629	-0.0003140			0.999701
d3	inaccessible	0.0587706	0.0242021	0.0251237	0.0035837			0.999783
e1	accessible	0.2644501	-0.0522830	0.0174514	-0.0007720			0.999830
e2	inaccessible	0.1045198	-0.0186340	0.0324746	-0.0016950			0.998851
e3	inaccessible	0.1929550	-0.0009060	0.0193245	-0.0014000			0.997713
e4	inaccessible	0.2405418	0.0525240	0.0185349	-0.0016430			0.999939
e5	inaccessible	0.1638797	0.0641514	0.0154803	-0.0005310			0.999804
f1	inaccessible	0.1739937	0.0635282	0.0203875	-0.0018780			0.999794
g1	inaccessible	0.1892287	0.0987825	0.0062653	-0.0058050			0.999944
g2	inaccessible	0.0931441	-0.0384050	0.0157411	0.0021989			0.999960
g3	inaccessible	0.1196003	0.0233847	0.0261085	0.0007707			0.998646
g4	inaccessible	0.0972376	-0.0013880	0.0094959	0.0001690			0.998850
g5	inaccessible	0.2316473	-0.0331400	0.0312490	0.0001196			0.997981
g6	accessible	0.2106971	-0.0757830	0.0120617	0.0015271			0.999957
g7	accessible	0.2546374	-0.1490120	0.0231255	0.0040611			0.999891
g8	accessible	0.1649075	-0.0784930	0.0184456	0.0011122			0.999834
h1	inaccessible	0.1833423	0.0610858	0.0196690	0.0000589			0.999859
h2	accessible	0.2419092	-0.0833240	0.0079686	0.0047524			0.999974
h3	accessible	0.3102993	-0.1440280	0.0280056	0.0029472			0.999769
h4	accessible	0.1063215	-0.0659230	0.0150567	0.0041203			0.999837
h5	inaccessible	0.1023829	0.0383831	0.0189366	-0.0002760			0.999769
h6	accessible	0.2876911	-0.0853110	0.0139287	0.0025948			0.999619

Having obtained the parameter estimates we can calculate the *LinkScore* of an item given a proficiency measure (Cz). For instance, participant No.57 made a 'v' (local parsing) response to items **a4v, a5, a6, b4, c1, c2, d2, e3, g3, g4, g7,** and **h3**. Because the participant's proficiency measure (θ) was -1.33646, the *LinkScore* of **a4v** at this proficiency measure was

$LinkScore_{a4v\theta}$ = Intercept + Parameter$_1$ × θ + Parameter$_2$ × θ^2 + Parameter$_3$ × θ^3
= 0.11203 + (−0.07736)(−1.33646) + (0.01399)(−1.33646)^2
+ (0.00490)(−1.33646)^3
= 0.22871

The aggregate *LinkScore* of this participant was

$LinkScore_\theta$ = $LinkScore_{a4v\theta}$ + $LinkScore_{a5\theta}$ + $LinkScore_{a6\theta}$ + $LinkScore_{b4\theta}$
+ $LinkScore_{c1\theta}$ + $LinkScore_{c2\theta}$ + $LinkScore_{d2\theta}$ + $LinkScore_{e3\theta}$
+ $LinkScore_{g3\theta}$ + $LinkScore_{g4\theta}$ + $LinkScore_{g7\theta}$ + $LinkScore_{h3\theta}$
= 0.22871 + 0.38002 + 0.41303 + 0.29444 + 0.27860 + 0.15786
+ 0.20933 + 0.23202 + 0.13314 + 0.11565 + 0.48540 + 0.54577
= 3.47398

This *LinkScore* reflects the test taker's tendency to take a local parsing strategy. We tested the correlation between the test takers' proficiency measures and their aggregate *LinkScores*. The result showed a significant reverse correlation (r = −0.18427, n = 1152, p < 0.0001), indicating that the lower the test taker's proficiency is, the stronger the tendency becomes to adopt a local parsing strategy. When the items were limited to 'v' responses in Core Cluster Level 1 (ie., **a5, g7**, and **h3**), there was even a stronger correlation (r = −0.58363, n = 898, p < 0.0001). This result also supported our Hypothesis 3:

3. Test takers with lower proficiency can deal with a relatively shorter span of text than test takers with higher proficiency.

4.3 Discussion

4.3.1 Unidimensionality in the C-test

We originally intended to represent test takers' proficiency by the logit scale of the C-test. The logit measures were obtained by conducting a Rasch analysis or one-parameter Item Response Theory. A Rasch analysis enables us to compare item difficulty with person ability on the same scale (Henning, 1984, 1987; Woods & Baker, 1985). It can also detect statistically misfitting items and persons (Henning, 1987). Despite these advantages, however, we abandoned the logit scale scheme because of the (1) local independence and (2) unidimensionality problem. First, items in a C-test do not generally exhibit local independence. An answer to a blank is found by referring to the context before and after the blank which also contains blanks. Because of its simple test structure, answers are often exact copies of some preceding answers. Therefore, unlike a normal cloze test, a C-test is hardly considered to be locally independent. Second, a Rasch analysis requires the data's being unidimensional (Henning, Hudson, & Turner, 1985; Spurling, 1987). However, this assumption may partly entail a logical fallacy — we may be pursuing a differential dimension in one's syntactic ability (to be measured by the GJ test) in terms of the unitary dimension in the general proficiency (to be measured by the C-test) of which the syntactic ability is a part. Since the general proficiency comprises the syntactic ability, the multidimensionality we expect to detect in the GJ test does not even exist from the beginning, strictly speaking. To avoid this question-begging we abandoned the logit scale scheme, and a more traditional z-score was adopted instead. Even if the z-score was multidimensional, we could still use it as the independent measure, as long as it was meaningful. As a result the psychometric construct became obscure, but the psychological construct — namely, the proficiency measure obtained by the C-test — was not affected. After all, our C-test proved out to be unidimensional, and was certainly more strongly so than our GJ test. So we could use it as a reliable measure.

4.3.2 The local parsing strategy

We shall consider here the significance of our observation. The fact that certain GJ items were more strongly associated with one another than other items did indicates that the test takers employed a common parsing strategy for these items. The fact that this association became stronger among low-proficiency test takers than among high-proficiency test takers indicates that the strategy is characteristic of low-proficiency test takers. We called the strategy *local parsing* — a strategy with which test takers regard a sequence as grammatical if the widest possible span of text that they can process at one time is meaningful. It is important that the test takers understood the meaning of the local context. The test takers who used this strategy forced interpretation from anomalous structures in **e1** and **h6**.

e1 ¶ #*For badly wounded*, the soldier stopped fighting.

h6 ¶ I watched the match because I knew some of the **playing*people*.

To them the information as to whether the sequence is grammatical or not was not provided; they simply interpreted the sequence where it was possible. Otherwise the high association scores of these items among low-proficiency test takers cannot be explained. They also ignored the phrase/clause boundary (as in **a4v**, **a5**, and **a6**), and disregarded the remote phrase/clause of the entire sentence (as in **b4** and **c1**).

a4v ¶ You will find the glasses with *red marks on both sides #are quite expensive*.
a5 ¶ The Department of *Foreign Languages *are not located* in the new building.
a6 ¶ To grow *several kinds of flowers *are the joy* of gardening.
b4 ¶ Mr Kawase, vice president of Tomato Bank, *#he will speak* to the press this afternoon.
c1 ¶ [When] *Most people hear "endangered species"*, they think of animals.

All these items showed a high degree of association by *LinkScores* in low proficiency levels and a drastic decrease in association measures as the proficiency level rose (Table 4.4). In other words, low-proficiency test takers tended to judge items in the 'accessible' category as grammatical but were not attracted by 'inaccessible' items. On the other hand, high-proficiency test takers were not affected by local parsing elements but judged the grammaticality of individual items on some other grounds.

It is evident that Frazier and others' syntax-dependent model (Frazier & Fodor, 1978; Fodor & Frazier,1980; Frazier & Rayner, 1982, 1987; Rayner & Pollatsek, 1989; Frazier & Flores-d'Arcais, 1989) is not appropriate for explaining these facts. Instead, Holmes' (1987: 598) view, quoted again, that "the slow average readers may be relying much more on semantic than syntactic information to understand written sentences", Upshur & Homburg's (1983: 199) view that "at lower ability levels most of the comprehension of a text depends upon knowledge of the meanings of content words employed in the text", and VanPatter's (1996: 21) model in which "learners prefer processing lexical items to grammatical items (eg., morphology) for semantic information" are more convincing in dealing with these meaning-oriented judgements.

We observed a clear contrast of *LinkScores* and their transition tendencies between the two item groups: 'accessible' and 'inaccessible'. In the group of items where local parsing was 'accessible' only 5 items out of 21 (23.8%) increased their *LinkScores* as the proficiency measure rose, whereas in the 'inaccessible' group 12 items out of 17 (70.6%) increased their *LinkScores*. Considering that items in the latter group do not allow interpretation in the local context and requires a syntactic judgement against a wider context, it can be concluded that high-proficiency test takers depend less on the interpretation available from local parsing but more on the interpretation available from global structural information than low-proficiency test takers do.

Yet a closer examination reveals a finer characterisation of local parsing strategy. In Figure 4.11 for 'accessible' items, four items exhibited exceptional transition tendencies:

a2 ¶ *Vivian knew the police officer* under suspicion had received the money.
a3 ¶ The fact that the dog hurt *the boy scared Linda*.
a4l ¶ *You will find the glasses* with red marks on both sides #are quite expensive.
b5 ¶ [That] You don't know *Russian is a pity*.

These items all show a flat transition, which might suggest they are not subject to the local parsing strategy. In items **a2** and **a4l** the likely 'local parsing' phrase is located at the beginning of the sentence. It was possible that by the time test takers reached the end of the sentence they had thrown away the comprehension of the initial part of the sentence due to the shortage of working memory capacity. This view of sequential processing may apply to a special circumstance of reading with a moving window (Rayner, 1975), but whether or not it is also true in a more natural paper test in which test takers can go back and forth in a sentence remains a question to be solved by further research. In terms of the processing capacity, items **a3** and **b5** may have been short enough for test takers to process a wider text span than the assumed 'local parsing' phrase. It is possible that the awareness of a larger structure blocked concentrating only on a part of a sentence.

On the other hand, in Figure 4.12 for 'inaccessible' items, one item exhibited a strong exceptional transition tendency:

g5 ¶ The policemen [were] surprised that the girls chased the man in the station.

The transition of this item looked like that of 'accessible' items, which might suggest that this item should belong to the 'accessible' category. The fact that test takers judged this item as grammatical indicates that they do not care whether the verb "surprised" is transitive or intransitive. In fact, the Japanese verb corresponding to this verb is intransitive. So the absence of distinction in transitivity may be the result of transfer from L1. We can infer that the initial part of the sentence "The policemen surprised" was grammatical in the test takers' interlanguage and they comprehended the sentence using the same strategy as for other sentences in the 'accessible' category without making a syntactic judgement.

4.3.3 The relationship between general proficiency and parsing ability

Our results suggest that at a low proficiency level a limited capacity is used for processing local parsing and the global parsing is beyond the learner's capacity. This view is endorsed by studies in working memory, in particular Zwaan & Brown (1996), Kadota & Noro (2001), and Yoshida (2003). They maintain that inefficient readers consume their working memory resources in processing lower order information such as vocabulary, syntax, and phonological coding, whereas efficient readers can assign their working memory capacity to higher order information processing such as semantic elaboration and inference as they automatise the lower order tasks.

It does not necessarily mean, however, that inefficiency in lower order processing is the cause of problematic parsing. Nor does it entail the reverse cause-effect order, ie., fumbling parsing consumes lower order capacity. Harrington & Sawyer's (1992) conclusion that there is a high correlation between the reading span test and the 'grammar' test is based on their TOEFL grammar, which involved a high degree of sentence-level reading. Therefore their claim needs a decent reservation. Harrington's (1991) study in which L2 reading span test scores, L2 vocabulary test scores, grammar test scores, and reading comprehension test scores were all significantly correlated is remarkable in the sense that after removing the common variance with L2 vocabulary and grammar scores the L2 reading scores still correlated with the L2 reading span test scores ($r = 0.51$). This finding suggests, according to Miyake & Friedman (1999: 345), that working memory "is an important factor in L2 reading comprehension ability, beyond knowledge of L2 vocabulary and grammar." In other words, the relevance of working memory is not so great for grammar and vocabulary as it is for reading comprehension. In Ikeno's (2002) study the correlation of the L2 reading span test scores (L2 RST) was not so high with the grammaticality judgement (GJ) test scores as with the lexical semantic judgement (SEM) test scores or with the sentence verification (SV) test scores (see Figures 2.5a and 2.5b). It may be premature at this stage to draw a solid conclusion about the relationship between the working memory capacity *as measured by a reading span test* and the proficiency as measured by a grammar test. In order to do so we need to first define 'grammatical proficiency', second clarify the domain of working memory relevant to syntactic processing, and third examine the validity of the measurement technique of working memory capacity/efficiency used for syntactic processing.

Most of the above-mentioned studies in the limitations of lower order processing, as well as King & Just (1991) who focused on comprehension of complex sentence structure, dealt with sentence-level processing. What we have found in the present study is the limitation in processing *within* a sentence. One possible senario is that learners use up the working memory resource in the lower order phonological loop during the ongoing process of reading so they have to throw away the past unit for the sake of the incoming unit (Kadota & Noro, 2001). In fact, between items **a4l** and **a4v** the latter was easier to cause local parsing.

a4l ¶ *You will find the glasses* with red marks on both sides #are quite expensive.
a4v ¶ You will find the glasses with *red marks on both sides #are quite expensive.*

The low-proficiency test takers judged **a4v** as correct with a strong association with other items (*LinkScore* = 0.2009 at Cz = -1.0), but they judged **a4l** as correct with a weak association with other items (*LinkScore* = 0.0345 at Cz = -1.0). It would seem as if they had forgotten the first segment (as indicated by italics in **a4l**) by the time they processed the second segment (as indicated by italics in **a4v**), and gave a final 'correct' judgement against this sentence. Other error examples in items **a1, b4, g7** seem to support this view, but it remains a mere speculation as the number of evidence is limited[3].

Yet another possible explanation concerns rather the 'central executive' (Baddeley & Hitch, 1974) than the phonological loop. Considering the fact that low proficiency learners *do* think of the meaning and accept the local parsing when the processing unit makes sense, be it grammatical or not, it is more likely that the phenomenon involves a higher order processing stage besides simply a phonological loop. Gilhooly (1998: 4) observes that "propositional reasoning strongly involves the central executive, with lesser roles for the articulatory loop and visuo-spacial scratch-pad," provided that the participants are not trained enough. By his study of how working memory affects propositional reasoning, he concludes "the 'central executive' holds information relevant for immediate processing and the result of recent processing. [...] It seems plausible that information in the central executive is in an abstract propositional code, whereas information in slave systems is in more literal, surface-based codes" (Gilhooly: 20). Thus it is assumed that the difference in proficiency is somehow related to the different degrees of efficiency of the logistic abstraction in the central executive. In other words, low-proficiency learners may have a unique processing style (presumably arousal/stimulation of proper semantic association) which affects the eventual efficiency of working memory resource.

4.3.4 Methodological reminders

The most critical feature of this research procedure is the use of logistic regression analysis for measuring the degree of association between responses. A logistic regression analysis is used for predicting the estimate probabilities of categorical responses at a point of a continuous measure. It is basically an analysis tool for a single item containing multiple responses. Like classical item analysis one logistic regression analysis for an item is independent of another analysis for another item. However, a combination of two sets of dichotomous responses has made it possible to connect the two items. In our study, in fact, the raw frequency of the 'local parsing' response *increased* as the proficiency measure rose. For example, take the top three core 'local parsing' items, **h3**, **g7**, and **a5**. The frequencies of these responses in three proficiency levels (N = 384; divided as in the classical item analysis) are as follows (Table 4.8).

[Table 4.8: Frequencies of local parsing responses in 3 proficiency levels for items **h3, g7**, and **a5**]

	h3	g7	a5
Upper	124 (36.6%)	266 (37.4%)	198 (38.3%)
Middle	127 (37.5%)	256 (36.0%)	183 (35.4%)
Lower	88 (26.0%)	189 (26.6%)	136 (26.3%)
Total	339 (100.0%)	711 (100.0%)	517 (100.0%)

The logistic regression analysis describes this tendency more precisely (see Figure 3.5 for item **a5** and Figure 3.6 for item **h3**, both in Section 3.3.1). It appears therefore to claim that the 'local parsing' strategy is more frequently used among high proficiency learners than among low proficiency learners. By the simple frequency size the answer is affirmative. Yet to recognise it as a single psychological phenomenon one must explain the reason behind the superficial rising frequencies; an increase in frequency in one item must be related to an increase in frequency in another item. Our rationale here is that qualitatively different parsing strategies must be reflected *in common* in a certain set of items. Hence we need the association measure between two items, using the probabilities of combined responses in different proficiency levels. Our result for these two items showed a *decreasing* tendency of 'local parsing' responses as the proficiency level rose (Section 3.3.2.2; see Table 3.6 (restated) below).

[Table 3.6 (restated): Association measures (phi) of **a5** and **h3** in 9 proficiency levels]

Cz	φ (**a5–h3**)
-2.0	0.302
-1.5	0.269
-1.0	0.232
-0.5	0.192
0.0	0.149
0.5	0.103
1.0	0.054
1.5	0.004
2.0	-0.047

To recapitulate, the absolute frequency does not reflect the inherent relations among items.

Still the procedure leaves us a question of the identity of association; given a strong association between responses A and B, and an equally strong association between responses B and C, are the three responses elicited by the same motive? Obviously they are syllogistically irrelevant. Even when there is a strong association between responses C and A, the three responses A, B, and C are not necessarily homogeneous. However, if correlated responses can be interpreted as sharing a similar linguistic (ie., syntactic and semantic) feature and if the responses are densely linked with other responses, we can infer a certain common factor behind superficial responses. This rationale is the same as that of exploratory factor analysis. The problem, then, is reduced to measuring the degree of links of individual responses with other responses.

Thus our next important issue is the conversion of association measures:

from measures between items to measures inherent to individual items. The association measure we have discussed above pertains to a *pair* of responses, whereas what we want is the association measure pertaining to individual responses. To solve this problem we applied Expression 4 (Section 4.1.5):

$$LinkScore_i = \sum_{k=1}^{n} (\varphi_{ik})^2 \quad \ldots(4)$$

This expression calculates the *LinkScore* of item i as the sum of association measures (φ) obtained from n combinations with other items where the association measure takes a positive value. Here the power coefficient is tentatively set at 2. It means a smaller weight of links for small phi values than for large phi values. Because of its simple structure and indiscreteness it helps us postulate a continuous function of the proficiency measure (θ).

4.4 Summary

In this chapter we have observed that our hypotheses cited again below are supported.

1. A cognitive constraint on processing works commonly across certain test items of grammaticality judgement.
2. The performance of test takers at a low proficiency level is more severely affected by the cognitive constraint than that of test takers at a high proficiency level.
3. Test takers with lower proficiency can deal with a shorter span of text than test takers with higher proficiency.

First, the matrices of association measures indicated an uneven distribution of association among test items. Since the responses we focused on among other options contained syntactic violations derived from cognitive constraints, the uneven distribution of association indicated that the cognitive constraint does not work on individual items independently but is potentially active for all items in the same way and is significantly strong against certain items.

Second, the contrast of *LinkScores* in the contour plot analysis (Section 4.1.5) confirmed that there is a strong association among certain item responses for low proficiency learners whereas the association diffuses as the proficiency level rises. Since the variable *LinkScore*, by definition, reflects the association between the item in question and other items linked with the item with at least the minimum association measures, and is a monotonic projection of the strength of cognitive constraint, the contrast in *LinkScores* between high- and low-proficiency test takers indicates the effectiveness of the cognitive constraint. Thus the lower-proficiency test takers are more susceptible to the cognitive constraint.

Third, items belonging to the core cluster which reflects the strength of association held by low-proficiency learners are interpretable in terms of 'local parsing'. Test takers using this strategy narrow down the span of text as the target of interpretation, and when it is interpretable by the reason of semantic configuration, rather than syntactic, they accept no further contextual information which may alter the initial interpretation. The rational categorisation of items as to whether or not they contain a sequence for local parsing was a good predictor of the strength of the *LinkScore*. The group of items with local parsing elements marked significantly higher *LinkScores* than the group of items without local parsing elements, and this tendency was stronger when the proficiency level was low. Thus low-proficiency test takers are considered, generally speaking, to be able only to focus on a limited span of interpretable context.

Chapter 5
Conclusion

In the present research we have explored the hypothesis that low-proficiency test takers use a specific parsing strategy. Our experiment shows that the strategy they use is heavily constrained by processing capacity. As a result the target text to be comprehended is restricted to the extent in which they can understand the meaning based on lexical-semantic information. We have also seen that this tendency is relative and indiscrete; the lower one's proficiency is the stronger this 'local parsing' strategy becomes. In this chapter we shall review our research and consolidate the discussions in the following steps.

    5.1 Summary of research
        5.1.1 Summary of research procedure
            5.1.1.1 Preparation
            5.1.1.2 Experiment
            5.1.1.3 Confirmation
        5.1.2 Summary of cognitive mechanism
        5.1.3 Limitations
    5.2 Originality
    5.3 Contributions to academic research
        5.3.1 Test development
        5.3.2 Data mining
        5.3.3 Research in second language development
        5.3.4 Suggestions for TEFL
    5.4 Future orientations

5.1 Summary of research

5.1.1 Summary of research procedure
Our research is made of three stages: (1) preparation of research framework and experimental materials, (2) experiment, and (3) confirmation.

5.1.1.1 Preparation
In the first preparatory stage, a general framework was structured in which a grammaticality judgement test was the instrument of eliciting expected responses and the difference in response was to be explained by the test takers' proficiency measures. This framework reflects one of our research questions:

Q1. What is characteristic of the sentence parsing strategy of low proficiency learners?

In order to clarify the characteristics of the sentence parsing strategy, a grammaticality judgement test was used. Since the parsing strategy was not directly observable it was sought through an association network of responses. When a cluster of responses shared a common cognitive feature it was considered to characterise a sentence parsing strategy. We assumed that the use of a particular sentence parsing strategy depends on the test taker's proficiency level. To measure a test taker's general proficiency, a C-test was used. We then developed an instrument which could predict the use of a particular parsing strategy by means of proficiency. This is a reflection of our second research question:

Q2. How is it possible to represent the characteristics of a sentence parsing strategy as a function of proficiency scale?

The strength of association among responses reflecting the use of a sentence parsing strategy must be represented as a continuous function of proficiency. Since individual data of proficiency measures were discrete, we could not use the raw data as the independent variable. To use the proficiency as a continuous scale, logistic regression analysis was employed. It enabled us to predict the probability of the occurrence of categorical responses (ie., judgement as 'correct' or 'incorrect') as a continuous function of the proficiency measure.

Having set up the framework, test materials were written. Based on the findings in the previous studies including the preliminary study, grammaticality judgement items and accompanying multiple-choice options were written in such a way that the differences in responses would reveal the cognitive constraint (Section 3.1.1). In order to solve the contradictory problem of avoiding the influence of other options in a multiple-choice format and decreasing a chance-level error in a dichotomous format at the same time, the judgement part was written in a dichotomous format followed by a question of identifying the location of error in a multiple-choice format. Further, in order to place an equal weight of work load on the judgement as correct and judgement as incorrect, a question was prepared of identifying a logical equivalent or implication of the stimulus when the judgement is 'correct'.

In the development of C-test, care was taken in adjusting the difficulty of the passages and increasing the reliability. It was found that the factor of reaching the end of the test affects the reliability and stability of test scores more seriously than items with low discrimination indices (Section 3.2.2.2.1). Therefore in the actual experiment, test takers were allowed to take the test paper home and complete it.

Additionally, a questionnaire was conducted to collect the information of the test takers' TOEFL scores by self report (Section 3.2.2.3). This information was to concurrently validate the C-test and to provide an index of difficulty corresponding to TOEFL scores.

5.1.1.2 Experiment

The two tests and one questionnaire were sent to participants in 21 universities in Japan. 1508 samples were collected, of which 1152 samples proved valid for our analyses. The rest were discarded by reason of incompleteness in either the grammaticality judgement test or the C-test (Section 4.1.1).

The scores of the C-test showed a clear normal distribution (Section 4.1.2.2). A factor analysis indicated that the data were unidimensional. Therefore the test data could be used as a reliable independent variable. The raw scores were normalised (0, 1) so the scores of the new scale Cz could be easily conceptualised.

On the other hand, the scores of the grammaticality judgement test were positively skewed (Section 4.1.2.1). A factor analysis indicated that the data were on the border of unidimensional and multidimensional distributions. This result was more supportive than defective, as we assume a multidimensional proficiency structure with a qualitative difference in parsing ability of learners in different proficiency levels.

The actual analysis involved several steps. First, we calculated a matrix of association measures between all pairs of items in the grammaticality judgement test (Section 4.1.3). Each association measure (φ) was calculated (Expression 2) using estimated probabilities of the occurrence of four combinations of response choices. The probabilities of occurrence of responses were calculated (Expression 1) using parameters estimated by logistic regression analysis (Sections 3.3.1). Logistic regression analysis was used in order to continuously estimate the parameters by any given value on a proficiency scale.

Second, we plotted the test items on a two-dimensional space by multidimensional scaling analysis using the data based on the matrix of association measures (Section 4.1.4). Since the raw phi statistics (φ) were not suitable for multidimensional scaling, they were converted into new statistics (Expression 3) so the data would fit a Euclidean space.

Third, we added the information of the strength of association of individual items as the third-dimension element in contour plot analysis (Section 4.1.5). This job was needed because multidimensional scaling does not provide a stable or at least gradient plotting of items; in other words the apparent distances between item plots can be deceptive. Therefore the plot of items was fixed at the proficiency level Cz = -0.5 and this plot was used throughout the nine levels in the contour plot analysis. The third-dimension statistic in the contour plot analysis represents the strength of association of individual items with other items (*LinkScore*). These statistics were converted from the matrix of association measures (Expression 4), since the matrix only provided information about pairs of items instead of individual items.

Finally, we drew model maps of items representing the association network in order to simplify the relations among items and to observe the members of the core cluster of association network (Section 4.1.6). Items were placed on a two-dimensional space and linked by lines representing the association measures (φ). This job was intended to double-check the relative locations of items using unconverted phi statistics.

5.1.1.3 Confirmation

The matrix of association measures among items and corresponding configurations of items in different proficiency levels was the source of interpretation of a common cognitive constraint affecting the items of the core cluster. Once an interpretation, 'local parsing' factor was postulated, all stimulus sentences were classified into two categories as to whether or not they allow local parsing. The mean values representing the strength of association of individual items (*LinkScores*) were compared between the two categories by analysis of variance (Section 4.2.2). The mean *LinkScore* in the category where local parsing is accessible was significantly higher than that in the category where local parsing is inaccessible when the proficiency level was up to Cz = -0.5 (Table 4.6). Further, graphs of transition of *LinkScores* of individual items clearly showed that the two categories are distinct (Figures 4.11 and 4.12).

Finally, we estimated the individual test taker's tendency to take a 'local parsing' strategy. The aggregate *LinkScore*, which represents this tendency, was calculated by the sum of the linear product of individual responses and item *LinkScores* corresponding to the proficiency measure of the test taker. We obtained a highly significant correlation between the test takers' proficiency and their aggregate *LinkScores*. This result further proved our hypothesis that low-proficiency test takers are more likely to take a 'local parsing' strategy (Section 4.2.2.2).

5.1.2 Summary of cognitive mechanism

The use of local parsing strategy by low-proficiency test takers appears to be related to the shortage of working memory capacity (Section 4.3.3). Theories in working memory have an explanatory adequacy over the phenomenon we have observed. Low-proficiency test takers may consume their working memory, presumably phonological representations of the written text and logical configuration among the conceptual units, before they take in a wider context for more elaborate processing. This scenario is, however, not beyond a plausible conjecture, and further research is required for confirming the relationship between erroneous parsing and working memory capacity/efficiency.

In our experiment we investigated the relationship between overall language proficiency as the independent variable and degrees of item association as the dependent variable. The proficiency was measured by a C-test performance. Since a C-test is claimed to be a reliable index of general language proficiency, our experimental design has a general and practical appeal.

5.1.3 Limitations

The current study has some limitations. First, the test material consisted of so wide a variety of sentences that it seemed difficult to draw a straightforward conclusion out of the results. In other words, if the test material had been prepared in such a way as to directly reflect the research hypotheses, in particular the working memory capacity/efficiency, the results could have been more easily interpreted. While this is one test design we followed another direction. One of our research questions was exploratory in nature; we wanted to know the types of syntactic structures learners are weak in, though the overall framework was to focus on cognitive constraints in sentence processing. Thus the selection of stimulus sentences was not restricted to one or a few types of artificial structures. We avoided making the stimulus sentences artefact as in Miyake & Friedman (1999) in which participants were asked to judge the grammatical subject of abnormal sentences. Nevertheless, having understood the nature of low proficiency learners' parsing strategy we might use more controlled stimuli in our next attempt. For example, items **a5**, **a6**, and **a4v** are all instances of violation of agreement, but their degrees of local parsing are slightly different. Whether they belong to the same cognitive category or not awaits further research. On the other hand, items **a2**, **a4l**, and **b2** are judged as outside the core cluster of local parsing. They share the same feature of having the local-parsing-with-error part at the beginning of the sentence. It is possible that low-proficiency test takers discarded the sentence-initial part at the moment they entered the later part, thus were more sensitive to sentence-final structures. The contrast between items **a4v** and **a4l** suggests this view, but we need a more precisely controlled study.

Our second possible limitation concerns the test procedure. In order to collect as many samples as possible we administered a paper test. However, having supervised some of the tests myself I noticed that most test takers spent much more time answering the GJ test than they would need for simply making a grammaticality judgement and choosing the locus of error or logical implication. It is conceivable that they read the options, both for the correct judgement and incorrect judgement, and chose the most plausible reason first. The grammaticality judgement was originally planned to be made **prior** to the reasoning, but in fact it may have been made **after** arriving at the reason. Though it does not seem to have seriously affected the result, this a posteriori judgement process, if at all, obviously repeats the defective nature of a multiple-choice question, namely, the tendency to choose the option which is relatively more plausible than the others. If so, the wording of options may have affected the final judgement to some extent. A think-aloud protocol would have been a solution to the question whether the grammaticality judgement was made a priori or a posteriori, but it was not designed as the main part of this research scheme. In any case, to solve this problem the only possible procedure is to administer a computer-based test. Participants are first presented with a stimulus sentence and asked to judge whether it is grammatically correct or not. Then depending on which judgement they have made they proceed to the next screen where they are asked to either locate the locus of error or indicate the logical implication. This procedure would certainly trace the intended route of judgement and reduce the administration time. However, in addition to the practicality problem of preparing computers for all test takers in all institutions, it may cause a reliability problem — motivation of particularly low-proficiency test takers. When the judgement task is felt as overload the work efficiency decreases and they lose hold of attention. Then their outcome may become inaccurate without correctly reflecting their interlanguage status. We would then commit the same fallacy that Sorace (1990) points out of forcing judgement on learners with indeterminacy. This dilemma would be mitigated if we remind ourselves that the problem is the degree of overload or difficulty and include easier items on purpose which will eventually be discarded.

5.2 Originality

There are several original ideas and procedures in our research. First, we used a multiple-choice grammaticality judgement format instead of a traditional dichotomous format. According to my related study (Amma, 2004), an internal reliability coefficient of the same grammaticality test items used in this research improved from $r = -0.213$ (N = 156) with the dichotomous format to $r = 0.559$ with the multiple-choice format (N = 156). The correlation with a C-test score also improved: the dichotomous format had $r = 0.141$ (N = 156; n.s.) while the multiple-choice format had $r = 0.406$ (N = 156; $p < 0.001$). Furthermore, the correlation with the self-reported TOEFL ITP score also improved, though not significantly: the dichotomous format had $r = 0.072$ (N = 26; n.s.) while the multiple-choice format had $r = 0.332$ (N = 26; n.s.). The advantage of the multiple-choice format over the dichotomous format is overwhelming; it reduces the chance-level error and increases the reliability.

Another innovation also concerns the grammaticality judgement test. When test takers judged a stimulus sentence as ungrammatical, they were asked to indicate the locus of error from among the variants of loci, instead of having to correct the error. Error correction is a completely different psychological construct from judgement, besides being far more demanding. A mere indication of the locus of error avoids the possible error of underestimating the judgement. When test takers judge a stimulus as grammatical, they, then, are asked to choose the most appropriate paraphrase or implication. This multiple-choice task is to balance the load of the task for the judgement as ungrammatical, and it reduces the error of overestimating the judgement which is given when people are simply asked to say 'correct'. These new features made the grammaticality judgement test more precise, reliable, and valid than preceding procedures.

Third, we used the output of a logistic regression analysis as the input data for a contingency table analysis. This was intended to predict the association measure (Expression 3) as a continuous function of the proficiency scale. The traditional 2x2 contingency table analysis requires *frequencies* of categories. It necessarily means that both variables in comparison must be categories with some band widths or of the aggregate sample. What it could do at best was to compare the high-proficiency group and low-proficiency group. By using *probabilities* instead of frequencies we are free from the range of test takers, and can continuously estimate the association measures. Though the actual association matrices were calculated in nine discrete proficiency levels for the purpose of simplifying the argument, we later extrapolated the formula with estimated coefficients that enabled us to calculate the association measure in any given proficiency level.

Fourth, we converted the association measures into distance measures for a multidimensional scaling analysis. We used a formula (Expression 4) to solve the problems of the ceiling effect and the negative values. There may be some other monotonic formula which better reflects the association measure with less stress, but the present formula at least produced meaningful results in the subsequent analyses.

Fifth, we converted the inter-item association measures into item-inherent association measures. We used a formula (Expression 4) in order to assign each item the degree of association with other items. This conversion enabled us to conduct contour plot analyses.

Our methodological innovations are considered as attempts at data mining. The conversion of the inter-item to item-inherent association measures means to seek differential item functioning (DIF), because we can identify items that work differentially from other items. Similarly, we can calculate 'differential person performance' by the linear product of item association measures (or *LinkScore* loadings) and person local parsing responses. We can thus identify learners who would need a special care.

5.3 Contributions to academic research

5.3.1 Test development

The result of this research offers several contributions to the related fields. Most directly, the new understanding of the nature of low-proficiency learners helps developing language tests with more validity and reliability. We have observed that there are two kinds of sentences in our test battery: those which invite local parsing and those which don't. It does not mean that low-proficiency learners misunderstand the former and correctly understand the latter, but it is evident that there are sentences with different degrees of DIF. A local parsing strategy may sometimes be helpful for partial comprehension, and at other times be harmful, but it is clear that a complete, precise comprehension is a long way. In actual test writing, inclusion of items with large DIF may result in distorted test results, as Ryan & Bachman (1992) suggest. Therefore, test items — and perhaps instructions — should be checked with reference to length, syntactic complexity, and semantic coherence.

We have also established a means of calculating the magnitude of DIF in terms of local parsing. Our newly invented statistic *LinkScore* measures the strength of association of individual items with other items. We have suggested that this statistic can be used to calculate the degree of tendency of test takers using a local parsing strategy. This information is an important profile of language learners in progress and can be added to the feedback report of a diagnosis test.

5.3.2 Data mining

Our research technique can be applied to other areas in humanities. One can discover a hidden pattern or latent trait of responses which is otherwise implicit to observers. The response format can either be multiple-choice or dichotomous. As long as the same test takers choose responses to multiple items, contingency can be calculated for any given pair of items. When the contingency information is networked across the entire set of items a cluster or clusters can possibly emerge. If the responses vary according to some continuous variable(s) the magnitude of the output cluster can be predicted as a function of the variable(s). One strong reservation for this procedure would be that the stimuli must be psychologically unidimensional; otherwise it would be very difficult to interpret the result. A simple application in EFL area is to knowledge learning. In such a test one is asked to show the knowledge of vocabulary or culture items. A certain cluster of responses may reflect her/his study history, background, or strength of motivation. Both the learner and teacher can benefit from the feedback of the result, as it can be used as a diagnosis for the learner's reflective study and for the teacher's backup classes and future curriculum design. This is a new approach in data mining and it can be widely used not only in language studies but also in other disciplines.

5.3.3 Research in second language development

The current research has indicated a particular difficulty that low-proficiency learners typically face. The fact that their performance is seriously affected by cognitive constraints cast new light upon the nature of second language development. The picture that low-proficiency learners are simply behind high-proficiency learners by several years is irrelevant; the two party's interlanguages are qualitatively different. It is not simply a difference in unidimensional proficiency as measured by test performance, but presumably a difference in the style of perceiving and processing language information. If working memory has anything to do with this difference, some extra- or para-linguistic practices should be effective in the more efficient processing of language.

The idea of indeterminacy in second language may need to change. Researchers (typically Sorace, 1990) claim that an early stage interlanguage is unstable and inconsistent. This phenomenon can partly be explained by cognitive constraints. It is like the 'end of test' factor in C-test (Section 3.2.3.2). We observed that when test takers do not reach the end of the test, the internal consistency of the test performance is severely damaged. Likewise, if learners' comprehension of test stimuli is limited to part of a sentence or passage because of some cognitive constraint, the result of the test is expected to be indeterminate.

5.3.4 Suggestions for TEFL
Our research findings provide suggestions for supporting low-proficiency learners' learning in the classroom in two ways: bottom-up awareness-oriented approach and top-down formulaic approach. We have observed that low-proficiency learners rely more on lexical-semantic than on syntactic information in comprehending sentences. One solution for correcting their strategy, if possible, is to train their analytic capacity. Activities for raising structural awareness (eg. Storch, 2001) are effective in 'noticing' structural clues in the text. The advantage of this noticing model is that knowledge of structure will provide a template (or 'exemplar' in Skehan's term (1998)) for comprehension, especially when learners under heavy cognitive constraints are kept from expanding a comprehensible span of text. This approach does not imply that we should introduce more rule-based teaching. Skehan (1998: 30–31) points out that a rule-based approach assumes (a) computation is 'cheap' and fast, and (b) memory systems should be compact, and organized efficiently and non-redundantly. Yet, "neither assumption is self-evidently valid" (p.31). Several studies indicate that real-life language use is memory-oriented (Bolinger, 1975), unsystematic (Pawley & Syder, 1983; Biber, Conrad, & Rippen, 1994; Carter & McCarthy, 1995), and of formulaic nature (Tannen, 1989). It is easily imaginable that an abstract manipulation of grammatical notions and terms would soon demoralise low-proficiency learners. Thus it is only in the sense that the input chunk is meaningful that noticing or explicit awareness works properly. In our research low-proficiency learners who used the local parsing strategy did so against a meaningful chunk in stimulus sentences, and did not apply it for a local sequence which did not form a meaningful unit. It is possible that if they are aware of a wider meaningful unit and its syntactic role, they can process a wider context with lower consumption of memory.

Another solution, a formulaic approach, which appears to contradict the first, is in fact another side of the same coin. Sinclair (1991) states that the language we use and understand is confined in the world of frequency of occurrence, and the combination of language units is not as open-ended as is predicted by grammarians. Thus learning patterns of language is a shortcut in language development. Admitting that low-proficiency learners have difficulty in analytic capacity, attempts should be made to directly expand a comprehensible span to be processed in the working memory. Practices of using formulaic expressions ease the memory load and save the memory resources for processing syntactic and discourse information. These chunks should gradually be expanded into a more elaborate communicative unit.

As for the efficiency of working memory, learners should learn an effective way of processing lower order information. One actual learning practice is shadowing. In shadowing learners repeat the words verbatim *as* they listen to the source text. Tamai (1992, 1999, 2000) suggests that this is an effective method of strengthening the phonological loop of working memory, because it requires the retention of phonological codes for a short time (Tamai, 1999: 53). He observed a dominantly positive effect of a shadowing practice on listening performance over a simple dictation practice (Tamai, 1992).

Apart from direct attempts to improve memory capacity/efficiency, we should consider the optimal learning environment for low-proficiency learners. Ando, et al. (1992) compared the effect of structural and communicative approaches in a Japanese EFL class in relation with the learners' working memory span. They found that the traditional grammar-oriented approach was more effective for large working memory span learners than the communicative approach; and the other way round for small working memory span learners. This observation suggests that abstract and formal handling of rules is beyond learners with small working memory capacity. The assumption of the current research is parallel to this phenomenon; low-proficiency learners find it difficult to deal with abstract syntactic information together with semantic processing, hence narrowing down the range of text to be comprehended, and depending more on lexical-semantic than syntactic information. Though Ando, et al.'s study had limitations in the sense that it was based on a short-term training, it is suggestive for a versatile learning/teaching orientation for learners in different proficiency levels.

5.4 Future orientations

We can extend our research findings and elaborate the research for the future.

(1) *Participants*

In the present research the participants were all Japanese university students of

EFL. This was because in the Japanese EFL context universities and colleges are where the gap between high proficiency learners and low proficiency learners are widest. If we can precisely diagnose the 'differential person performance' our technique should be applied to learners in earlier stages for early treatment. The local parsing strategy having been identified with participants with homogeneous background (ie., L1 and study history), we could use participants with heterogeneous background. The first thing would be to place the research in other countries representing different cultural and language types.

(2) *Materials*

The main experimental material, the grammaticality judgement test, needs further refinement. We could not precisely predict the categorisation of stimulus sentences at the planning stage. In addition, the two categories, (local parsing) 'accessible' and 'inaccessible', do not have a clear-cut contrast, despite statistical significance. The effect of the locus of quasi-sentential unit on the occurrence of local parsing is unsolved (cf. Section 4.3.3). Other possible variables affecting the magnitude of local parsing would be vocabulary items (in particular, in terms of difficulty and familiarity), structural complexity (ie., density of modification, word order, etc.), idiosyncratic morpho-syntactic rules, and background knowledge. It is possible to identify the cause of local parsing by controlling these variables .

(3) *Experimental design*

Two things need further consideration. The first topic concerns working memory. Though working memory appears to play an important part in low proficiency learners' performance, its relationship with text parsing was only suggestive. If we conducted a direct memory capacity/efficiency test along with a grammaticality judgement test, we could know what constitutes the cognitive constraint in more detail. Whether we can use a reading span test used widely in psychological analyses in reading needs reconfirmation, however. Since the local parsing phenomenon we have observed concerns a limitation in processing within a sentence, it is yet unknown whether or not a reading span test is a suitable measure as it focuses on the limitation in holding and processing information of multiple sentences.

Second, there is only one independent variable in our research, namely, the general proficiency measure represented by a Cz score. For a precise model of language performance, however, a multilevel regression analysis can be more appropriate. In other words, given the proficiency measure as x_1, the degree of local parsing can be expressed as

[Local parsing] = $f_1(x_1) + f_2(x_2) + ... + f_n(x_n)$

where $x_2, ... x_n$ can be working memory capacity, overseas stay experience, motivational factors, and cognitive/metacognitive strategy uses.

(4) *Analytical procedure*

As we reviewed in Section 5.2 above the application of *LinkScores* to 'differential person performance' will be an interesting incentive to deeper understanding of low language performance. But whether the conversion formula is as straightforward as a simple product of the *LinkScores* and an individual test taker's response requires further statistical investigation. Since the absolute frequencies of local parsing responses increase (Table 4.8) and the probabilities of these responses increase (Figures 3.5 and 3.6) as the proficiency measure rises, a simple product might predict a higher local parsing tendency for high-proficiency test takers than for low-proficiency test takers. We also need to elaborate the *LinkScore* formula (Expression 4) so it will be a continuous function of proficiency scale. One application of using the 'differential person performance' measure is to compare it with individual test takers' portfolio report including test scores, experience of overseas stay, and learning activities. A structural equation modelling technique would clarify the relationship between the cognitive constraint on text parsing and cognitive and metacognitive learning strategies.

(5) *Research goal*

We still don't know what precisely is syntactic proficiency and what is engaged in grammaticality judgement. It is one thing to understand that some learners parse sentences incorrectly; it is quite another to consider what activates their intuition in judging a sentence grammatical. The current research does not delve into this question. As long as the participants were sincere and did their best, they all considered their choice more grammatical than other options and fit to their intuition, whatever kind it is. One possible explanation is the awareness of rules; are they aware of syntactic and morphological rules? how strongly? and how correctly? Our research result suggests that high-proficiency test takers are more sensitive to syntactic anomaly (Section 4.2.2.1). Yet we are not sure whether it is because they have efficient dynamic capacity in working memory or because they have reliable static knowledge in long-term memory. Unfortunately, grammaticality judgement test does not distinguish these two components. We may have to conduct an efficiency test and knowledge test separately. At least, from our research results we understand that the problem of low-proficiency learners lies in (1) the narrow text span to be processed and (2) the semantic processing strategy. As for Skehan's model (1998), whether or not noticing is the only factor that affects these two memory components leaves a question, but it is certain that various factors influence processing: intelligence (in the sense of the capacity of abstract manipulation), aptitude, processing style, and formal teaching/learning. Research in these learner factors will deepen our understanding of the nature of individualised proficiency.

Notes

1 Universities and colleges in Japan normally have a rank of reputation widely accepted in the society, especially among high school students wishing to receive higher education. As a result of the competition, a limited number of notable schools collect students with relatively high academic proficiency while others collect students whose academic proficiency correspond to the school's level of reputation. Therefore within a school students tend to be homogeneous in proficiency. The universities and colleges were selected in the present study without any intention of using participants at schools of a particular reputation rank. It turned out that the proficiency levels (as measured by the C-test scores) of the schools varied widely. (p.69)

2 Logistic regression is applied as an alternative to item analyses, ie., classical item analysis and item response theory. The main concern here is to identify misfit items, so the items are independent of one another. No prior research — as far as language studies are concerned — has attempted to apply logistic regression to identify inter-item relationships. (p.86)

3 In view of Pavesi's (1984, 1986) studies the false judgement against our item **g7** may also be described as nonmastery of pronominalisation. As we examined in Section 2.3.2 the phenomenon can be considered as an example of local parsing, as long as we discuss it in terms of cognitive constraint. (p.126)

Bibliography

Abney, Steven P. and Mark Johnson. (1991) Memory requirements and local ambiguities of parsing strategies. *Journal of Psycholinguistic Research*, 20(3), pp.233–250.
Absy, A. Conceicao. (1995) The use of inference in EFL text comprehension. *Trabalhos em Linguistica Aplicada*, 26, pp.5–16.
Altmann, Gerry T., Kathy Y. van Nice, Alan Garnham, and Judith-Ann Hestra. (1998) Late closure in context. *Journal of Memory and Langugage*, 38, pp.459–484.
Amma Kazuo. (1983) *Comprehension of parenthetical clauses with prosodic contours in English.* MA thesis, Graduate School of Languages and Linguistics, Sophia University.
Amma Kazuo. (1984) Reading strategy formation and comprehension of parenthetical clauses. *Sophia Linguistica*, XIV, pp.79–88.
Amma Kazuo. (1997) Reliability in language testing: is it a unitary concept? *Ronso (Bulletin of the Faculty of Arts and Education, Tamagawa University)*, 37, pp.99–119.
Amma Kazuo. (2001) Variations of parsing strategies among EFL learners of different proficiency levels. *Ronso (Bulletin of the Faculty of Humanities, Tamagawa University)*, 41, pp.79–115.
Amma Kazuo. (2004) Development of multiple-choice grammaticality judgement tests. *JLTA Journal* (Japanese Language Testing Association), 6.
Anderson, J. (1983) *The Architecture of Cognition*. Cambridge, Massachusetts: Harvard University Press.
Anderson, J. (1985) *Cognitive Psychology and Its Implications, 2nd ed.* New York: Freeman.
Ando, J., N. Fukunaga, J. Kurahashi, T. Suto, T. Nakano, and M. Kage. (1992) A comparative study on the two EFL teaching methods: the communicative and the grammatical approach. *Japanese Journal of Educational Psychology*, 40, pp.247–256.
Arthur, B. (1980) Gauging the boundaries of second language development: a study of learners' judgments. *Language Learning*, 30, pp.177–194.
Asao Kojiro. [2000] Corpus of Japanese Learners of English. http://www.lb.u-tokai.ac.jp/lcorpus/. [No longer available.]
Ayaduray, Jeyalaxmy and George M. Jacobs. (1997) Can learner strategy instruction succeed? The case of higher order questions and elaborated responses. *System*, 25(4), pp.561–570.
Bachman, Lyle. (1990) *Fundamental Considerations in Language Testing*. Oxford: Oxford University Press.
Baddeley, A. D. (1986) *Working Memory*. Oxford: Oxford University Press.
Baddeley, A. D. and G. J. Hitch. (1974) Working memory. G. Bower (ed) *The Psychology of Learning and Motivation*, 8, pp.47–90. New York: Academic Press.
Baddeley, A. D. and R. H. Logie. (1999) Working memory: the multiple-component model. A. Miyake and P. Shah (eds) *Models of Working Memory: Mechanisms of Active Maintenance and Executive Control*, pp.28–61. Cambridge: Cambridge University Press.
Bever, Thomas G. (1970) The influence of speech performance on linguistic structure.

G. B. Flores d'Arcais and W. J. M. Levelt (eds) *Advances in Psycholinguistics*, pp.4–30. Amsterdam: North-Holland.

Biber, D., S. Conrad, and R. Rippen. (1994) Corpus-based approaches to issues in applied linguistics. *Applied Linguistics*, 15(2), pp.169–189.

Bolinger, Dwight. (1975) Meaning and memory. *Forum Linguisticum*, 1, pp.2–14.

Bradshaw, Jenny. (1990) Test-takers' reactions to a placement test. *Language Testing*, 7(1), pp.13–30.

Bremner, Stephen. (1999) Language learning strategies and language proficiency: investigating the relationship in Hong Kong. *Canadian Modern Language Review*, 55(4), pp.490–514.

Britt, M. Anne, Charles A. Perfetti, Simon Garrod, and Keith Rayner. (1992) Parsing in discourse: context effects and their limits. *Journal of Memory and Language*, 31(3), pp.293–314.

Cadierno, T. (1995) Formal instruction from a processing perspective: an investigation into the Spanish pst tense. *Modern Language Journal*, 79, pp.179–193.

Canale, Michael. (1983a) From communicative competence to communicative language pedagogy. Jack C. Richards and Richard W. Schmidt (eds) *Language and Communication*. Harlow, Essex: Longman.

Canale, Michael. (1983b) On some dimensions of language proficiency. John W. Oller, Jr. (ed) *Issues in Language Testing Research*, pp.333–342. Rowley, Massachusetts: Newbury House.

Canale, Michael and Merrill Swain. (1980) Theoretical bases of communicative approaches to second language teaching and testing. *Applied Linguistics*, 1(1), pp.1–40.

Carpenter, P. A. and M. A. Just. (1989) The role of working memory in language comprehension. D. Klahr and K. Ktovsky (eds) *Complex Information Processing*. Hillsdale, NJ: Lawrence Erlbaum Associates.

Carreiras, Manuel and Charles Clifton, Jr. (1993) Relative clause interpretation preferences in Spanish and English. *Language and Speech*, 36(4), pp.353–373.

Carrell, Patricia L. (1991) Strategic reading. *Georgetown University Round Table on Languages and Linguistics*. pp.167–178.

Carter, R. and M. McCarthy. (1995) *Language as Discourse: Perspectives for Language Teaching*. London: Longman.

Chamot, Anna Uhl. (1987) The learning strategies of ESL students. Anita Wenden and Joan Rubin (eds) *Learner Strategies in Language Learning*, pp.71–84. Prentice Hall International.

Chamot, Anna Uhl. (1990) Cognitive instruction in the second language classroom: the role of learning strategies. *Georgetown University Round Table on Languages and Linguistics*, pp.496–513.

Chapelle, Carol A. (1994) Are C-tests valid measures for L2 vocabulary research? *Second Language Research*, 10(2), pp.157–187.

Chapelle, Carol A. and Roberta G. Abraham. (1990) Cloze method: what difference does it make? *Language Testing*, 7(2), pp.121–146.

Chomsky, Noam. (1981) *Lectures on Government and Binding*. Dordrecht: Foris.

Clancy, Patrica M., Hyeonjin Lee, and Myeong Han Zoh. (1986) Processing strategies in the acquisition of relative clauses: universal principles and language-specific realizations. *Cognition*, 24(3), pp.225–262.

Clark, Herbert H. and Eve Clark. (1977) *Psychology and Language*. New York: Hercourt, Brace, Jovanovich.

Cohen, Andrew D. (1987) Studying learner strategies: how we get the information. Anita Wenden and Joan Rubin (eds) *Learner Strategies in Language Learning*, pp.31–42. Prentice Hall International.

Connelly, Michael. (1997) Using C-tests in English with post-graduate students. *English for Specific Purposes*, 16(2), pp.139–150.

Coppieters, R. (1987) Competence differences between native and fluent nonnative speakers. *Language*, 63, pp.544–573.

Corder, S. P. (1967) The significance of learner's errors. *International Review of Applied Linguistics*, 5, pp.161–170.

Corder, S. P. (1981) *Error Analysis and Interlanguage*. London: Oxford University Press.

Cromer, W. (1970) The difference model: a new explanaion for some reading difficulties. *Journal of Educational Psychology*, 61, pp.471–483.

Cuetos, Fernando and Don C. Mitchell. (1988) Cross-linguistic differences in parsing: restrictions on the use of the late closure strategy in Spanish. *Cognition*, 30(1), pp.73–105.

Cummins, Jim. (1983) Language proficiency and academic achievement. John W. Oller, Jr. (ed) *Issues in Language Testing Research*, pp.108–129. Rowley, Massachusetts: Newbury House.

Daneman, M. and P. Carpenter. (1980) Individual differences in working memory and reading. *Journal of Verbal Learning and Verbal Behavior*, 19, pp.450–466.

Daneman, M. and P. Carpenter. (1983) Individual differences in integrating information between and within sentences. *Journal of Experimental Psychology: Learning, Memory and Cognition*, 9, pp.561–583.

Daneman, M. and P. M. Merikle. (1996) Working memory and language comprehension: a meta-analysis. *Psychonomic Bulletin and Review*, 3, pp.422–433.

de Jong, John H. A. L. and Lieneke W. van Ginkel. (1992) Dimensions in oral foreign language proficiency. Ludo Verhoeven and John H. A. L. de Jong (eds) *The Construct of Language Proficiency: Applications of Psychological Models to Language Assessment*, pp.187–205. John Benjamins.

de Vincenzi, Marica and Remo Job. (1993) Some observations on the universality of the late-closure strategy. *Journal of Psycholinguistic Research*, 22(2), pp.189–206.

de Vincenzi, Marcia and Remo Job. (1995) An Investigation of late closure: the role of syntax, thematic structure, and pragmatics in initial and final interpretation. *Journal of Experimental Psychology: Learning, Memory, and Cognition*, 21(5), pp.1303–1321.

Dixon, P., et al. (1988) Word knowledge and working memory as predictors of reading skill. *Journal of Educational Psychology*, 80, pp.465–472.

Dornyei, Zoltan and Lucy Katona. (1992) Validation of the C-test amongst Hungarian EFL learners. *Language Testing*, 9(2), pp.187–206.

Doughty, Catherine. (1991) Second language instruction does make a difference: evidence from an empirical study of SL relativization. *Studies in Second Language Acquisition*, 13(4), pp.431–469.

Dušková, L. (1983) On the sources of errors in foreign language learning. B. Robinett and J. Schachter (eds) *Second Language Learning: Contrastive Analysis, Error Analysis, and Related Aspects*, pp.215–233. Ann Arbor: University of Michigan Press.

Ehrman, Madeline E. and Rebecca L. Oxford. (1990) Adult language learning styles and strategies in an intensive training setting. *The Modern Language Journal*, 74(3), pp.311–327.

Ellis, Rod. (1990) *Instructed Second Language Acquisition: Learning in the Classroom*. (Applied Language Studies). Oxford: Blackwell.

Ellis, Rod. (1991) Grammaticality judgments and second language acquisition. *Studies in Second Language Acquisition*, 13(2), pp.161–186.

Ellis, Rod, David Crystal, and Keith Johnson. (1990) *Instructed Second Language Acquisition: Learning in the Classroom* (Applied Language Studies). Oxford: Blackwell.

Everitt, Brian S. and Graham Dunn. (1991) *Applied Multivariate Data Analysis*. London: Edward Arnold.

Faustino, Isabel Patricia M. de. (1996) Learning strategies in language learning. *CTJ Journal*, 33, pp.11–19.

Flaitz, J., C. Feyten, S. Fox, and K. Mukherjee. (1995) Raising general awareness of language learning strategies: a little goes a long way. *Hispania*, 78(2), pp.337–348.

Fodor, Janet Dean. (1998) Learning to parse? *Journal of Psycholinguistic Research*, 27(2), pp.285–319.

Fodor, Janet Dean and Lyn Frazier. (1980) Is the human sentence parsing mechanism an ATN? *Cognition*, 8, pp.417–459.

Fowler, Christopher. (1981) Some aspects of language perception by eye: the beginning reader. Ovid J. L. Tzeng and H. Singer (eds) *Perception of Print: Reading Research in Experimental Psychology*, pp.171–196. Hillsdale, NJ.: Lawrence Erlbaum Associates.

Frazier, Lyn and Giovanni B. Flores d'Arcais. (1989) Filler driven parsing: a study of gap filling in Dutch. *Journal of Memory and Language*, 28(3), pp.331–344.

Frazier, Lyn and Janet Dean Fodor. (1978) The sausage machine: a new two-stage parsing model. *Cognition*, 6, pp.291–325.

Frazier, Lyn and Keith Rayner. (1982) Making and correcting errors during sentence comprehension: eye movements in the analysis of structurally ambiguous sentences. *Cognitive Psychology*, 4, pp.178–210.

Frazier, Lyn and Keith Rayner. (1987) Resolution of syntactic category ambiguities: eye movements in parsing lexically ambiguous sentences. *Journal of Memory and Language*, 26(5), pp.505–526.

Frenck-Mestre, C. and J. Pynte. (1997) Syntactic ambiguity resolution while reading in second and native languages. *Quarterly Journal of Experimental Psychology, Section A: Human Experimental Psychology*, 50A(1), pp.119–148.

Gass, Susan M. (1983) The development of L2 intuitions. *TESOL Quarterly*, 17, pp.273–291.

Gass, Susan M. (1994) The reliability of second-language grammaticality judgments. Elaine E. Tarone, Susan M Gass, and Andrew D. Cohen (eds) *Research Methodology in Second-Language Acquisition*, pp.263–286. Hillsdale, NJ: Lawrence Earlbaum Associates.

Gass, Susan M. and Larry Selinker. (1994) *Second Language Acquisition: an Introductory*

Course. Hillsdale, New Jersey: Lawrence Erlbaum Associates.

Gathercole, Susan E. and Alan D. Baddeley. (1993) *Working Memory and Language.* Hove: Lawrence Erlbaum Associates.

Gilboy, Elizabeth, Josep-Maria Sopena, Charles Clifton, Jr., and Lyn Frazier. (1995) Argument structure and association preferences in Spanish and English complex NPs. *Cognition,* 54(2), pp.131–167.

Gilhooly, Kenneth J. (1998) Working memory, strategies, and reasoning tasks. R. H. Logie and K. J. Gilhooly (eds) *Working Memory and Thinking,* pp.7–22. Hove, East Sussex: Psychology Press.

Goh, Christine C. M. and Kwah Poh Foong. (1997) Chinese ESL students' learning strategies: a look at frequency, proficiency, and gender. *Hong Kong Journal of Applied Linguistics,* 2(1), pp.39–53.

Green, John M. and Rebecca Oxford. (1995) A closer look at learning strategies, L2 proficiency, and gender. *TESOL Quarterly,* 29(2), pp.261–297.

Greenbaum, S. and R. Quirk. (1990) *A Student's Grammar of the English Language.* Longman.

Grotjahn, Rudiger. (1986) Test validation and cognitive psychology: some methodological considerations. *Language Testing,* 3(2), pp.159–185.

Grotjahn, Rudiger. (1987) How to construct and evaluate a C-test: a discussion of some problems and some statistical analyses. *Quantitative Linguistics,* 34, pp.219–253.

Grotjahn, Rudiger. (1993) Der C-Test. Grundlagentheoretische und Anwendungsbezogene Untersuchungen [The C-test. theoretical and applicational studies]. *ZFF: Zeitschrift fur Fremdsprachenforschung,* 4(2), pp.77–87.

Grotjahn, Rudiger. (1995) Der C-Test: state of the art [The C-test: state of the art]. *ZFF: Zeitschrift fur Fremdsprachenforschung,* 6(2), pp.37–60

Guthrie, John T., Peggy Van Meter, Ann Dacey McCann, Allan Wigfield, Lois Bennett, Carol C. Poundstone, Mary Ellen Rice, Frances M. Faibisch, Brian Huntl, and Ann M. Mitchel. (1996) Growth of literacy engagement: changes in motivations and strategies during concept-oriented reading instruction. *Reading Research Quarterly,* 31(3), pp.306–332.

Guttman, L. (1954) Some necessary conditions for common factor analysis. *Psychometrika,* 19, pp.149–163.

Halbach, Ana. (2000) Finding out about students' learning strategies by looking at their diaries: a case study. *System,* 28(1), pp.85–96.

Harrington, M. (1991) Indivitual differences in L2 reading: processing capacity versus linguistic knowledge. Paper presented at the Annual Meeting of the American Association of Applied Linguistics, New York, NY.

Harrington, M. and M. Sawyer. (1992) L2 working memory capacity and L2 reading skill. *Studies in Second Language Acquisition,* 14, pp.25–38.

Hastings, Robert P. (1986) *SUGI Supplemental Library User's Guide, Version 5 Edition.* Cary, NC.: SAS Institute Inc.

Heffernan, Peter J. (1998) Promoting the development of strategic competence in the language classroom. *Mosaic,* 5(4), pp.1–5.

Henning, Grant H. (1984) Advantages of latent trait measurement in language testing.

Language Testing, 1(2), pp.123–133.
Henning, Grant H. (1987) *A Guide to Language Testing*. Newbury House.
Henning, Grant H. (1992) Dimensionality and construct validity of language tests. *Language Testing*, 9, pp.1–11.
Henning, Grant H., Thom Hudson, and Jean Turner. (1985) Item response theory and the assumption of unidimensionality for language tests. *Language Testing*, 2(2), pp.141–154.
Holland, Paul W. and Dorothy T. Thayer. (1988) Differential Item Performance and the Mantel-Haenszel Procedure. Wainer, Howard and Henry I. Braun (eds) *Test Validity*, pp.129–145. Hillsdale, NJ: Lawrence Erlbaum.
Holmes, S. E. (1982) Unidimensionality and vertical equating with the Rasch Model. *Journal of Educational Measurement*, 19, pp.139–147.
Holmes, V. M. (1987) Syntactic parsing: in search of the garden path. Max Coltheart (ed) *The Psychology of Reading* (Attention and Performance XII), pp.587–599. Hove, Sussex: Lawrence Erlbaum Associates.
Hsia, Sopie. (1993) The role of metalinguistic judgments in reading comprehension: evidence from Euro-Latin, Japanese, Korean and Hong Kong Cantonese-speaking adult learners of English as a second language. *Research Report: City Polytechnic of Hong Kong, Department of English*
Hyltenstam, Kenneth. (1982) Data types and second language variability. Paper presented at a conference 'Psycholinguistics and Foreign Language Learning' (Stockholm and Åbo, October 25–26, 1982). ERIC ED 276 313; FL 016 295.
Hymes, Dell. (1972) On communicative comptence. J. Pride and J. Holmes (eds) *Sociolinguistics*. Harmondsworth: Penguin.
Ikeno Osamu (2002) Text structure prediction in L2 reading and working memory. *JACET Bulletin*, 35, pp.105–116.
Ingram, David E. (1985) Assessing proficiency: an overview of some aspects of testing. Kenneth Hyltenstam and Manfred Pienemann (eds) *Modelling and Assessing Second Language Acquisition*, pp.215–276. Clevedon: Multilingual Matters.
Ito Akihiro. (1997) Japanese EFL learners' test-type related interlanguage variability. *JALT Journal*, 19(1), pp.89–105.
Ito Akihiko. (1998) The author responds: more on test-types. *JALT Journal*, 20(1), pp.89–90.
Jafarpur, Abdoljavad. (1995) Is C-testing superior to cloze? *Language Testing*, 12(2), pp.194–216.
Jafarpur, Abdoljavad. (1999a) Can the C-test be improved with classical item analysis? *System*, 27(1), pp.79–89.
Jafarpur, Abdoljavad. (1999b) What's magical about the rule-of two for constructing C-tests? *RELC Journal*, 30(2), pp.86–100.
James, Carl. (1998) *Errors in Language Learning and Use: Exploring Error Analysis*. Longman.
Johnson, Jacqueline. S. and Elissa. L. Newport. (1989) Critical period effects in second language learning: the influence of maturational state on the acquisition of English as a second language. *Cognitive Psychology*, 21, pp.60–99.
Johnson, Jacqueline S., Kenneth D. Shenkman, Elissa L. Newport, and Douglas L. Medin. (1996) Indeterminacy in the grammar of adult language learners. *Journal of Memory and*

Language, 35(3), pp.335–352.
Juffs, Alan. (1998) Main verb versus reduced relative clause ambiguity resolution in L2 sentence processing. *Language Learning,* 48(1), pp.107–147.
Juffs, Alan and Michael Harrington. (1995) Parsing effects in second language sentence processing. *Studies in Second Language Acquisition,* 17, pp.483–516.
Kaan, Edith. (1998) Sensitivity to np-type: processing subject-object ambiguities in Dutch. *Journal of Semantics,* 15(4), pp.335–354.
Kadota Shuhei and Noro Tadashi. (2001) *Eigo Reading no Ninchi Mechanism: How the Mind Works in EFL Reading.* Tokyo: Kuroshio.
Kagan, J. and N. Kogan. (1970) Individuality and cognitive performance. P. H. Mussen (ed) *Carmichael's Manual of Child Psychology, 3rd ed.*, 1, pp.1273–1365. John Wiley and Sons.
Kayne, R. (1984) *Connectendess and Binary Branching.* Dordrecht, the Netherlands: Foris.
King, J. and M. A. Just. (1991) Individual differences in syntactic processing: the role of working memory. *Journal of Memory and Language,* 30, pp.580–602.
Klein-Braley, Christine. (1984) Advance prediction of difficulty with C-tests. *Occasional Papers: University of Essex, Department of Language and Linguistics,* 29, pp.97–112.
Klein-Braley, Christine. (1985) A cloze-up on the C-test. *Language Testing,* 2, pp.76–104.
Klein-Braley, Christine. (1997) C-tests in the context of reduced redundancy testing: an appraisal. *Language Testing,* 14(1), pp.47–84.
Klein-Braley, Christine and Ulrich Raatz. (1994) Vergleichende Untersuchungen zur Effektivitat des Fremdsprachenunterrichts in Schule und Universitat in mehreren Landern Europas [Comparative studies of the effectiveness of second-language instruction at schools and universities in several european count]. *ZFF: Zeitschrift fur Fremdsprachenforschung,* 5(1), pp.57–61.
Köberl, Johann and Günther Sigott. (1994) Word frequency, transitional probability, and item facility in C-tests. *Language Testing* Update, 16, pp.56–62.
Köberl, Johann and Günther Sigott. (1996) Deletion patterns in C-tests: native speakers vs. foreign learners. *Language Testing* Update, 20, pp.45–48.
Kojic-Sabo, Izabella and Patsy M. Lightbrown. (1999) Students' approaches to vocabulary learning and their relationship to success. *Modern Language Journal,* 83(2), pp.176–192.
Kokkota, V. (1988) Letter-deletion procedure: a flexible way of reducing text redundancy. *Language Testing,* 5(1), pp.115–119.
Krashen, Stephen D. (1985) *The Input Hypothesis: Issues and Implications.* London: Longman.
Krashem, Stephen D. and Tracy D. Terrell. (1983) *The Natural Approach: Language Acquisition in the Classroom.* Oxford: Pergamon.
Leow, Ronald P. (1996) Grammaticality judgment tasks and second-language development. *Georgetown University Round Table on Languages and Linguistics,* pp.126–139.
Lewis-Beck, Michael S. (ed.). (1993) *Basic Statistics.* (International Handbooks of Quantitative Applications in the Social Sciences, Vol.1) London: Sage Publications..
Lin, Yue-Hong and John Hedgcock. (1996) Negative feedback incorporation among high-proficiency and low-proficiency Chinese-speaking learners of Spanish. *Language Learning,* 46(4), pp.567–611.
Littlemore, Jeannette. (1995) Cognitive style dimensions and learning strategy: preference in an L2 context. *Universite Libre de Bruxelles Rapport d'Activites de l'Institut des Langues*

Vivantes et de Phonetique, 31, pp.43–61.

MacDonald, Maryellen C., Marcel Adam Just, and Patricia A. Carpenter. (1992) Working memory constraints on the processing of syntactic ambiguity. *Cognitive Psychology*, 24(1), pp.56–98.

MacIntyre, Peter D. and Kimberly A. Noels. (1996) Using social-psychological variables to predict the use of language learning strategies. *Foreign Language Annals*, 29(3), pp.373–386.

Mantel, Nathan and William Haenszel. (1959) Statistical aspects of the analysis of data from retrospective studies of disease. *Journal of the National Cancer Institute*, 22, pp.719–748.

McElree, Brian. (1993) The locus of lexical preference effects in sentence comprehension: a time-course analysis. *Journal of Memory and Language*, 32(4), pp.536–571.

McNamara, Tim. (1996) *Measuring Second Language Performance*. London: Longman.

Milanovic, M. (1988) *The construction and validation of a performance-based battery of English language progress tests*. Unpublished PhD dissertation, University of London.

Mitchell, Richard. (1991) Validating language tests: a Hong Kong case study. *Research Report: City Polytechnic of Hong Kong, Department of English*, 10, pp.1–101.

Miyake, A. and N. P. Friedman. (1999) Individual differences in second language proficiency: working memory as 'language aptitude'. A. F. Healy and L. E. Bourned (eds) *Foreign Language Learning: Psycholinguistic Studies on Training and Retention*, pp.339–364. Mahwah, NJ.: Lawrence Erlbaum Associates.

Mochizuki Akihiko. (1999) Language learning strategies used by Japanese university students. *RELC Journal*, 30(2), pp.101–113.

Mohammed, Abdel Moneim M. (1993) Towards a learner-centred technique of teaching grammar. *Language Learning Journal*, 7, pp.59–63.

Mollica, Anthony and Frank Nuessel. (1997) The good language learner and the good language teacher: a review of the literature and classroom applications. *Mosaic*, 4 (3), pp.3–16.

Moran, Chris. (1991) Lexical inferencing in EFL reading coursebooks: some implications of research. *System*, 19(4), pp.389–400.

Morrison, Louise. (1996) Talking about words: a study of French as a second language learners' lexical inferencing procedures. *Canadian Modern Language Review*, 53(1), pp.41–75.

Naiman, N., M. Fröhlich, H. H. Stern, and A. Todesco. (1978) *The Good Language Learner*. The Ontario Institute for Studies in Education.

Naiman, N., M. Fröhlich, H. H. Stern, and A. Todesco. (1995) *The Good Language Learner* (Modern Languages in Practice 4). Clevedon, Avon: Multilingual Matters.

Nation, Robert and Barry McLaughlin. (1986) Novices and experts: an information processing approach to the good language learner problem. *Applied Psycholinguistics*, 7 (1), pp.41–55.

Nyikos, Martha and Rebecca Oxford. (1993) A factor analytic study of language learning strategy use: interpretations from information processing theory and social psychology. *The Modern Language Journal*, 77(1), pp.11–22.

Oller, John W. Jr. (1979) *Language Tests at School*. Harlow, Essex: Longman.

Oller, John W. Jr. (1983) Evidence for a general language proficiency factor: an expectancy grammar. John W. Oller, Jr. (ed) *Issues in Language Testing Research*, pp.3–10. Rowley, Massachusetts: Newbury House.

Oltman, P. K., L. J. Sticker, and T. Barrows. (1988) *Native Language, English Proficiency and the Structure of the Test of English as a Foreign Language*. TOEFL Research Reports, 27. Princeton: Educational Testing Service.

O'Malley, J. Michael and Anna Uhl Chamot. (1990) *Learning Strategies in Second Language Acquisition*. Cambridge University Press.

Osaka, M and N. Osaka. (1992) Language-independent working memory as measured by Japanese and English reading span tests. *Bulletin of the Psychometiric Society*, 30, pp.287–289.

Oscarson, Mats. (1991) Item response theory and reduced redundancy techniques: some notes on recent developments in language testing. Kees de Bot, Ralph B. Ginsberg, and Claire Kramsch (eds) *Foreign Language Research in Cross-cultural Perspective*, pp.95–111. Amsterdam: John Benjamins.

Oxford, Rebecca L. (1990) *Language Learning Strategies: What Every Teacher Should Know*. New York: Newbury House.

Oxford, Rebecca L. (1992) Language learning strategies in a nutshell: update and ESL suggestions. *TESOL Journal*, 2(2), pp.18–22.

Oxford, Rebecca L. (1993a) Individual differences among your ESL students: why a single method can't work. *Journal of Intensive English Studies*, 7, pp.27–42.

Oxford, Rebecca L. (1993b) Research on second language learning strategies. *Annual Review of Applied Linguistics*, 13, pp.175–187.

Oxford, Rebecca L. and Judith A. Burry-Stock. (1995) Assessing the use of language learning strategies worldwide with the ESL/EFL version of the strategy inventory for language learning (SILL). *System*, 23(1), pp.1–23.

Oxford, Rebecca L. and Madeline E. Ehrman. (1995) Adults' language learning strategies in an intensive foreign language program in the United States. *System*, 23(3), pp.359–386.

Oxford, Rebecca L., Young Park-Oh, Sukero Ito, and Malenna Sumrall. (1993) Japanese by satellite: effects of motivation, language learning styles and strategies, gender, course level, and previous language learning experience on japanese language achievement. *Foreign Language Annals*, 26(3), pp.359–371.

Palacios-Martínez, Ignacio M. (1995) A study of the learning strategies used by secondary school and university students of English in Spain. *Refista Alicantina de Estudios Ingleses*, 8, pp.177–193.

Park, Gi Pyo. (1997) Language learning strategies and English proficiency in Korean University students. *Foreign Language Annals*, 30(2), pp.211–221.

Pawley, A. and F. Syder. (1983) Two puzzles for linguistic theory: nativelike selection and nativelike fluency. J. C. Richards and R. Schmidt (eds) *Language and Communication*. London: Longman.

Payne, M. C. and T. Holtzman. (1983) Auditory short-term memory and digit span: normal versus poor readers. *Journal of Educational Psychology*, 75(3), pp.424–430.

Pearlmutter, Neal J. and Maryellen C. MacDonald. (1995) Individual differences and probabilistic constraints in syntactic ambiguity resolution. *Journal of Memory and*

Language, 34(4), pp.521–542.
Pickering, Martin J. (1999) Sentence comprehension. S. Garrod and M. J. Pickering (eds), *Language Processing*, pp.123–153. Hove, East Sussex: Psychology Press.
Prapphal, Kanchana. (1994) A study of the C-test and the X-test performed by first-year science-oriented university students. *PASAA* (Thailand), 24, pp.16–23.
Purpura, James Enos. (1998) Investigating the effects of strategy use and second language test performance with high- and low-ability test takers: a structural equation modelling approach. *Language Testing*, 15(3), pp.333–379.
Pyle, Michael A. and Mary Ellen Muñoz. (1986) *Test of English as a Foreign Language Preparation Guide*. Lincoln, Nebraska: Cliffs Notes.
Quigley, S. P., M. W. Steinkamp, D. J. Power, and B. W. Jones. (1978) *Test of Syntactic Abilities*. Dormac.
Raatz, Ulrich. (1984) The factorial validity of C-tests. *Occasional Papers: University of Essex, Department of Language and Linguistics*, 29, pp.124–139.
Raatz, Ulrich and Christine Klein-Braley. (1981) The C-Test: a modification of the cloze procedure. T. Culhane, C. Klein-Braley, and D. K. Stevenson (eds) *Practice and Problems in Language Testing (University of Essex Occasional Paper)*, pp.113–148. Colchester: University of Essex.
Rayner, Keith. (1975) The perceptual span and peripheral cues in reading. *Cognitive Psychology*, 7(1), 65–81.
Rayner, Keith and Alexander Pollatsek. (1989) *The Psychology of Reading*. Hilsdale, NJ: Lawrence Erlbaum Associates.
Rayner, Keith and Sara C. Sereno. (1994) Regressive eye movements and sentence parsing: on the use of regression-contingent analyses. *Memory and Cognition*, 22(3), pp.281–285.
Reckase, Mark D. (1979) Unifactor latent trait models applied to multifactor tests: results and implications. *Journal of Educational Statistics*, 4, pp.207–230.
Rees-Miller, Janie. (1993) A critical approach of learner training: theoretical bases and teaching implications. *TESOL Quarterly*, 27 (4), pp.679–687.
Reiss, Mary-Ann. (1983) Helping the unsuccessful language learner. *The Canadian Modern Language Review*, 39, pp.257–266.
Reves, Thea. (1978) The ability to imitate — as a characteristic of the good language learner. Paper presented at the Fifth International Congress of Applied Linguistics (AILA).
Reynolds, H. T. (1993) Analysis of Nominal Data. Michaes S. Lewis-Beck (ed) *Basic Statistics, Volume 1 (Part III)* (International Handbooks of Quantitative Applications in the Social Sciences), pp.159–234. SAGE Publications/Toppan Publishing.
Richards, J. C. (ed.). (1974) *Error Analysis*. London: Longman.
Richards, Jack C. and Theodore Rogers. (1986) *Approaches and Methods in Language Teaching*. Cambridge University Press.
Ridley, Jennifer. (1997) The relationship between language learning awareness and language using awareness among university-level ab initio learners of German. *ZFF: Zeitschrift für Fremdsprachenforschung*, 8 (2), pp.267–280.
Rösler, Frank, Thomas Pechman, Judith Streb, Brigitte Röder, and Erwin Henninghausen. (1998) Parsing of sentences in a language with varying word order: word-by-word variations of processing demands are revealed by event-related brain potentials. *Journal of*

Memory and Language, 38, pp.150–176.
Romney, A. Kimball, Roger N. Shepard, and Sara Beth Nerlove. (1972) *Multidimensional Scaling: Theory and Applications in the Behavioral Sciences, Volume II: Applications*. New York: Seminar Press.
Rubin, Joan. (1975) What the 'Good Language Learner' can teach us. *TESOL Quarterly*, 9(1), pp.41–51.
Rubin, Joan. (1981) Study of cognitive processes in second language learning. *Applied Linguistics*, 11, pp.117–131.
Rubin, Joan. (1987) Learner strategies: theoretical assumptions, research history and typology. Anita Wenden and Joan Rubin (eds) *Learner Strategies in Language Learning*, pp.15–30. Prentice Hall International.
Ryan, Katherine E. and Lyle F. Bachman. (1992) Differential item functioning on two tests of EFL proficiency. *Language Testing*, 9(1), pp.12–29.
Sang, F., B. Schmitz, H. J. Vollmer, J. Bauert, and P. M. Roeder. (1986) Models of second language competence: a structural equation approach. *Language Testing*, 3(1), pp.54–79.
SAS Institute. (2002) *Statistics and Graphics Guide* (JMP Version 5). Cary, NC: SAS Institute.
Sasaki, Miyuki. (2000) Effects of cultural schemata on students' test-taking processes for cloze tests: a multiple data source approach. *Language Testing*, 17(1), pp.85–114.
Scevak, Jill and Phillip Moore. (1997) The strategies students in years 5, 7 and 9 use for processing texts and visual aids. *The Australian Journal of Language and Literacy*, 20(4), pp.280–289.
Schachter, J. (1974) An error in error analysis. *Language Learning*, 24, pp.205–214.
Schachter, J. (1983) A new account of language transfer. Gass and Selinker (eds) *Language Transfer in Language Learning*, pp.98–111. Rowley, MA: Newbury House.
Schachter, J. (1992) A new account of language transfer. Gass and Selinker (eds) *Language Transfer in Language Learning*, pp.32–46. Amsterdam: John Benjamins.
Schachter, J., A. Tyson, and F. Diffley. (1976) Learners' intuitions of grammaticality. *Language Learning*, 26, pp.67–76.
Schachter, J and M. Celce-Murcia. (1971) Some reservations concerning error analysis. *TESOL Quarterly*, 11, pp.441–451.
Schachter, Jacquelyn and Virginia Yip. (1990) Grammaticality judgments: why does anyone object to subject extraction? *Studies in Second Language Acquisition*, 12, pp.379–392.
Schmidt, Richard. (1990) The role of consciousness in second language learning. *Applied Linguistics*, 11, pp.129–158.
Schmidt, Richard. (1993a) Awareness and second language acquisition. *Annual Review of Applied Linguistics*, 13, pp.206–226. Cambridge University Press.
Schmidt, Richard. (1993b) Consciousness, learning and interlanguage pragmatics. G. Kasper and S. Blum-Kulka (eds) *Interlanguage Pragmatics*, pp.21–42. New York: Oxford University Press.
Schriefers, Herbert, Angela D. Friederici, and Katja Kuhn. (1995) The processing of locally ambiguous relative clauses in German. *Journal of Memory and Language*, 34(4), pp.499–520.
Schütze, Carson T. and Edward Gibson. (1999) Argumenthood and english prepositional

phrase attachment. *Journal of Memory and Language*, 40(3), pp.409–431.
Selinker, Larry. (1972) Interlanguage. *IRAL*, X(3), pp.209–231.
Shepard, Roger N, A. Kimball Romney, and Sara Beth Nerlove. (1972) *Multidimensional Scaling: Theory and Applications in the Behavioral Sciences, Volume I: Theory*. New York: Seminar Press.
Sheorey, R. (1999) An examination of language learning strategy use in the setting of an indigenized variety of English. *System*, 27(2), pp.173–190.
Simmons, Diana. (1996) A study of strategy use in independent learners. Pemberton, Richard, Edward S. L. Li, Winnie W. F. Or, and Herbert D. Pierson (eds) *Taking Control: Autonomy in Language Learning*, pp.61–75. Hong Kong: Hong Kong U Press.
Sinclair, John. (1991) *Corpus, Concordance, Collocation*. Oxford: Oxford University Press.
Sirkin, R. Mark. (1995) *Statistics for the Social Sciences*. Thousand Oaks, CA: SAGE Publications.
Skehan, Peter. (1988) Language testing. Part I. (State of the art article) *Language Teaching*, 21(4), pp.211–221.
Skehan, Peter. (1989) Language testing. Part II. (State of the art article) *Language Teaching*, 22(1), pp.1–13.
Skehan, Peter. (1998) *A Cognitive Approach to Language Learning*. Oxford: Oxford University Press.
Sorace, Antonella. (1990) Indeterminacy in first and second languages: theoretical and methodological issues. Jong, John H. A. L. de and Douglas K. Stevenson, *Individualizing the Assessment of Language Abilities*, pp.127–153. Clevedon, Avon: Multilingual Matters.
Spurling, Steven. (1987) Questioning the use of the Bejar method to determine unidimensionality. *Language Testing*, 4(1), pp.93–95.
Stern, H. H. (1975) What can we learn from the good language learner? *Canadian Modern Language Review*, 30, pp.244–254.
Stern, H. H. (1976) What can we learn from the good language learner? *Modern Languages in Scotland*, 11, pp.71–85.
Stolz, W. (1967) A study of the ability to decode grammatically novel sentences. *Journal of Verbal Learning and Verbal Behavior*, 6, pp.867–873.
Storch, N. (2001) Comparing ESL learners' attention to grammar on three different classroom tasks. *RELC Journal*, 32(2), pp.104–124.
Suh Sungki. (1991) Constituent structure processing in Korean. *Proceedings: Eastern States Conference on Linguistics*, 8, pp.347–358.
Swaminathan, Hariharan and H. Jane Rogers. (1990) Detecting differential item functioning using logistic regression procedures. *Journal of Educational Measurement*, 27(4), pp.361–370.
Swan, Michael. (1995) *Practical English Usage, 2nd ed*. Oxford: Oxford University Press.
Taillefer, Gail F. (1996) L2 reading ability: further insight into the short-circuit hypothesis. *The Modern Language Journal*, 80(4), pp.461–477.
Tamai K. (1992) Follow-up no chôkairyoku kôjô ni oyobosu kôka oyobi follow-up nôryoku to chôkairyoku no kankei [The effect of follow-up on improving listening skills and the relationship between ability of follow-up and listening skills]. *STEP Bulletin*, 4, pp.48–62.
Tamai K. (1999) Eigo kyôiku ni ikasu tsûyaku kunrenhô [Translation practice for English

language teaching]. *Jiji Eigo Kenkyû*, March, pp.51–53. [In Japanese]
Tamai K. (2000) Strategic effect of shadowing on listening ability. A paper presented at the 4th Conference on Foreign Language Education and Technology. Kobe, Japan.
Tannen, D. (1989) *Talking Voices: Repetition, Dialogue and Imagery in Conversational Discourse*. Cambridge: Cambridge University Press.
Tarone, Elaine. (1988) *Variation in Interlanguage*. Arnold.
Trueswell, John C. and Albert E. Kim. (1998) How to prune a garden path by nipping it in the bud: fast priming of verb argument structure. *Journal of Memory and Language*, 39, pp.102–123.
Trueswell, J., M. K. Tanenhaus, and C. Kello. (1993) Verb-specific constraints in sentence processing: separating effects of lexical preference from garden-paths. *Journal of Memory and Language*, 33, pp.285–318.
Truscott, John. (1998) Noticing in second language acquisition: a critical review. *Second Language Research*, 14(2), pp.103–135.
Tsuda Atsuko and George Yule. (1985) The confidence factor: an exploratory study of the interaction of self-confidence and accuracy in test performance among a group of Japanese learners of English. *JALT Journal*, 7(1), pp.93–106.
Upshur, J. A. and T. J. Homburg. (1983) Some relations among language tests at successive ability levels. John W. Oller, Jr. (ed) *Issues in Language Testing Research*, pp.188–202. Rowley, Massachusetts: Newbury House.
van Susteren, Timothy J. (1997) *The comparative reliability and validity of alternate-choice and multiple-choice tests*. PhD dissertation, Michigan State University, 1986. Ann Arbor: University Microfilms International.
VanPatten, Bill. (1996) *Input Processing and Grammar Instruction*. New York: Ablex.
VanPatter, B. and T. Cadierno. (1993) Explicit instruction and input processing. *Studies in Second Language Acquisition*, 15, pp.225–243.
Walter, Helen Catherine. (2000) *The involvement of working memory in reading in a foreign language*. PhD dissertation, University of Cambridge.
Wenden, Anita L. (1987) How to be a successful language learner: insights and prescriptions from L2 learners. Anita Wenden and Joan Rubin (eds) *Learner Strategies in Language Learning*, pp.103–118. Prentice Hall International.
Wenden, Anita L. (1991) *Learner Strategies for Learner Autonomy: Planning and Implementing Learner Training for Language Learners*. Prentice Hall.
Woods, Anthony and Rosemary Baker. (1985) Item response theory. *Language Testing*, 2(2), pp.117–140.
Yoshida Mami. (2003) Working memory capacity and the use of inference in L2 reading. *JACET Bulletin*, 36, pp.1–17.
Yoshitake, Sonia Sonoko. (1991) Grammaticality judgment test as a research instrument. *ICU Language Research Bulletin*, 6(1), pp.103–122.
Young, A. Robert and Ann O. Strauch. (1994) *Nitty Gritty Grammar: Sentence Essentials for Writers*. St. Martin's Press.
Zagar, Daniel, Joel Pynte, and Sylvie Rativeau. (1997) Evidence for early-closure attachment on first-pass reading times in French. *Quarterly Journal of Experimental Psychology* (Section A: Human Experimental Psychology), 50A, pp.421–438.

Zwaan, R. A. and C. M. Brown. (1996) The influence of language proficiency and comprehension skill on situation-model construction. *Discourse Processes*, 21, pp.289–327.

Statistical packages
JMP 5.0. (2002) SAS Institute Inc.
SPSS 6.1.1. (1995) SPSS Inc.

Appendix A

Parsing strategies (Amma, 2001)

—Classification of Incorrect Parsing Strategies—

A1. Seek a simple structure
A1a. *Make a smallest local closure. Avoid embedding and complementation.*

<Definition> Identify a finite clause within the stimulus which constitutes a minimal meaningful unit. A grammatically incomplete clause can be the clause for local closure as long as it is taken for a clause by the learner. Embedded or complemented structures should be reduced to simple structures locally, ie, disregarding the overall structural configuration.

<Examples>
The little girls who ate with <u>Cathy loved ice cream</u>.
The dress, <u>the material was silk</u>, pleased her.

A1b. *Find local familiarity.*

<Definition> Identify any small collocation unit within the stimulus which is familiar to the learner. If the unit agrees to the learner's knowledge, acknowledge the unit as correct. In case of dichotomous judgement, repeat the process with the rest of the units. If all the acknowledged units are correct, the stimulus is regarded as correct. In case of multiple-choice judgement, if the focused unit is correct, the stimulus is regarded as correct.

<Examples>
You won't be <u>laughed at</u> the audience.
I talked to the girls <u>which Anne knew</u>.

A2~6. Follow developmental stages
A2. *Avoid inflections.*

<Definition> Any inflected elements of verbs and auxiliaries should be disregarded. The stimulus is not regarded as incorrect because of the lack of inflections.

<Example>
Catherine <u>not come</u> over here, because she's got a cold.

A3. *Avoid case agreement.*

<Definition> Any case agreement should be disregarded. The stimulus is not regarded as incorrect because of the lack of case agreement.
<Example>
"Can I see Harriet?" "I'm sorry, her gone to school."

A4. *Avoid pronouns/reflexives.*
<Definition> Any obligation for pronominalisation or reflex- ivisation should be disregarded. The stimulus is not regarded as incorrect because of the lack of pronouns or reflexive pronouns.
<Example>
When the girls arrived, Bill came downstairs to see the girls.

A5. *Avoid determiners.*
<Definition> Determiners should be disregarded. The stimulus is not regarded as incorrect because of the lack of determiners.
<Example>
What I want is cup, not glass.

A6. *Skip arguments.*
<Definition> Obligatory arguments commanded by the verb, or the verb itself, should be disregarded. The stimulus is not regarded as incorrect because of the lack of these arguments.
<Example>
"How do you like your coffee?" "No want sugar."

B. Prefer a lexical meaning
<Definition> If the meaning of the content words (or part of them), disregarding function words, is conceivable, the stimulus is regarded as correct. If the detected meaning is inconceivable, the application of this strategy is avoided.
<Example>
The envelope was written "To Anne".

C. Resort to a structural reinforcement
<Definition> Be sensitive to structural rules. Make semantic elements structurally explicit so the meaning becomes marked. Any local or overall structure violating the familiar structural rules makes the stimulus incorrect.
<Examples>
For badly wounded, he stopped fighting.
We went to the lake to swimming.
He was seeing her at the time. [judged as incorrect]

Appendix B

Test material (Grammaticality judgement test)

[Correct answers are shown by asterisks, and 'local parsing' interpretations are shown in italics.]

② ② ② ② ② ② ②　文法問題　② ② ② ② ② ②
Test form =

　この問題はみなさんの英語理解力がどのような能力から成り立っているのかを研究するためのものです．授業の成績には影響しませんが，気を抜かずに時間内に終えるようにがんばってください．
　解答はマークシートに記入してください．1～38桁に記入してください．鉛筆を使用し，間違えたときは消しゴムでよく消して下さい．
　最初に，この問題用紙の右上に書いてあるTest formの番号をマークシート右端のW桁に記して下さい．
　次の文を読み，文法的に正しいか誤っているかを判断し，それぞれの指示に沿って解答してください．まず例題をやってみましょう．

【例題】This picture paints by a famous artist in 1765.
　　正しいと思う場合，この文から言えることを選んでください．
　　　1. ある有名な画家がこの絵を1765年に描いた．
　　　2. 多くの画家がこの絵を1765年に一緒に描いた．
　　　3. ある有名な画家が1765年に一連の絵を描いた．
　　　4. この絵はある画家を1765年に有名にした．
　　誤りだと思う場合，どこを直せば正しい文になるかを選んでください．下線部分は訂正あるいは削除すべき場所を示し，< >には何らかの語／句が入るものとします．
　　　5. This picture < > paints by a famous artist in 1765.
　　*6. This picture <u>paints</u> by a famous artist in 1765.
　　　7. This picture paints < > by a famous artist in 1765.
　　　8. This picture paints <u>by</u> a famous artist in 1765.

　この例題の場合，This picture <u>was painted</u> by a famous artist in 1765. としなければならないので6が正解です．この場合下線部分を書き直しましたが，下線部分を削除したい場合にもその下線部分を解答としてください．誤りだと思う場合は1～4の意味解釈は選ぶ必要はありません．
　< >には1つ以上の語が入る可能性があります．また，問題によっては1つの文に< >が2ヶ所ある場合もあります．
　それでは本番です．( )内の問題番号はマークシートの桁番号(1～38)に対応します．解答はそれぞれの桁の中のマーク位置の番号で示してください．

a1 The letter kept by the old woman who we met when we were looking for the boy disappeared.
   正しいと思う場合，この文から言えることを選んでください．
   *1. 手紙がなくなった．
   2. 老婦人がいなくなった．
   3. 少年がいなくなった．
   4. 私たちは老婦人を捜していた．
   誤りだと思う場合，どこを直せば正しい文になるかを選んでください．下線部分は訂正あるいは削除すべき場所を示し，< >には何らかの語／句が入るものとします．
   5. The letter kept by the old woman <u>who</u> we met when we were looking for the boy disappeared.
   6. The letter kept by the old woman who we met < > when we were looking for the boy disappeared.
   7. The letter kept by the old woman who we met when we were looking for < > the boy disappeared.
   8. The letter kept by the old woman who we met when we were looking for the boy < > disappeared.

a2 Vivian knew the police officer under suspicion had received the money.
   正しいと思う場合，この文から言えることを選んでください．
   1. 警察官はビビアンのことを知っていた．
   *2. 警察官はお金をもらっていた．
   3. ビビアンには嫌疑がかかっていた．
   4. ビビアンは警察官を知っていた．
   誤りだと思う場合，どこを直せば正しい文になるかを選んでください．下線部分は訂正あるいは削除すべき場所を示し，< >には何らかの語／句が入るものとします．
   5. Vivian knew the police officer < > under suspicion had received the money.
   6. Vivian knew the police officer <u>under suspicion</u> had received the money.
   7. Vivian knew the police officer under suspicion < > had received the money.
   8. Vivian knew the police officer under suspicion <u>had received</u> the money.

a3 The fact that the dog hurt the boy scared Linda.
   正しいと思う場合，この文から言えることを選んでください．
   1. 少年はリンダを怖がらせた．
   2. 犬がけがをし，リンダは少年を怖がらせた．
   *3. 犬が少年にけがをさせたのでリンダは怖くなった．
   4. 少年が犬を怖がらせたのでリンダは傷ついた．
   誤りだと思う場合，どこを直せば正しい文になるかを選んでください．下線部分は訂正あるいは削除すべき場所を示し，< >には何らかの語／句が入るものとします．
   5. <u>The fact</u> that the dog hurt the boy scared Linda.
   6. The fact <u>that</u> the dog hurt the boy scared Linda.
   7. The fact that the dog hurt < > the boy scared Linda.
   8. The fact that the dog hurt the boy < > scared Linda.

a4 You will find the glasses with red marks on both sides are quite expensive.
　　正しいと思う場合，この文から言えることを選んでください．
　　　　1. 眼鏡そのものよりあなたが眼鏡を見つけられるかどうかが重要です．
　　　　2. 赤い印がついているのであなたは眼鏡を見つけられるでしょう．
　　　　3. あなたが眼鏡を見つけると赤い印の価値が上がります．
　　　　4. 眼鏡がとても高価であることがわかるでしょう．
　　誤りだと思う場合，どこを直せば正しい文になるかを選んでください．下線部分は訂正あるいは削除すべき場所を示し，< >には何らかの語／句が入るものとします．
　　　　5. You will find the glasses <u>with</u> red marks on both sides are quite expensive.
　　　　6. You will find the glasses with red marks on <u>both sides</u> are quite expensive.
　　　　7. You will find the glasses with red marks on both sides < > are quite expensive.
　　　*8. You will find the glasses with red marks on both sides <u>are</u> quite expensive.

a5 The Department of Foreign Languages are not located in the new building.
　　正しいと思う場合，この文から言えることを選んでください．
　　　　1. 外国語学科は新しい建物にはありませんよ．
　　　　2. 外国語学科の建物は新しくはありません．
　　　　3. 新しい学科は外国語学科ではありません．
　　　　4. 外国語学科の新しい建物はここにはありません．
　　誤りだと思う場合，どこを直せば正しい文になるかを選んでください．下線部分は訂正あるいは削除すべき場所を示します．
　　　　5. The Department of Foreign <u>Languages</u> are not located in the new building.
　　　*6. The Department of Foreign Languages <u>are</u> not located in the new building.
　　　　7. The Department of Foreign Languages are not <u>located</u> in the new building.
　　　　8. The Department of Foreign Languages are not located <u>in</u> the new building.

a6 To grow several kinds of flowers are the joy of gardening.
　　正しいと思う場合，この文から言えることを選んでください．
　　　　1. 園芸にはいろいろな楽しみ方があります．
　　　　2. いろいろな花を育てることこそ園芸の楽しみです．
　　　　3. 園芸ではいろいろな花を育てることを学びます．
　　　　4. いろいろな園芸を学ぶことは楽しいものです．
　　誤りだと思う場合，どこを直せば正しい文になるかを選んでください．下線部分は訂正あるいは削除すべき場所を示します．
　　　　5. <u>To grow</u> several kinds of flowers are the joy of gardening.
　　　　6. To grow several <u>kinds</u> of flowers are the joy of gardening.
　　　*7. To grow several kinds of flowers <u>are</u> the joy of gardening.
　　　　8. To grow several kinds of flowers are the joy <u>of</u> gardening.

b1 I think that gardening is wash the human heart.
　　正しいと思う場合，この文から言えることを選んでください．
　　　　1. 園芸のことを考えると心が安らかになります．
　　　　2. 園芸ではいろいろなものを水で洗います．
　　　　3. 園芸は人々の心を清めてくれます．

　　　　4. 園芸には心の持ち方が大事です．
　　誤りだと思う場合，どこを直せば正しい文になるかを選んでください．下線部分は訂正
　　あるいは削除すべき場所を示し，< >には何らかの語／句が入るものとします．
　　　　5. I think that gardening is wash the human heart.
　　　*6. I think that gardening is wash the human heart.
　　　　7. I think that gardening is < > wash the human heart.
　　　　8. I think that gardening is wash < > the human heart.

b2　Half of the people were invited to the party didn't turn up.
　　正しいと思う場合，この文から言えることを選んでください．
　　　　1. パーティーでは半分の人がひっくり返った．
　　　　2. 半分の人しか招待されなかった．
　　　　3. 半分のパーティーは閑散としていた．
　　　　4. 招待された人の半分しか来なかった．
　　誤りだと思う場合，どこを直せば正しい文になるかを選んでください．下線部分は訂正
　　あるいは削除すべき場所を示します．
　　　　5. Half of the people were invited to the party didn't turn up.
　　　　6. Half of the people were invited to the party didn't turn up.
　　　*7. Half of the people were invited to the party didn't turn up.
　　　　8. Half of the people were invited to the party didn't turn up.

b3　Take this flight which I think that is least expensive.
　　正しいと思う場合，この文から言えることを選んでください．
　　　　1. この飛行機が安いからお乗りなさいよ．
　　　　2. 最も安い飛行機のチケットはすぐに売れてしまう．
　　　　3. 安上がりに済ますには飛行機に乗るのが一番だ．
　　　　4. 飛行機の便は安ければ安いほどよい．
　　誤りだと思う場合，どこを直せば正しい文になるかを選んでください．下線部分は訂正
　　あるいは削除すべき場所を示し，< >には何らかの語／句が入るものとします．
　　　　5. Take this flight which I think that is least expensive.
　　　　6. Take this flight which I think that is least expensive.
　　　*7. Take this flight which I think that is least expensive.
　　　　8. Take this flight which I think that is least expensive.

b4　Mr Kawase, vice president of Tomato Bank, he will speak to the press this afternoon.
　　正しいと思う場合，この文から言えることを選んでください．
　　　　1. 川瀬氏はトマト銀行副頭取にもかかわらず記者に情報を流すでしょう．
　　　　2. トマト銀行副頭取の川瀬氏が午後記者会見をします．
　　　　3. 川瀬氏がトマト銀行副頭取になったので，彼(別の人)が午後記者会見をするこ
　　　　　とになった．
　　　　4. トマト銀行の副頭取になった川瀬氏はいろいろ発言する機会が多い．
　　誤りだと思う場合，どこを直せば正しい文になるかを選んでください．下線部分は訂正
　　あるいは削除すべき場所を示し，< >には何らかの語／句が入るものとします．
　　　　5. < > Mr Kawase, vice president of Tomato Bank, he will speak to the press this

Appendix B   167

  afternoon.
 6. Mr Kawase, < > vice president of Tomato Bank, he will speak to the press this afternoon.
 7. Mr Kawase, vice president of Tomato Bank, < > he will speak to the press this afternoon.
 *8. Mr Kawase, vice president of Tomato Bank, <u>he</u> will speak to the press this afternoon.

b5 You don't know Russian is a pity.
 正しいと思う場合，この文から言えることを選んでください．
  1. ロシア人はかわいそうな人たちだってことを知らないのね．
  2. ロシア人がどのくらいかわいそうかを知らないのね．
  3. ロシア語を知らないなんて．
  4. ロシア人がかわいそうかどうかを知る必要はありません．
 誤りだと思う場合，どこを直せば正しい文になるかを選んでください．下線部分は訂正あるいは削除すべき場所を示し，< >には何らかの語／句が入るものとします．
  *5. < > you don't know Russian is a pity.
  6. You don't know < > Russian is a pity.
  7. You don't know Russian < > is a pity.
  8. You don't know Russian <u>is</u> a pity.

b6 His attacker was described a tall man with a beard.
 正しいと思う場合，この文から言えることを選んでください．
  1. 彼が襲撃犯で背が高くひげを生やしていた．
  2. 彼は背が高くひげを生やしていたので襲撃犯と間違えられた．
  3. 背が高くひげを生やした男が襲われた．
  4. 襲撃犯は背が高くひげを生やしていた．
 誤りだと思う場合，どこを直せば正しい文になるかを選んでください．下線部分は訂正あるいは削除すべき場所を示し，< >には何らかの語／句が入るものとします．
  5. < > his attacker was described a tall man with a beard.
  6. His attacker was <u>described</u> a tall man with a beard.
  *7. His attacker was described < > a tall man with a beard.
  8. His attacker was described a tall man <u>with</u> a beard.

b7 I was having such a nice time I didn't want to leave.
 正しいと思う場合，この文から言えることを選んでください．
  *1. とても楽しかったので帰りたくなかった．
  2. 私が帰ったらもう楽しみがないことはわかっていた．
  3. こんなに楽しいことは今まで経験したことがなかった．
  4. 楽しくなかったので早めに帰った．
 誤りだと思う場合，どこを直せば正しい文になるかを選んでください．下線部分は訂正あるいは削除すべき場所を示し，< >には何らかの語／句が入るものとします．
  5. < > I was having such a nice time I didn't want to leave.
  6. I <u>was having</u> such a nice time I didn't want to leave.

7. I was having such a nice time I didn't want to leave.
8. I was having such a nice time < > I didn't want to leave.

c1 Most people hear "endangered species", they think of animals.
正しいと思う場合，この文から言えることを選んでください．
1. 人々は「絶滅に瀕した種」のことを考えてばかりで動物のことを考えません．
2.「絶滅に瀕した種」というと動物のことを思い浮かべます．
3. 動物は一般に「絶滅に瀕した種」ではありません．
4. 多くの人にとって「絶滅に瀕した種」は縁遠いものです．
誤りだと思う場合，どこを直せば正しい文になるかを選んでください．下線部分は訂正あるいは削除すべき場所を示し，< >には何らかの語／句が入るものとします．
*5. < > most people hear "endangered species", they think of animals.
6. Most people hear "endangered species", they think of animals.
7. Most people hear "endangered species", they think of animals.
8. Most people hear "endangered species", they think of animals.

c2 I'm worried about you are happy.
正しいと思う場合，この文から言えることを選んでください．
1. 私に心配事があるとあなたは幸せなのね．
2. あなたが幸せだと私は心配だわ．
3. あなたが幸せかどうかが気がかりだわ．
4. あなたが幸せであってもなくても私は気になるわ．
誤りだと思う場合，どこを直せば正しい文になるかを選んでください．下線部分は訂正あるいは削除すべき場所を示し，< >には何らかの語／句が入るものとします．
5. < > I'm worried about you are happy.
6. I'm worried about you are happy.
*7. I'm worried about < > you are happy.
8. I'm worried about you are happy.

d1 Diane's nose got extremely cold, running home through the snow.
正しいと思う場合，この文から言えることを選んでください．
1. 雪が降って鼻が冷たくならないうちにダイアンは急いでうちに帰りました．
2. ダイアンは鼻が冷たくなっても雪の中を走りました．
3. ダイアンの鼻は冷たかったけれどそれは雪のせいじゃない．
4. 雪の中を走ってきたのでダイアンの鼻はすっかり冷えてしまいました．
誤りだと思う場合，どこを直せば正しい文になるかを選んでください．下線部分は訂正あるいは削除すべき場所を示し，< >には何らかの語／句が入るものとします．
5. Diane's nose < > got extremely cold, running home through the snow.
6. Diane's nose got extremely cold, running home through the snow.
*7. Diane's nose got extremely cold, < > running home through the snow.
8. Diane's nose got extremely cold, running home through the snow.

d2 The activity I liked most in the Gardening Club was planted many seeds.
正しいと思う場合，この文から言えることを選んでください．

Appendix B   169

   1. *私が園芸クラブで一番好きだったのは種を植えたことです.*
   2. 園芸クラブではほとんどの人が種を植えるのが好きでした.
   3. 私の好きな活動が園芸クラブの中で根付いてゆきました.
   4. 私の好きな園芸クラブは種植えばかりやっていました.
  誤りだと思う場合，どこを直せば正しい文になるかを選んでください．下線部分は訂正あるいは削除すべき場所を示し，< >には何らかの語／句が入るものとします．
   5. The activity < > I liked most in the Gardening Club was planted many seeds.
   6. The activity I liked most in the Gardening Club < > was planted many seeds.
   7. The activity I liked most in the Gardening Club <u>was</u> planted many seeds.
   *8. The activity I liked most in the Gardening Club was <u>planted</u> many seeds.

d3 Hiromi is difficult to learn mathematics.
  正しいと思う場合，この文から言えることを選んでください．
   1. ヒロミは数学のことを考えると気難しくなる.
   2. ヒロミは数学を敬遠している.
   3. ヒロミは数学とは馬が合わない.
   4. ヒロミは数学が嫌いなわけじゃない.
  誤りだと思う場合，どこを直せば正しい文になるかを選んでください．下線部分は訂正あるいは削除すべき場所を示し，< >には何らかの語／句が入るものとします．
   *5. < > is difficult < > to learn mathematics.
   6. Hiromi <u>is</u> difficult to learn mathematics.
   7. Hiromi is < > difficult to learn mathematics.
   8. Hiromi is difficult <u>to learn</u> mathematics.

e1 For badly wounded, the soldier stopped fighting.
  正しいと思う場合，この文から言えることを選んでください．
   1. 兵士はひどくけがをしなければ戦わなかった.
   2. 兵士は戦うのをやめたとたんけがをしてしまった.
   3. 兵士は重傷を負ったので戦いをやめた.
   4. 重傷を負ってもなお，兵士は戦わなかった.
  誤りだと思う場合，どこを直せば正しい文になるかを選んでください．下線部分は訂正あるいは削除すべき場所を示し，< >には何らかの語／句が入るものとします．
   *5. <u>For</u> badly wounded, the soldier stopped fighting.
   6. For badly <u>wounded</u>, the soldier stopped fighting.
   7. For badly wounded, < > the soldier stopped fighting.
   8. For badly wounded, the soldier stopped <u>fighting</u>.

e2 I can't think of anybody whom to invite.
  正しいと思う場合，この文から言えることを選んでください．
   1. 誰も私を招待してくれないんだわ.
   2. 誰に招待されるのかわからないわ.
   3. 誰を招待しても同じことよ.
   4. 誰を招待したらよいのかわからないわ.
  誤りだと思う場合，どこを直せば正しい文になるかを選んでください．下線部分は訂正

あるいは削除すべき場所を示し，< >には何らかの語／句が入るものとします．
    5. I can't think of <u>anybody</u> whom to invite.
    6. I can't think of anybody < > whom to invite.
   *7. I can't think of anybody <u>whom</u> to invite.
    8. I can't think of anybody whom <u>to invite</u>.

e3　I hate insects - it is the reason that I don't like to gardening.
    正しいと思う場合，この文から言えることを選んでください．
    1. 虫が嫌いなので園芸はやりたくありません．
    2. 虫は嫌いだけど園芸はやりたいです．
    3. 園芸は嫌いなので虫も嫌いです．
    4. 園芸は虫が好かない．
    誤りだと思う場合，どこを直せば正しい文になるかを選んでください．下線部分は訂正
    あるいは削除すべき場所を示し，< >には何らかの語／句が入るものとします．
    5. I hate insects - it is the reason <u>that</u> I don't like to gardening.
    6. I hate insects - it is the reason that I don't <u>like</u> to gardening.
    7. I hate insects - it is the reason that I don't like < > to gardening.
   *8. I hate insects - it is the reason that I don't like <u>to</u> gardening.

e4　I showed the little boys how to jumping.
    正しいと思う場合，この文から言えることを選んでください．
    1. 私は子供たちは跳ぶだろうと思った．
    2. 私は子供たちに跳び方の手本を示した．
    3. 私は子供たちの跳び方に疑問を持った．
    4. 私は子供たちに跳ぶ許可を与えた．
    誤りだと思う場合，どこを直せば正しい文になるかを選んでください．下線部分は訂正
    あるいは削除すべき場所を示し，< >には何らかの語／句が入るものとします．
    5. I showed the little boys <u>how</u> to jumping.
    6. I showed the little boys how < > to jumping.
    7. I showed the little boys how <u>to</u> jumping.
   *8. I showed the little boys how to <u>jumping</u>.

e5　Yamane visited Kyoto to meeting an old friend of his.
    正しいと思う場合，この文から言えることを選んでください．
    1. 山根は京都で偶然昔の友達に出会った．
    2. 山根は京都での会議で昔の友達を見かけた．
    3. 山根は京都に旧友を訪ねた．
    4. 山根とその旧友は京都の会議に出席した．
    誤りだと思う場合，どこを直せば正しい文になるかを選んでください．下線部分は訂正
    あるいは削除すべき場所を示し，< >には何らかの語／句が入るものとします．
    5. Yamane visited Kyoto to < > meeting an old friend of his.
   *6. Yamane visited Kyoto to <u>meeting</u> an old friend of his.
    7. Yamane visited Kyoto to meeting <u>an old friend of his</u>.
    8. Yamane visited Kyoto to meeting an old friend of <u>his</u>.

f1 "Can I see Harriet?" "I'm sorry her gone to school."
　　正しいと思う場合，この文から言えることを選んでください．
　　　　1. ハリエットは学校はやめたよ．
　　　　2. ハリエットは学校から帰ったよ．
　　　　3. ハリエットは学校には来ていないよ．
　　　　4. ハリエットは学校に出かけたよ．
　　誤りだと思う場合，どこを直せば正しい文になるかを選んでください．下線部分は訂正あるいは削除すべき場所を示し，< >には何らかの語／句が入るものとします．
　　　　5. "Can I see Harriet?" "I'm sorry < > her gone to school."
　　　*6. "Can I see Harriet?" "I'm sorry <u>her</u> gone to school."
　　　　7. "Can I see Harriet?" "I'm sorry her < > gone to school."
　　　　8. "Can I see Harriet?" "I'm sorry her <u>gone</u> to school."

g1 Catherine not come here anymore, because her mother is ill in bed.
　　正しいと思う場合，この文から言えることを選んでください．
　　　　1. キャサリーンはお母さんの具合が悪いのでここには来ません．
　　　　2. キャサリーンのお母さんは具合が悪いのでここには来ません．
　　　　3. キャサリーンがここに来ないとお母さんの具合が悪くなるわ．
　　　　4. キャサリーンが来ても来なくてもお母さんの具合が悪いことに変わりはないの．
　　誤りだと思う場合，どこを直せば正しい文になるかを選んでください．下線部分は訂正あるいは削除すべき場所を示し，< >には何らかの語／句が入るものとします．
　　　　5. < > Catherine not come here anymore, because her mother is ill in bed.
　　　*6. Catherine < > not come here anymore, because her mother is ill in bed.
　　　　7. Catherine not <u>come</u> here anymore, because her mother is ill in bed.
　　　　8. Catherine not come < > here anymore, because her mother is ill in bed.

g2 It is my mother to like arranging little trees in the garden.
　　正しいと思う場合，この文から言えることを選んでください．
　　　　1. 庭木は母に世話をされるのが好きです．
　　　　2. 庭木の世話をするのはもっぱら母です．
　　　　3. 母は庭木の世話しか関心がありません．
　　　　4. 母の世話をするのは私たちのつとめです．
　　誤りだと思う場合，どこを直せば正しい文になるかを選んでください．下線部分は訂正あるいは削除すべき場所を示し，< >には何らかの語／句が入るものとします．
　　　　5. <u>It is</u> my mother to like arranging little trees in the garden.
　　　　6. It is < > my mother to like arranging little trees in the garden.
　　　*7. It is my mother <u>to like</u> arranging little trees in the garden.
　　　　8. It is my mother to like <u>arranging</u> little trees in the garden.

g3 The children thanked Jim for come.
　　正しいと思う場合，この文から言えることを選んでください．
　　　　1. 子供たちはジムのおかげでやって来ることができた．
　　　　2. 子供たちはジムがくることを待ち望んだ．
　　　　3. 子供たちはジムに来てくれてありがとうと言った．

　　　　4. ジムは子供たちに呼んでくれてありがとうと言った.
　　誤りだと思う場合，どこを直せば正しい文になるかを選んでください．下線部分は訂正
　　あるいは削除すべき場所を示し，< >には何らかの語／句が入るものとします．
　　　　5. The children thanked < > Jim for come.
　　　　6. The children thanked Jim for come.
　　　　7. The children thanked Jim for < > come.
　　　*8. The children thanked Jim for come.

g4　I was very interesting in the lesson.
　　正しいと思う場合，この文から言えることを選んでください．
　　　　1. 私はおもしろい講義をすることができました．
　　　　2. 私はその講義をおもしろくしようと思いました．
　　　　3. おもしろい講義は好きです．
　　　4. その講義はとてもおもしろいと思いました．
　　誤りだと思う場合，どこを直せば正しい文になるかを選んでください．下線部分は訂正
　　あるいは削除すべき場所を示し，< >には何らかの語／句が入るものとします．
　　　　5. I was very interesting in the lesson.
　　　　6. I was very interesting in the lesson.
　　　*7. I was very interesting in the lesson.
　　　　8. I was very interesting < > in the lesson.

g5　The policemen surprised that the girls chased the man in the station.
　　正しいと思う場合，この文から言えることを選んでください．
　　　1. 少女たちが男を追いかけていたのでお巡りさんはびっくりしました．
　　　　2. お巡りさんが少女たちをびっくりさせたので男は逃げてしまいました．
　　　　3. お巡りさんが男を追いかけていたので少女たちはびっくりしました．
　　　　4. 男が少女たちを追いかけていたのでお巡りさんはびっくりしました．
　　誤りだと思う場合，どこを直せば正しい文になるかを選んでください．下線部分は訂正
　　あるいは削除すべき場所を示し，< >には何らかの語／句が入るものとします．
　　　*5. The policemen < > surprised that the girls chased the man in the station.
　　　　6. The policemen surprised < > that the girls chased the man in the station.
　　　　7. The policemen surprised that the girls chased the man in the station.
　　　　8. The policemen surprised that the girls chased the man in the station.

g6　What I want is cup, not glass.
　　正しいと思う場合，この文から言えることを選んでください．
　　　　1. ほしいのはコップじゃなくてグラスだぜ．
　　　2. ほしいのはグラスじゃなくてコップだぜ．
　　　　3. コップもグラスもいらねえと言ってるんだ．
　　　　4. いくらコップをほしがってもグラスは出て来やしない．
　　誤りだと思う場合，どこを直せば正しい文になるかを選んでください．下線部分は訂正
　　あるいは削除すべき場所を示し，< >には何らかの語／句が入るものとします．
　　　　5. What I want is cup, not glass.
　　　　6. What I want < > is cup, not glass.

Appendix B   173

   *7. What I want is < > cup, not < > glass.
    8. What I want is cup, < > not glass.

g7 When the magician appeared, Bill came downstairs to see the magician.
   正しいと思う場合，この文から言えることを選んでください．
    1. 奇術師が現れるのがわかっていたかのようにビルは下におりてきた．
    2. 奇術師が現れる前からビルは下の階にいた．
    3. 奇術師が現れるとビルは見にやってきた．
    4. 奇術師が現れるとビルは別の奇術師だと思っておりてきた．
   誤りだと思う場合，どこを直せば正しい文になるかを選んでください．下線部分は訂正あるいは削除すべき場所を示します．
    5. <u>When</u> the magician appeared, Bill came downstairs to see the magician.
    6. When the magician <u>appeared</u>, Bill came downstairs to see the magician.
    7. When the magician appeared, Bill came downstairs <u>to see</u> the magician.
   *8. When the magician appeared, Bill came downstairs to see <u>the magician</u>.

g8 We did not know what to do with us.
   正しいと思う場合，この文から言えることを選んでください．
    1. 私たちが知っていたことを他の誰も知らなかった．
    2. 私たちのほかに誰がいるのかわからなかった．
    3. 私たち以外には誰も私たちのことを知らなかった．
    4. 私たちだけではどうしたらいいのかわからなかった．
   誤りだと思う場合，どこを直せば正しい文になるかを選んでください．下線部分は訂正あるいは削除すべき場所を示します．
    5. We did not know <u>what</u> to do with us.
    6. We did not know what <u>to do</u> with us.
    7. We did not know what to do <u>with</u> us.
   *8. We did not know what to do with <u>us</u>.

h1 All the students were looking forward spending their free time on the beach.
   正しいと思う場合，この文から言えることを選んでください．
    1. 生徒たちはみな自由に浜辺を見つめていた．
    2. 生徒たちはみな浜辺では自由に行動した．
    3. 生徒たちはみな浜辺での自由行動を楽しみにしていた．
    4. 生徒たちはみな浜辺では思い思いに捜し物をした．
   誤りだと思う場合，どこを直せば正しい文になるかを選んでください．下線部分は訂正あるいは削除すべき場所を示し，< > には何らかの語／句が入るものとします．
    5. All the students <u>were looking</u> forward spending their free time on the beach.
    6. All the students were looking <u>forward</u> spending their free time on the beach.
   *7. All the students were looking forward < > spending their free time on the beach.
    8. All the students were looking forward < > <u>spending</u> their free time on the beach.

h2 Mr Peters used to think of hisself as the only president of the company.
   正しいと思う場合，この文から言えることを選んでください．

1. ピーターズ氏は社長だけは彼を理解してくれると思っていた.
2. ピーターズ氏は社長にだけは胸の内をうち明けたいと思っていた.
3. ピーターズ氏は社長だけは本物だと思っていた.
4. ピーターズ氏は自分こそが社長だと思っていた.
誤りだと思う場合，どこを直せば正しい文になるかを選んでください．下線部分は訂正あるいは削除すべき場所を示します．
5. Mr Peters <u>used to think</u> of hisself as the only president of the company.
*6. Mr Peters used to think of <u>hisself</u> as the only president of the company.
7. Mr Peters used to think of hisself <u>as</u> the only president of the company.
8. Mr Peters used to think of hisself as the <u>only</u> president of the company.

h3 When I last saw Janet, she hurried to her next class on the other side of the campus.
正しいと思う場合，この文から言えることを選んでください．
1. ジャネットはキャンパスのはずれの教室に急いでいた.
2. ジャネットはキャンパスのはずれにいたので急がなければならなかった.
3. ジャネットは次の授業に急いでいたらキャンパスの端まで来てしまった.
4. ジャネットはキャンパスのはずれで小走りに駆けていた.
誤りだと思う場合，どこを直せば正しい文になるかを選んでください．下線部分は訂正あるいは削除すべき場所を示します．
5. When I <u>last saw Janet</u>, she hurried to her next class on the other side of the campus.
*6. When I last saw Janet, she <u>hurried</u> to her next class on the other side of the campus.
7. When I last saw Janet, she hurried to her <u>next class</u> on the other side of the campus.
8. When I last saw Janet, she hurried to her next class on <u>the other</u> side of the campus.

h4 Carl was upset last night because he had to do too many homeworks.
正しいと思う場合，この文から言えることを選んでください．
1. カールは宿題は決して終わらないことがわかっていた.
2. カールは宿題がたくさんあったのでプリプリしていた.
3. カールは休んでいたので宿題がたまってしまった.
4. カールは山のような宿題に気が遠くなった.
誤りだと思う場合，どこを直せば正しい文になるかを選んでください．下線部分は訂正あるいは削除すべき場所を示します．
5. Carl was <u>upset</u> last night because he had to do too many homeworks.
6. Carl was upset last night because <u>he had</u> to do too many homeworks.
7. Carl was upset last night because he had to <u>do</u> too many homeworks.
*8. Carl was upset last night because he had to do too <u>many homeworks</u>.

h5 This is Naomi, that sells the tickets.
正しいと思う場合，この文から言えることを選んでください．
1. この人がナオミさんであの人はチケットを売る人です.

2. ナオミさんはチケットだけを売ります．
3. この人がチケット係のナオミさんです．
4. ナオミ，ここに来てチケットを売りなさい．

誤りだと思う場合，どこを直せば正しい文になるかを選んでください．下線部分は訂正あるいは削除すべき場所を示し，< >には何らかの語／句が入るものとします．

5. <u>This is</u> Naomi, that sells the tickets.
*6. This is Naomi, <u>that</u> sells the tickets.
7. This is Naomi, that <u>sells</u> the tickets.
8. This is Naomi, that sells < > the tickets.

b6　I watched the match because I knew some of the playing people.
　　正しいと思う場合，この文から言えることを選んでください．
1. 試合を見たので選手のことがわかるようになった．
2. 選手のことを知っていたら試合はもっとおもしろかっただろうに．
3. 試合を見ても知っている選手のことしか眼中になかった．
4. 少しは選手を知っていたので試合を見た．

誤りだと思う場合，どこを直せば正しい文になるかを選んでください．下線部分は訂正あるいは削除すべき場所を示します．

5. I <u>watched</u> the match because I knew some of the playing people.
6. I watched the match <u>because I knew</u> some of the playing people.
7. I watched the match because I knew <u>some of</u> the playing people.
*8. I watched the match because I knew some of the <u>playing people</u>.

時間内にできた人はパート③(C-test)を始めて下さい．

Sources:

a1 original
a2 original
a3 after Quigley
a4 original
a5 after Cliffs: 363
a6 after Asao: g2
b1 Asao: g1
b2 Swan: 495
b3 original
b4 original
b5 Greenbaum: 306
b6 Swan: 610
b7 Swan: 589
c1 after NittyGrity: 33
c2 after Swan: 456
d1 original
d2 Asao: g1
d3 Swan: 271

e1 Quigley
e2 Swan: 494
e3 after Asao: g2
e4 Quigley
e5 original
f1 after Quigley
g1 after Quigley
g2 after Asao: g2
g3 Quigley
g4 Swan: 409
g5 after Quigley
g6 Quigley
g7 after Quigley
g8 original
h1 after Cliffs: 277
h2 Cliffs: 277
h3 after Cliffs: 362
h4 Cliffs: 256
h5 Swan: 490
h6 Swan: 405

Asao: Corpus of Japanese Learners of English. [2000]. http://www.lb.u-tokai.ac.jp/lcorpus/

Cliffs: Pyle, Michael A. & Mary Ellen Muñoz. 1986. *Test of English as a Foreign Language Preparation Guide*. Lincoln, Nebraska: Cliffs Notes. ISBN: 0-8220-2018-1.

Greenbaum: Greenbaum, S. & R. Quirk. 1990. *A Student's Grammar of the English Language*. Longman. ISBN: 0-582-05971-2.

NittyGrity: Young, A. Robert & Ann O. Strauch. 1994. *Nitty Gritty Grammar: Sentence Essentials for Writers*. St. Martin's Press. ISBN: 0-312-06743-7.

Quigley: Quigley, S. P., M. W. Steinkamp, D. J. Power, & B. W. Jones. 1978. *Test of Syntactic Abilities*. Dormac.

Swan: Swan, Michael. 1995. *Practical English Usage, 2nd ed*. Oxford: Oxford University Press. ISBN: 0194311988.

Appendix C

Test material (C-test)

[Correct answers are shown in bold letters. Passage [0] was used as a practice passage and was not counted in the actual experiment.]

C-test
このテストは英語の総合的な能力を短時間で測るために考案されたものです。文章を読み，文脈に合うように単語の後半を完成させてください。_ に 1 文字が入ります。アポストロフィー(')も 1 文字に数えます。
では例題をやってみましょう．

[example]
　　Welcome to the City of Tampa! We a**re** proud o**f** this sun-b**lessed** paradise. Sure**ly**, you can**'t** enjoy t**he** pleasure t**oo** much h**ere**. In t**he** middle o**f** the to**wn** is a b**ig** shopping ma**ll** where y**ou** can b**uy** almost anyt**hing** in t**he** world.
　　答は順に the, of, town, big, mall, you, buy, anything, the になります．
　　答は直接空欄に書き込んで下さい．

[0] (PainlessG: 242)
　　Last night I was hungry as a bear. I to**ld** my m**om** wan**ted** a real**ly** big din**ner** because I kn**ew** I cou**ld** eat like a p**ig**. She sa**id**, "Let's g**o** to McDon**ald's**."

[1] (HtoH:57)
　　Yoshiko flew to L.A. to see her cousin. On t**he** airplane, s**he** wanted t**o** listen t**o** music t**o** relax bu**t** found th**at** her hea**dset** was no**t** working prop**erly**. No mu**sic** came o**n**. So s**he** called a fli**ght** attendant an**d** told h**er** the pro**blem**. The fli**ght** attendant smi**led** and sa**id**, "Oh, yo**u** can mo**ve** to a**ny** unoccupied se**at** you'd li**ke**." She did**n't** say "I'**m** sorry" bec**ause** SHE did**n't** break t**he** headset.

[2] (RdgPwr:103)

Diamonds are very expensive for several reasons. First, they_ _ are difficult_ _ _ _ _ to find_ _ . They are_ _ only found_ _ _ in a few_ _ places in_ the world_ _ _ . Second, they_ _ are useful_ _ _ . People use_ _ diamonds to_ cut other_ _ _ stones. Third_ _ _ , diamonds do_ not change_ _ _ . They stay_ _ the same_ _ for millions_ _ _ _ of years_ _ _ . And finally_ _ _ _ , they are_ _ very beautiful_ _ _ _ _ .

[3] (Rate Builder 2B brown 6)

Penguins are birds. They live where it's very cold. Most have_ _ black and_ _ white feathers_ _ _ _. The feathers_ _ _ _ are oily_ _ and keep_ _ the penguins_ _ _ _ dry and_ _ warm.

Penguins_ _ _ _ can't fly_ _, but they_ _ can swim_ _. And they_ _ stand on_ two little_ _ _ legs. They_ _ can't walk_ _ fast. They_ _ like to_ slide on_ the snow_ _ and ice_ _ . When they_ _ get tired_ _ _ , they stand_ _ _ still and_ _ sleep.

[4] (2B blue 4)

Mr Glen was driving his car down a busy city street. There was_ _ a big van_ _ in front_ _ _ of him_ _ . Suddenly the_ _ van began_ _ _ to go_ faster. Its_ _ back door_ _ flew open_ _ , and out_ _ fell a big_ _ white pig_ _ ! The poor_ _ pig landed_ _ _ on its_ _ back with_ _ its feet_ _ in the_ _ air. It_ just lay_ _ there.

"Oh_ , dear," Mr_ Glen said_ _ _ . "I hope_ _ it's not_ _ hurt."

He_ got out_ _ of his_ _ car and_ _ ran up_ to the_ _ pig.

"Are_ _ you all_ _ right?" he_ asked. The_ _ pig did_ _ not answer_ _ _ . Its eyes_ _ were closed_ _ _ . Mr Glen_ _ patted the_ _ pig on_ its fat_ _ tummy. In a minute the pig opened its eyes.

Sources:
2B blue 4: Parker, Don H. 1973b. *SRA Reading Laboratory, 2B*. Chicago: Science Research Associates.
HtoH: Yoshida, Kensaku & Sophia University Applied Linguistics Research Group. 2000. *Heart to Heart: Overcoming Barriers in Cross-Cultural Cummunication*. Tokyo: Macmillan Languagehouse. ISBN: 4-89585-322-5.
PainlessG: Elliott, Rebecca. 1997. *Painless Grammar*. Macmillan Language House. ISBN: 4-89585-370-5.
RdgPwr: Mikurecky, Beatrice S. & Linda Jeffries. 1986. *Reading Power*. Addison-Wesley. ISBN: 0-20115865-5.
Rate Builder 2B brown 6: Parker, Don H. 1973a. *SRA Rate Builder, 2B*. Chicago: Science Research Associates.

Appendix D

Contour plots of LinkScores at Cz = -2.0 to +2.0

[Circles and crosses indicate the locations of items calculated by MDS at Cz = -0.5. Circles: 'accessible' items. Crosses: 'inaccessible' items.]

[Table D1: Common levels of contour plot of LinkScores]

LinkScore
- <= 0.100
- <= 0.150
- <= 0.200
- <= 0.250
- <= 0.300
- <= 0.350
- <= 0.400
- <= 0.450
- <= 0.500
- > 0.500

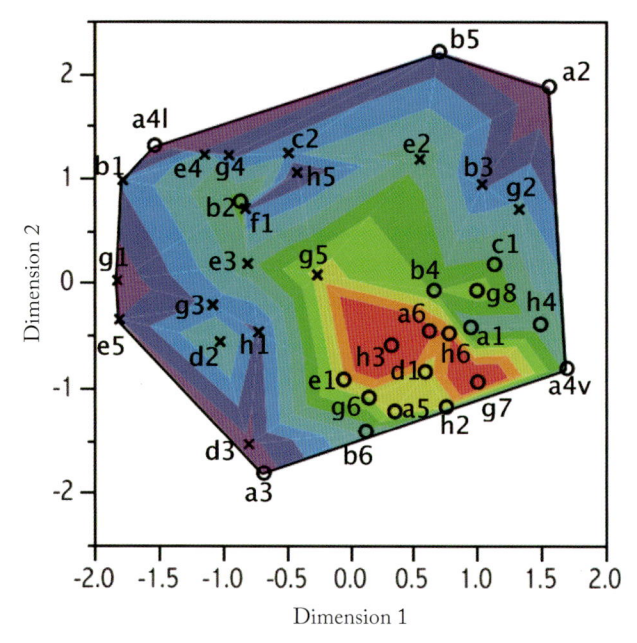

[Figure D1: Contour plot of LinkScores at Cz = -2.0]

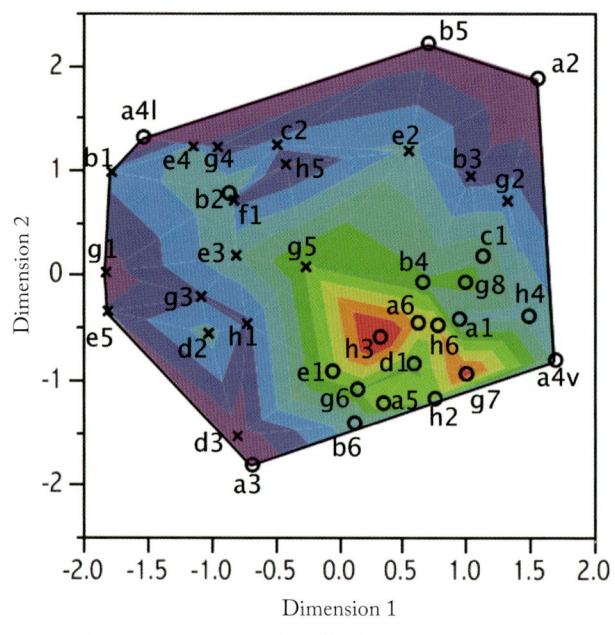

[Figure D2: Contour plot of LinkScores at Cz = -1.5]

Appendix D 181

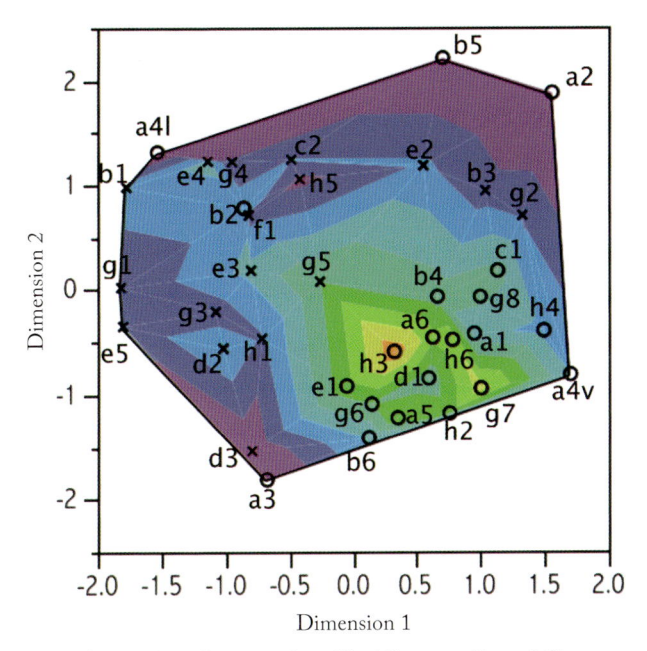

[Figure D3: Contour plot of LinkScores at Cz = -1.0]

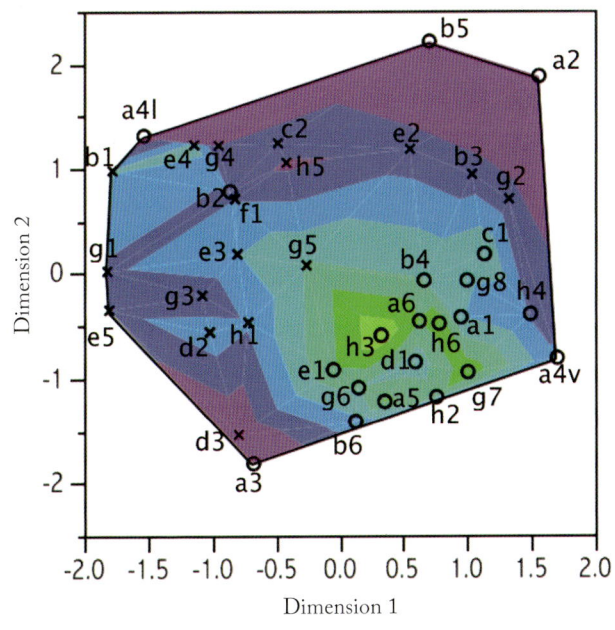

[Figure D4: Contour plot of LinkScores at Cz = -0.5]

182

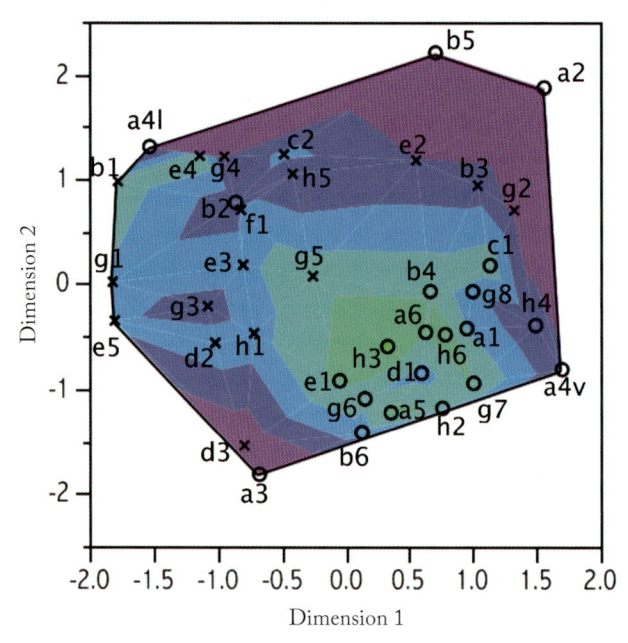

[Figure D5: Contour plot of LinkScores at Cz = 0.0]

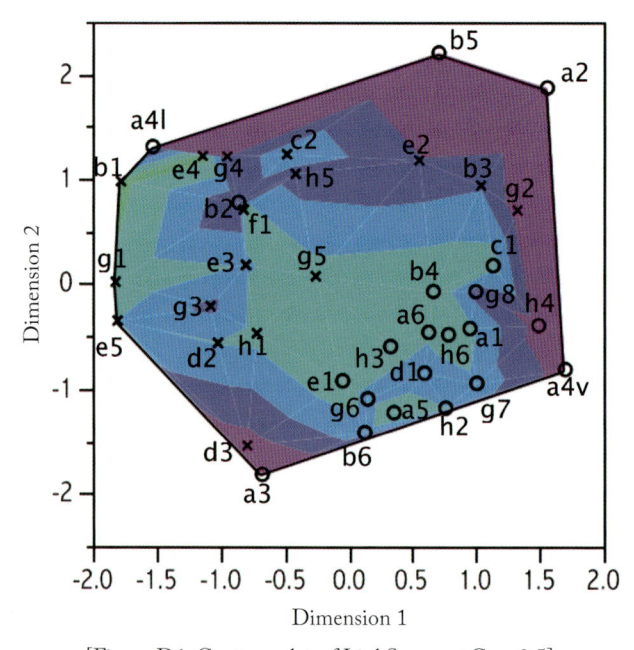

[Figure D6: Contour plot of LinkScores at Cz = 0.5]

Appendix D 183

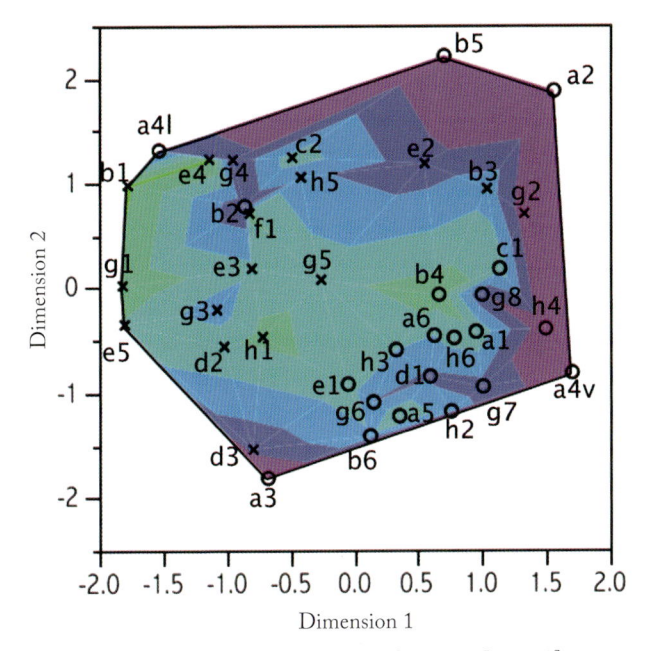

[Figure D7: Contour plot of LinkScores at Cz = 1.0]

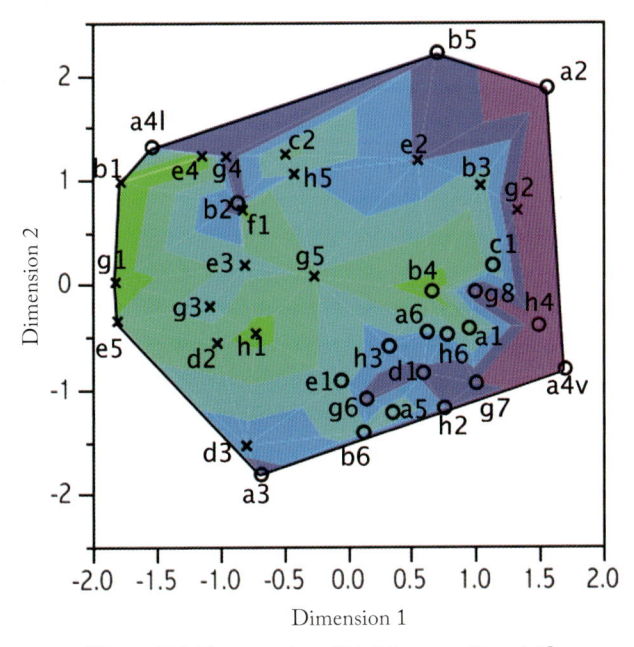

[Figure D8: Contour plot of LinkScores at Cz = 1.5]

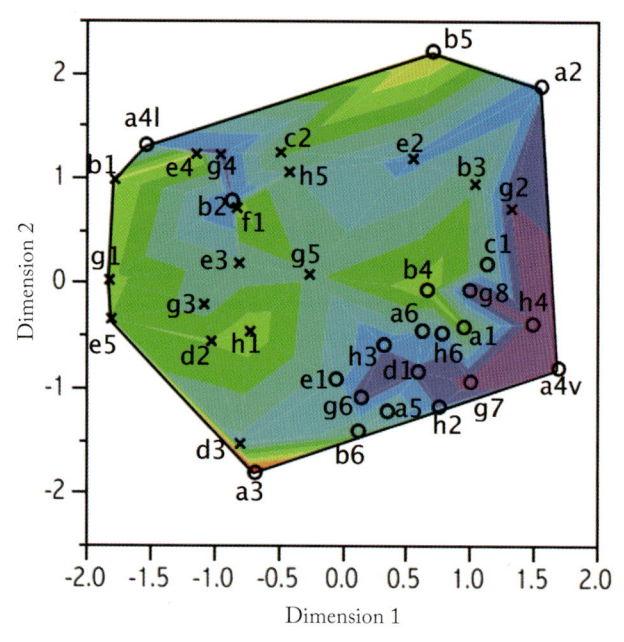

[Figure D9: Contour plot of LinkScores at Cz = 2.5]

【著者紹介】

安間 一雄（あんま かずお）

1956年生まれ。愛知県出身。2003年英国レディング大学博士課程修了(PhD)。玉川大学講師・助教授・教授を経て獨協大学国際教養学部教授。
（主要論文）『〈実践〉言語テスト作成法』（大修館書店、2000年、共訳）、Development of multiple-choice grammaticality judgement tests (2004年, *JLTA Journal*, 6), Scoring of sequential items (2004年, *Language Testing Update*, 35)。

Parsing Strategies of Japanese Low-proficiency EFL Learners

発行	2009年2月20日　初版1刷
定価	8900円＋税
著者	ⓒ 安間一雄
発行者	松本 功
印刷・製本所	ディグ株式会社
発行所	株式会社 ひつじ書房

〒112-0011 東京都文京区千石2-1-2 大和ビル2F
Tel.03-5319-4916　Fax.03-5319-4917
郵便振替 00120-8-142852
toiawase@hituzi.co.jp　http://www.hituzi.co.jp/

ISBN978-4-89476-437-8　C3080

造本には充分注意しておりますが、落丁・乱丁などがございましたら、小社かお買上げ書店にておとりかえいたします。ご意見、ご感想など、小社までお寄せ下されば幸いです。

刊行案内

Chunking and Instruction: The Place of Sounds, Lexis, and Grammar in English Language Teaching　中森誉之 著　菊判上製　定価 8,800 円＋税

The Development of the Nominal Plural Forms in Early Middle English
堀田隆一 著　菊判上製　定価 13,000 円＋税

Detecting and Sharing Perspectives Using Causals in Japanese
宇野良子 著　菊判上製　定価 12,000 円＋税

Discourse Representation of Temporal Relations in the So-Called Head-Internal Relatives　石川邦芳 著　菊判上製　定価 9,400 円＋税

Features and Roles of Filled Pauses in Speech Communication: A corpus-based study of spontaneous speech
渡辺美知子 著　菊判上製　定価 11,000 円＋税

言葉と認知のメカニズム —山梨正明教授還暦記念論文集
児玉一宏・小山哲春 編　A5 判上製　定価 17,000 円＋税

講座社会言語科学 第 3 巻　関係とコミュニケーション
大坊郁夫・永瀬治郎 編　A5 判上製　定価 3,200 円＋税

講座社会言語科学 第 4 巻　教育・学習
西原鈴子・西郡仁朗 編　A5 判上製　定価 3,200 円＋税

ことばの宇宙への旅立ち 2 —10 代からの言語学
大津由紀雄 編　四六判並製　予価 1,500 円＋税

The Proceedings of the Ninth Tokyo Conference on Psycholinguistics (TCP2008)　大津由紀雄 編　菊判上製　定価 9,800 円＋税